SMART MONEY

SMART MONEY

How digital currencies will win
the New Cold War – and why the
West needs to act now

BRUNELLO ROSA
WITH CASEY LARSEN

BLOOMSBURY PUBLISHING
LONDON · OXFORD · NEW YORK · NEW DELHI · SYDNEY

BLOOMSBURY PUBLISHING
Bloomsbury Publishing Plc
50 Bedford Square, London, WC1B 3DP, UK
29 Earlsfort Terrace, Dublin 2, Ireland

BLOOMSBURY, BLOOMSBURY PUBLISHING and the Diana logo are
trademarks of Bloomsbury Publishing Plc

First published in Great Britain 2024

A catalogue record for this book is available from the British Library

ISBN: HB: 978-1-5266-7587-3; TPB: 978-1-5266-7847-8; EBOOK: 978-1-5266-7851-5;
EPDF: 978-1-5266-7850-8

2 4 6 8 10 9 7 5 3 1

Typeset by Newgen KnowledgeWorks Pvt. Ltd., Chennai, India
Printed and bound in Great Britain by CPI Group (UK) Ltd, Croydon CR0 4YY

To find out more about our authors and books visit www.bloomsbury.com
and sign up for our newsletters

Contents

Introduction

On 18 January 2024, Donald Trump was giving a stump speech at a campaign stop in New Hampshire – home to the Bretton Woods resort, where the post-war monetary order was born eighty years earlier. After a series of campaign pledges, the former president made a dramatic pause. He was, so he informed the excitable audience, intent on making 'a promise to protect Americans from tyranny'. But this was not a tirade against '*Chay-na*', nor was it a pledge to end the war in Ukraine. It wasn't even another bombastic attack on North Korea.

Rather, the Republican nominee was referring to an entirely new threat: 'As your president, I will never allow the creation of a *central bank digital currency*, do you know about—' Before Trump could even finish his sentence, the crowd was whooping and cheering. The former president was visibly impressed. 'Ooh … I didn't know you knew so much,' he said, as the crowd cheered even louder. 'Well, New Hampshire! Very SMART PEOPLE! Very *current* – you know what they're doing? A central [bank digital] currency would give our federal government absolute control over your money. They could take your money, and you wouldn't even know it was gone. This would be a dangerous threat to freedom, and I will stop it from coming to America.'[1]

Central bank digital currencies – or 'CBDCs' – are digital versions of state-issued cash. For those in the West who have heard talk of

CBDCs, Mr Trump's position is unlikely to come as a surprise. In the public sphere, CBDCs are widely regarded to represent 'a solution in search of a problem' at best. At worst, they are suspected to be tools of state surveillance and government overreach.

Indeed, the prevailing prejudice surrounding CBDCs in the West seems to be that they are inherently designed to invade privacy and infringe upon civil liberties. After all, in China, the widely piloted digital yuan is likely to become closely tied to the country's dystopian social credit system. It is said that CBDCs will be programmed to ensure that your money is not spent on the 'wrong' things, or that you do not emit too much carbon in the process of spending your money.

CBDCs are also the worst nightmare of libertarian cryptocurrency enthusiasts – an attempt to co-opt the blockchain revolution to the benefit of the centralised state and the detriment of decentralised finance ('de-fi'). To others – mostly central bankers and management consultants – they are an exciting new means of making payments faster and cheaper and increasing financial inclusion. But what if – paradoxically – they are also an indispensable means of safeguarding Western values in the digital age?

The truth of the matter is that CBDCs can be all or none of these things. As with any technological revolution – from the internet to artificial intelligence (AI) – when it comes to bringing money into the digital age, we are still in the process of discovering the opportunities and challenges. Similarly, the stakes are monumental.

In the case of the AI race, the West is seeking to lead the way. In November 2023, for example, Rishi Sunak – then Prime Minister of the UK – hosted 'The AI Safety Summit', which was widely praised for bringing together the international community and public and private sectors to discuss the need to properly regulate AI, while simultaneously harnessing its enormous and as yet unimaginable opportunities.

Meanwhile, at the time of writing, 134 countries – representing over 98 per cent of global gross domestic product (GDP) – are either researching or developing a CBDC. But, unlike with AI, the conversation in the West is entirely different in tone. Far from leading the CBDC race, the West seems unsure if it even wants to take part. After all, what's wrong with paper money? Isn't money digital already? Why not continue punching credit card numbers into unfamiliar websites? But make no mistake: this is a race for the future of money.

We seem to be hopelessly confused, unable to see the forest for the trees. In the West, a narrow set of issues – namely, privacy and the programmable capabilities of CBDCs – have captured the popular imagination, issues which became prominent features of the US presidential election in 2024. We are hyper alert to these specific risks, but apparently oblivious to the costs of withdrawing from the race. This is a generationally important conversation, and it risks being hijacked by political slogans.

When this book speaks of 'the West', we are referring primarily – but not exclusively – to the United States, the United Kingdom and the member states of the European Union. This is not intended to diminish or dismiss other, smaller economies that also belong to the West in cultural and political terms, but because these three economies and currency unions are the most significant with regards to the topics explored in this book. They are also simply the jurisdictions we know best and therefore feel most comfortable writing about.

There is no question that a technological revolution is underway. Just as the advent of telecommunications in the 1980s and 1990s revolutionised the exchange of information, so the advent of distributed ledger technologies such as blockchain have transformed the exchange of monetary value. Money has become digital in a whole new way. This isn't just about digitally *representing* coins or paper notes on a website or an app, it's about transforming notes and coins into computer code. Thanks to blockchain, money can move at the same speed as information and without the need of trusted third parties, ripping up the twentieth century's financial playbook. The world's existing payment institutions and infrastructure – and the reserve currencies that run through them – risk becoming as redundant as the telephone box and the fax machine.

It was the invention of Bitcoin in 2008, and its subsequent and seemingly unstoppable rise, that first switched governments around the world onto the possibilities of digital money. China was the first major power to grasp the full magnitude of money's transition to the digital age. This should perhaps not come as a surprise. Given that paper currency originated under the Tang dynasty in the seventh century, this wasn't the first time China had spotted the next big thing in money before anyone else. So, the People's Bank of China (PBOC) began to research and develop a digital yuan (or e-CNY) in 2014, eventually launching it eight painstaking years later, at the Beijing Winter Olympics in 2022.

At the start of this process, many dismissed it as a fool's errand, an abstract curiosity for the tech savvy. But CBDCs are coming – and they have a critical role to play in the New Cold War that is presently unfolding between the United States and China. The US-led monetary order which has been in place since the end of the Second World War is falling apart; meanwhile, China is ushering in a digital alternative that can be controlled from Beijing.

This should be concerning for a number of reasons. To be sure, not every country has a dog in this fight, but the United States certainly does. Ever since the Bretton Woods Conference in 1944, the US dollar has acted as the global reserve currency, and today is the currency in which approximately 89 per cent of global trade is conducted and 59 per cent of the world's foreign reserves are held.[2] After the end of the gold standard in 1971, the United States struck an agreement with Saudi Arabia to ensure that global oil trade would continue to be denominated in dollars in exchange for military protection. In the words of former French president Valéry Giscard d'Estaing, the US dollar has enjoyed 'exorbitant privilege'.[3]

Essentially, for the past eighty years, the US has controlled the world's *payment rails*: metaphorically speaking, Washington has been able to choose who is allowed to use the tracks, how much freight they can carry, the speed at which they can travel and the direction in which they can go. And these arrangements have enabled the United States to simultaneously run a vast deficit and to uphold and reinforce its status as the world's largest economy and greatest military power.

Meanwhile, as China has exponentially grown in recent decades, with its economy now close to the size of that of the United States, it has become frustrated by its dependence on the US-dominated global trade system. This reliance is seen by China as a chronic weakness, given that it ties China's economic fortunes closely to the US and the US dollar.

In recognition of this, China has made significant efforts to increase the prominence of its own currency, the yuan, in international markets. Here, however, China faces a tough challenge. Competing with the economic might of the United States is no small task, especially given the global dominance of the US dollar.

One of the key strategies employed by China to protect its economy is capital controls. These effectively stop large sums of money from leaving the country too quickly. On the flip side, however, these controls also make it difficult for China to fully open up its economy in a way that would support the internationalisation of its currency. What's more, China's economic model is heavily focused on manufacturing and works best when it exports more than it imports, creating a trade surplus. This isn't compatible with having a big current account deficit, where a country spends more on foreign trade than it earns. So, in a nutshell, China's existing economic and manufacturing policies make it hard for the country to both safeguard its economy and promote its currency to a status that rivals the US dollar.

In order to challenge American control of the global financial system, China knew it would have to play an entirely different game. And with the arrival of digital money, a new game was afoot. This was exactly what China had been waiting for, and it wasted no time in establishing the rules.

In cyberspace, China knew that it could circumvent and overwrite the old American playbook. It wouldn't need to flood the international market with yuan, run vast deficits or phase out capital controls in order to dominate the global financial system of the twenty-first century. The Chinese understood that creating a digital currency wasn't the endgame. Rather, the key was to build new *digital payment rails* on which the digital currencies of its allies and dependent states would run. In other words, and to paraphrase Bill Clinton's former political advisor James Carville, 'it's the infrastructure, stupid'. And, as the world's largest manufacturer and biggest exporter of advanced technology, China is ideally placed to build this infrastructure – complex telecommunications infrastructure, cloud hosting services, 5G capability and more – across the globe.

China foresaw the potential of digital money, money that would be able to move through the internet rather than myriad financial institutions, allowing for faster and cheaper trade and simplified monetary policy. The Chinese knew that no forward-thinking country would choose to remain in the analogue world forever. What's more, by establishing first-mover advantage in this sphere, by building 'digital financial market infrastructure' that is internationally scalable, but ultimately controlled by Beijing, China knew that it could win the race for the future of money. This was not just about de-dollarisation, this was about *digital de-dollarisation*.

It is useful to make an analogy here with the transition from mail to email. Imagine that, in the twentieth century, the United States came to control the international distribution of paper mail, and that governments across the world could only communicate with each other on paper mail with a specially designated US letterhead printed by the US mail service. In this hypothetical situation, most cross-border mail would take days to arrive and usually incur significant costs, but the US monopoly on the global mail service ensured that this system continued to prevail.

Now let's imagine that, in the twenty-first century, China invented a system equivalent to email, allowing mail to take a digital form, cross borders instantly and travel much more cheaply for all parties involved. Imagine that, naturally, various countries around the world began to develop their own email applications. But imagine that the computers on which their programmes ran, as well as the software which was installed on them, were all built by China. In this world, we are all using email, but China is Microsoft. Unlike Microsoft, however, China is able and eager to read your mail, gather data from its contents and block your ability to correspond entirely. Beyond this, the Chinese are also able to install system updates from Beijing and programme how the correspondence is distributed.

This is the world we are rapidly moving towards, a world in which a significant portion of the world's trade – especially that of the developing world – will be conducted on Chinese-controlled digital payment rails. These rails will run on Chinese – not American – rules, with far-reaching consequences for the ethical norms that govern global trade.

Over the course of the last decade, China has taken a number of carefully calibrated steps to bring this vision into reality. In 2013, President Xi launched China's Belt and Road Initiative (BRI), the country's flagship infrastructure project designed to shore up supply chains through which to export its surplus goods to the developing world. The following year, in 2014, it started research on the digital yuan. The year after that, in 2015, it launched the Digital Silk Road (DSR), aimed at building telecommunications networks, 5G offerings and other digital infrastructure.

For almost a decade, the West has remained largely unfazed by these developments. In fact, many Western countries have collaborated with the BRI and DSR. To be sure, Chinese tech products have been met with some suspicion, with the United States banning Huawei from bidding on US government contracts in 2014, a ban which President Trump extended in 2020. The UK and Europe soon followed suit. However, Western leaders did not seem to cotton on to China's broader ambitions along the DSR until very recently.

While it has long been clear that the United States and China are locked into a New Cold War, digital money has not taken centre stage. This New Cold War has been evolving along three dimensions.

Firstly, global supply chains are becoming increasingly balkanised, as the world's two major powers seek greater control over key trade routes and trade partners. As a result, we are seeing the emergence of trade blocs and trade corridors reminiscent of the first Cold War. Secondly, through a trade war – taking place via these bifurcated trade routes – and thirdly, a tech war, as part of this broader trade war.

However, what has not been evident to the United States or its allies is what all three of these separate aspects have in common: they all point towards de-dollarisation; the gradual erosion of the influence of the US dollar on global trade, with widespread implications not just for the United States but the liberal democratic world order. The tech war is inextricably linked to the new world of digital money, while control of supply chains is critical to the establishment and proliferation of reserve currencies.

The far-reaching geopolitical implications of China's manoeuvres only began to dawn on the West in February 2022, when President Xi used the occasion of the Beijing Winter Olympics to mark the beginning of two groundbreaking developments. The first was a renewed alliance with Russia, announced through a pact of 'limitless cooperation' between the two countries, according to which Presidents Xi and Putin promised to back each other in Ukraine and Taiwan, and to collaborate against the West in general.[4] Two weeks later, Russian forces crossed the Ukrainian border. The second was the official launch of its digital yuan, as previously mentioned.

The two announcements were inextricably linked; the first signifying the dawn of a new era of international relations, and the second planting the seeds of a new monetary paradigm on which it would run.

Waking at last from its complacent slumber, the US reacted with a heady mix of decisive action and reckless abandon, which at once shattered the residual, unwritten consensus of the Bretton Woods system and seriously accelerated the digital currency wars.

When the United States and its allies froze $300 billion of $643 billion of Russian foreign reserves in the aftermath of the invasion on 28 February 2022, the US effectively weaponised the dollar's global reserve status and unambiguously signalled to Beijing that the US would seize foreign central bank reserves for political reasons, meaning they could no longer be considered unconditionally sovereign.

What's more, on 9 March, the White House hurriedly issued an executive order on 'Ensuring Responsible Development of Digital Assets', in which President Biden stated his intention to 'elevate the importance of these topics and expand engagement with our critical international partners, including through fora such as the G7, G20, FATF [Financial Action Task Force], and FSB [Financial Stability Board]';[5] then, on 4 April, the UK government announced plans to become a 'global hub' for the crypto industry.[6] Although marketed as spontaneous calls for private-sector innovation, in reality these developments represented long overdue geostrategic manoeuvres.

Few episodes in recent history so perfectly demonstrate Vladimir Lenin's old adage: 'There are decades where nothing happens, and there are weeks when decades happen.'

Twelve months later, Presidents Putin and Xi put any remaining doubts as to the seriousness of their pact to permanent rest. In March 2023, to mark the pact's first anniversary, President Xi made a two-day 'journey of friendship, cooperation and peace' to Moscow. During the visit, President Putin called for the internationalisation of the Chinese yuan and effectively announced that Russia would be adopting the currency for its international reserves, overseas trade and even some personal banking services. Claiming that around two-thirds of trade between Russia and China already uses the yuan and ruble, Putin also declared that Russia was strongly in favour of using the yuan in its dealings with the countries of Asia, Africa and Latin America.[7]

With all this in mind, it's hard to dispute that almost eight decades of US-dollar dominance could be on the way out and that a new global monetary trajectory has been set in place. That doesn't, however, make it any less astounding.

And money's digital revolution is not just unfolding against the backdrop of shifting geopolitical alliances. Even more significantly, it is unfolding against a paradigm shift in the nature of geopolitical power itself. As we approach a bottleneck in the history of global energy markets, with the era of cheap oil potentially coming to an end, the nature of power is being redefined. Superpowers can no longer rely on vast economic output and military might in order to maintain their status, because neither can be sustained without access to affordable sources of energy.

In the twenty-first century, power lies in the hands of commodity-rich nations, which have access to the world's remaining fossil fuel reserves as well as the rare metals required to power the energy transition. Notably, a significant proportion of these natural resources are in the hands of the world's autocracies: China, Russia, Saudi Arabia, Venezuela and Iran.

In recent decades, the US has unwittingly shot itself in the foot by deliberately ostracising and alienating many of the countries that could give it access to the cheap energy it needs. Now, although their differences largely outweigh their similarities, the world's commodity-rich autocracies are united in their mutual disdain for the exorbitant privilege of the US dollar, which is coupled with their rising mistrust of the global dollar-denominated system. Accordingly, they are all the more likely to pivot east, coalescing around China, the world's alternative economic superpower.

What else do these countries have in common? They are all developing their own CBDCs, which can run on Chinese digital payment rails, and which can therefore bypass the dollar system entirely.

In simple terms, the world's most important natural resources (which are rapidly depleting) and the new digital monetary order could soon fall under the control of Beijing, rather than Washington, D.C.

We are already beginning to see the early results of this. As economist Zoltan Pozsar wrote in the *Financial Times* in January 2023, 'CBDCs are spreading like fast-growing kudzu vines', which 'could enable central banks in the global east and south to serve as foreign exchange dealers to intermediate currency flows between local banking systems, all without referencing the dollar or touching the western banking system'.[8]

To add insult to injury, these developments are taking place at a time when confidence in the US dollar is plummeting at home. To name just one example, the collapse of Silicon Valley Bank in March 2023 was a sign that America's banks are undercapitalised to the tune of hundreds of billions of dollars.[9] And on the macro level, the US government has the highest level of sovereign debt of any country in the history of the world. It is more than arguable – as some economists already claim – that the United States is functionally insolvent. Needless to say, China and its allies have economic problems of their own, but America's power is declining on a relative basis, and its invincible aura fading.

Indeed, untethered from the gold standard since 1971 and with the petrodollar system increasingly challenged by the petroyuan, you could argue that the United States has only been able to maintain the US dollar's status thanks to the payment institutions which uphold it.

But these can no longer be relied upon. With the advent of digital money, countries and companies will be able to swap their payment rails at the click of a button. They will be able to exchange their foreign reserves of US dollars for digital yuan or the digital currencies of other countries – or indeed for Bitcoin and other cryptocurrencies – as quickly as depositors at Silicon Valley Bank wired their savings to J. P. Morgan.

While many argue that we are pivoting towards a multipolar world order, it is more accurate to say that we are racing towards a bipolar monetary order. The G7 – the group of the world's most wealthy and industrialised countries, founded in 1975 – will stick with the United States and the US dollar, while most of the commodity-rich autocracies of the BRICS+ group look increasingly likely to side with China.

But what are the ramifications of this? That's what this book intends to find out.

Many argue that talk of the dollar's demise is greatly exaggerated, or that CBDCs will make little difference to how we use money. To counter such claims, it is useful to reflect again on the evolution of modern communications, from paper letters to the telegram and telephone, to the internet and email. In the early days of the internet, many people didn't really see the point. In a famous interview with the British pop singer David Bowie from the year 1999, the acerbic journalist Jeremy Paxman asked Bowie why he was so fascinated by the emergence of the internet:

PAXMAN: You don't think that some of the claims being made for the internet are hugely exaggerated? I mean, when the telephone was invented people made amazing claims for it.

BOWIE: Yes, the president at the time said outrageous things – he said he foresaw the day when every town in America would have a telephone in it … I don't think we've even seen the tip of the iceberg, I think the potential of what the internet is going to do to society, both good and bad, is unimaginable. I think we're actually on the cusp of something that is both exhilarating and terrifying.

PAXMAN: It's just a tool, isn't it?

BOWIE: No, it's not. It's an *alien lifeform*.[10]

Few people today would dispute that Bowie has been proven emphatically right. In many ways, to this day, we are still only exploring the tip of the iceberg when it comes to the internet.

The internet allowed information and communication to take digital form. When email was invented, there were still people questioning its necessity, but it soon became obvious why instant communication would revolutionise the world as we know it.

CBDCs mean that money, and the global monetary system, is becoming truly digital for the first time: in other words, *monetary and economic value* is moving into the age of the internet in the same way that information did in the early 2000s. And the truth is that we cannot yet know the full range of possibilities offered by these new technologies – we can barely begin to imagine how digital, state-issued and state-backed money will enable governments to build, project, manipulate and weaponise monetary networks in ways never seen before. CBDCs could also become positive tools of economic, political and cultural leverage – deployed as a hedge against financial repression on a global scale and a means through which billions of unbanked citizens across the world will be able to access digital property rights.

By going digital, money takes on new properties. In addition to being a medium of exchange, a store of value and a unit of account, digital money can be used as a system of *control* – of both information and people – and a tool for faster and cheaper economic empowerment.

In the coming years, as China's digital monetary paradigm begins to take shape and gain strength, the G7 – led by the United States, the United Kingdom and the European Union – will have to make a choice. They can either abstain from issuing state-backed digital currencies and thereby withdraw from the race, ceding all territory to China and its allies, or they can choose to engage, developing an alternative vision for the future of money.

But we can't help questioning: what if it's already too late? Given China's ten-year head start, and the significant inroads it has made in that time with regard to digital infrastructure, can the West catch up, even if it wants to? Does the West have the technological know-how and capacity to build comparable digital financial infrastructure? Does the West have the political will and public support required to invest in it? Can the West rely on the residual effects of the legacy US-led system? Or do we need to drag ourselves kicking and screaming into the digital age?

And who else will we be racing against? Who is likely to join the emerging Sino-Russian axis? Will the US succeed in loosening China's grip on Africa? Which camp will the likes of India, Brazil and Argentina fall into? Will others follow El Salvador and the Central African Republic down the Bitcoin route? And what will all of this mean for the future global order and for populations around the world? What will it mean for energy prices and global living standards? Will the profit motive always prevail over geopolitics, or will the US and Europe get shut out of global energy markets as its former allies turn eastward?

Finally, what even is money? Most people today, including the vast majority of political, business and even financial leaders, do not spend much time thinking about what money is. Most people work to earn money and most people save some of it. Others, fewer in number, are able to make money and then invest it. All of us are able to spend it, politicians better than most. But who creates, defines and controls it? And what are the repercussions of this?

It is the contention of this book that these questions, which are already raging in certain interested circles and beginning to percolate into the mainstream, will come to dominate our social, cultural and political discourse in the years to come. And if they don't, they should. Because the answers to them – and there must be answers – will define human civilisation for many years after that.

This book is broad in scope and does not pretend to have all the answers. Rather, we are seeking to ask the right questions. The West is on the verge of sleepwalking into a new reality because it is blind to many of these issues, or else assumes it already knows the answers. Things are moving at a frightening pace in this sphere, with critical developments likely to unfold by the time the paperback version of this book is published next year, and even between the time of writing and the time of publication of this hardback. In the crucial years ahead, it is imperative that we have a frank conversation about the nature of money on an international – and not just domestic – scale.

As emerging technologies gradually render the global financial institutions of the twentieth century obsolete, it is imperative that we ask ourselves how the global monetary order works, who controls it and through what tools and technologies. We must endeavour to understand how the monetary order interacts with – or even controls – energy and commodities, and who stands to gain and to lose at the intersection of the race for digital money and the race to conquer the world's depleting natural resources.

This book offers a roadmap for what we consider to be the most important conversations of our time, but it cannot provide an exhaustive account of each of them. We urge Western governments and populations to start interrogating and reshaping their conception of what money is – after all, the race for the future of money has already begun.

From the perspective of anyone born after 1945, who has lived through eight decades of US dollar-denominated monetary hegemony, CBDCs are uncharted territory. They are 'fast-growing kudzu vines'; an *alien life form*. This is the brave new world of *smart money*.

Part I

Old Money, New Money and Smart Money

1

The Washington Consensus: Leadership, Innovation and International Engagement

'We're the United States of America for God's sake, the most
powerful nation in the history of the world.'

JOE BIDEN[1]

President Biden's bold assertion – made to insist that the US could
sustain its support for both Ukraine and Israel following the attacks by
Hamas on 7 October 2023 – invites some further examination of the
historical record, and of what constitutes 'power' in a global context.

Let's consider for a moment the scale and influence of various
historical empires. At its zenith in the late nineteenth and early
twentieth century, the British Empire, fuelled by the technological
advancements of its time, could boast an unprecedented global reach.
Prior to this, the Roman Empire dominated the Mediterranean
and much of Europe for several hundred years; longer than the
relatively brief ascendancy of modern superpowers.

Yet Biden's claim holds a certain weight: the United States does
stand as something of a colossus when it comes to military might,
economics and culture.

Its military prowess is unmatched, with defence spending
outstripping the next ten countries combined, including

heavyweights like China, Russia and Saudi Arabia. This unparalleled military reach underpins its global influence.

Economically, the US continues to be a juggernaut. As of the end of 2023, it was responsible for 26.1 per cent of the whole world's GDP.[2] This economic dominance is undergirded by a spirit of innovation: in 2023 alone, a total of 346,152 patents were granted at the US patent and trademark office, an increase from 182,218 in the year 2000, a testament to its relentless pursuit of technological advancement.[3]

The US's financial and industrial sectors are also formidable. Financial institutions like J. P. Morgan, Citi, Goldman Sachs, Blackrock and Blackstone not only dominate domestically but also cast a long shadow on the global stage. The US is also the world's pre-eminent soft power, whose film and music industries shape global tastes and trends.

In light of all this, President Biden's assertion is not just a proud display of patriotism; it is arguably an accurate description of the United States' standing in the annals of global superpowers. But history teaches us that all great empires, like pride, rise and fall.

To understand what is at stake in the race for the future of money, we need to understand how the United States came to enjoy its 'exorbitant privilege' in the first place. This story is not just about sheer economic expansion or military might; it's also about cultural reach, technological innovation and the shaping of international norms and institutions.

In each of these realms, the US has sought to lead the world, buttressed by the most important norm and institution of all: the emergence of the US dollar as the world's global reserve currency.

Crucially, the rise of the United States has been a story of strategic adaptation, a chess game at a global level in which America has consistently stayed one move ahead of its adversaries. It is a story of *engagement, leadership and innovation* on the international stage, characterised by foresight, resilience and a determination to maintain an upper hand against rivals in the realms of industry, technology and international finance.

The significance of the US dollar extends far beyond its status as the global reserve currency. The dollar represents America and the American century: it is a symbol of political liberty, economic opportunity, cultural primacy and technological prowess.

The dollar does not just represent Washington and Wall Street, but Hollywood and Silicon Valley. It embodies James Dean as much as it denotes Jerome Powell. For millions beyond the borders of the United States, the dollar represents 'Life, Liberty and the pursuit of Happiness', to quote the spirit of the US Declaration of Independence. Perhaps these are reasons enough to avoid tampering with the dollar's defining features. Perhaps the dollar is as foundational to the US as its constitution: to revisit its foundations would be to risk undermining the entire superstructure.

The difference is that, unlike the US Constitution, the properties of the dollar have never been fixed. They have evolved and mutated over time, enabling it to survive and thrive on the global stage. For the better part of the American century, the dollar has dominated the international financial system through its symbiotic relationship first with gold and then with oil. But in a twenty-first century marked by the rise of a superpower challenger, the digital transformation of money, depleting natural resources and shifting geopolitical alliances, can the United States maintain the dollar's status without adapting accordingly? And, if the dollar were to retreat from the world stage, what would this mean for the United Kingdom, Europe and the developing world across which the United States and China are both vying for control?

AMERICAN 'WELTGEIST'

At the dawn of the twentieth century, the United Kingdom was the unchallenged global superpower, presiding over the largest empire ever seen in human history. The UK, at this juncture, saw itself as embodying what the German philosopher Georg Wilhelm

Friedrich Hegel called 'Weltgeist' or 'world spirit'[4] – a cultural, intellectual and moral force that drives human progress and reflects the prevailing values and orthodoxies of the day. The UK was not only the largest economic power but arguably the world's foremost cultural influence during its reign. In Europe, historical powers like Spain and France, which had embodied the 'Weltgeist' during the sixteenth and seventeenth centuries respectively, were witnessing a relative decline in their influence. Meanwhile, Germany and Italy were just emerging from their national unification processes. Further afield, the UK's relationship with China had been defined by the nineteenth-century Opium Wars, and India, often referred to as the 'jewel in the crown', played a pivotal role in the British Empire.

However, the United States was a nation on the rise. Politically, it had solidified its institutional framework following the Civil War (1861–5) and, economically, it was experiencing rapid industrial growth. This period saw the burgeoning of key industries and the establishment of monopolies, which were subsequently regulated by the Sherman Antitrust Act of 1890, a landmark piece of legislation aimed at maintaining fair competition. Furthermore, the US was enjoying a current account surplus – a classic indicator of a flourishing economy that meant the country was exporting more than it imported – reflecting its economic vitality and growing global presence.

Demographically, the US was also experiencing a significant surge: the population grew at an astonishing rate of 25–30 per cent per decade. By the 1900 census, the population had reached over 76 million, including nearly 10 million immigrants (around 14 per cent of the total).[5] This melting pot of cultures contributed to the vibrant and dynamic character of the nation, though it could not yet measure up to the influence of the UK, its former coloniser.

The outbreak of the First World War in 1914, shortly followed by the seismic Russian Revolution, drastically altered the global landscape. After three years of fighting, the UK was financially depleted, and the Russian Empire had begun to collapse, eventually being replaced by the Soviet Union. The Allies were arguably teetering on the brink of defeat – until the intervention of the US.

Initially inclined towards isolationism, the US became involved in the war in April 1917, just as the Allies began to falter in terms of both morale and finances. While US isolationism shouldn't be overstated – it took part in the 1884 Berlin Conference to discuss the future partitioning of Africa – this was nevertheless a definitive moment that contradicted the Monroe Doctrine, which had established the 'Americas to the Americans, Europe to the Europeans'. In other words, separate spheres of influence for the US and for Europe. Beyond this, however, America's entry into the war, precisely 140 years after the nation fought to gain its independence from Britain, shifted the balance in favour of the Allies, establishing the US as a global power with a decisive role to play.

This heralded the beginning of a new era in global geopolitics. The period that followed was extremely turbulent, marked indelibly by the Great Depression that started in 1929. This global economic crisis led to the widespread abandonment of the gold standard and its variant, the gold-exchange standard, by nations that had previously been wedded to it. Concurrently, Europe witnessed the alarming rise of authoritarian regimes, which eventually morphed into dictatorships, setting the stage for the Second World War. Initially, the United States maintained its traditional isolationist stance, hesitant to become entangled in what it viewed as another European conflict. However, the Japanese attack on Pearl Harbor in December 1941 dramatically altered the American mindset, mirroring the transformative impact of the sinking of RMS *Lusitania* in May 1915 during the First World War. These events galvanised American public opinion and precipitated another shift from isolationism to interventionism.

By the early 1940s, it had become obvious that the United States would need to embrace its role as the 'leader of the free world', a responsibility it had previously been reluctant to accept. But by taking on a leading role at key conferences during this period, including Tehran (1943), Yalta (1945) and Potsdam (1945), the US began to signal that it was ready to lead. Meanwhile, the UK lost its global role. Wartime prime minister Winston Churchill was replaced in the middle of the Potsdam Conference by the newly elected Clement Attlee, signalling a changing of the guard and the effective end of the British Empire. By electing Attlee, the British public were making a crucial choice to adopt a leader who was overtly committed to the delivery of the welfare state – a reward to itself for its suffering – which had taken on a higher priority than maintaining the colonial empire, and whose framework had been developed during the war, with the Beveridge Report on the National Health Service (NHS) of 1942 and the Butler Education Act of 1944.

In the aftermath, the UK emerged as a leading nation within the newly formed Commonwealth. But its role on the world stage was totally different to what it had been just a few decades earlier. No longer the empire it once was, the UK found itself instead acting as a satellite nation to the US, while the US headed a new bloc of countries (which countered another bloc headed by the Soviet Union). This shift represented a significant realignment in global power structures, shaping international relations for the remainder of the twentieth century.

Amidst all these geopolitical reconfigurations, the Bretton Woods Conference, held in July 1944 in New Hampshire, USA, stands out as a defining moment in the establishment of the post-war economic order. The choice of a location within its own borders for this conference was itself a statement of intent by the United States, as underscored by historical precedent and signifying a newly concretised and elevated status: the Congress of Vienna in 1814 heralded the restoration of the Austrian Empire after the Napoleonic Wars, while the Congress of Berlin in 1878 publicly rubber-stamped the new, powerful German state following its unification in 1870, as well as its victorious conflicts with Denmark (1864), Austria (1866) and France (1870).

Bretton Woods not only laid the economic foundations for the rest of the twentieth century, but positioned the United States at the helm of the new world order – a role it was ready and determined to embrace.

BRETTON WOODS AND THE GOLD STANDARD

Between 1–22 July 1944, 730 delegates from forty-four Allied nations convened at the Mount Washington Hotel in Bretton Woods, New Hampshire, for the United Nations Monetary and Financial Conference; this followed a preliminary gathering in Atlantic City in mid-June. The conference sought to establish the economic and financial framework for the post-war era. And while representatives from dozens of countries participated, it was only the delegations of two nations that really mattered – that of the United States, led by Harry Dexter White, special assistant to the US Secretary of the Treasury, and that of the United Kingdom, led by the economist John Maynard Keynes, an advisor to the British Treasury.

The backdrop to Bretton Woods was a world economy ravaged by the Great Depression and the Second World War. Both White and Keynes, recognising the disastrous consequences of the 1930s protectionist policies that had crippled global trade and fanned the flames of war, had independently devised plans to prevent future economic catastrophes. Their proposals aimed to provide financial support to countries facing deficits, discouraging them from resorting to destructive trade and monetary policies.

But in spite of their shared goal, the visions of White and Keynes diverged significantly. Keynes was pushing for the establishment of an 'International Clearing Union', a mechanism to regulate global trade balances. He was concerned about the vicious cycle of debt and stagnation that hamstrung deficit-running countries, and to address this, he wanted the union to introduce its own currency, the 'bancor', pegged to national currencies at a fixed rate, which would be used for international transactions. The bancor was envisaged as a way to measure national trade imbalances and to stabilise the global economy.[6]

However, Harry Dexter White firmly opposed Keynes's concept. He didn't think the world needed an artificial new currency. Instead, he wanted the US dollar to be the linchpin of the new global financial system, taking over the role historically played by the British pound. White recognised the immense strategic advantage of positioning the US dollar as the world's reserve currency, a currency that nations would need to stockpile for international trade and could use in place of gold.[7]

The opposing views of White and Keynes at Bretton Woods therefore represented more than an academic policy debate. The American vision stood for a symbolic handover of global economic leadership. The United Kingdom had been the pre-eminent force in world trade since the end of the Napoleonic era in 1815, but now, after two prolonged wars, which had weakened the UK but bolstered the US, the Americans held the home-field advantage and ultimately prevailed.

Nonetheless, even if Keynes's ideas were not adopted as policy, they undeniably influenced other outcomes from the conference, such as the formation of the International Monetary Fund (IMF), a key institution for managing global financial stability. Bretton Woods also saw the birth of the Bank for Reconstruction and Development (now known as the World Bank). These new institutions were to be strategically headquartered in Washington, D.C., away from the financial tumult of New York, which had been the epicentre of the 1929 crisis. Their positioning in the political capital of the US reflected the increasing clout of the American government.

Another ambitious proposal that emerged from Bretton Woods, the creation of the International Trade Organization to regulate international trade, stalled at the time; the US Senate's failure to ratify its charter led to its non-realisation. Instead, the more modest General Agreement on Tariffs and Trade (GATT) was established. It wasn't until 1995, after the Uruguay Round of GATT negotiations, that the World Trade Organization (WTO) was finally created as GATT's successor, with a mandate to oversee and expand its principles and agreements.

Today, these three institutions – the IMF, the World Bank and the WTO – stand as the enduring legacies of the Bretton Woods Conference. They represent the foundational pillars of the international economic system, reflecting both Keynes's internationalist ideas and White's US-centred approach. Together, they continue to shape the contours of global finance and trade. Despite their differences, both White and Keynes envisaged a world where fixed exchange rates would prevail, believing this would foster global trade more effectively than fluctuating rates. At the heart of this system were two critical components: the US dollar as the principal reserve currency and the gold standard as the system's anchor. Keynes, who famously argued against the gold standard in the 1920s, and who thought that pegging the pound to gold after the war would be fatal to Britain – as a debtor nation – and its empire, accepted that the US dollar was the only currency strong enough to anchor the new international monetary system by being pegged to gold, and yielded to White's plan and America's position of comparative strength as a creditor nation.

Under the new arrangement, each participating nation was required to peg its currency to the US dollar within a 1 per cent margin, and the US was obligated to ensure that the dollar could be converted to gold at the rate of $35 per ounce for all foreign governments and central banks.

From its inception in 1944 until its dissolution in the early 1970s, this system anchored international finance, facilitating a period of remarkable economic growth, trade expansion, reduced inflation and a decrease in national debt levels. Economist Barry Eichengreen attributed the success of the Bretton Woods system during this period to three key factors: limited international capital mobility, stringent financial regulation and the dominant economic and financial position of the United States and the US dollar.[8] This triad created an environment conducive to stability and growth, underpinning one of the most prosperous periods in global economic history.

THE END OF THE GOLD STANDARD

However, as much as the Bretton Woods system supported global economic prosperity, it was also beset by various challenges throughout its existence, which ultimately led to its downfall. These included the emergence of new economic powerhouses, a surge in international capital mobility, rising inflation in the United States and an increasing global demand for gold.

This all came to a head in the early 1970s. By this point, the US deficit had been growing for several years, in large part due to extensive military spending in the Vietnam War alongside significant foreign investment and aid. The US government's solution was simply to print more dollars; in turn, however, this began to jeopardise the value of the dollar relative to the gold by which it was theoretically backed.

Foreign governments soon found themselves drowning in a surplus of US dollars, which raised concerns about its stability. Accordingly, a number of countries began to question the continued viability of the Bretton Woods system.

French president Charles de Gaulle was particularly critical of the US's position, railing against the injustice of the Americans printing dollars while other countries accumulated dollar reserves without an equivalent increase in their gold reserves.[9] The French government, foreseeing potential devaluation of dollar holdings and aiming to protect its own economic interests, started to convert its dollar reserves back into gold.

A number of others followed suit, leading to a rush. This in turn put significant strain on US gold reserves. To make matters worse, with rising inflation and increasingly divergent economic policies across the globe, the US was struggling to maintain the fixed gold conversion rate ($35 per ounce).

In response, in August 1971, President Nixon made a pivotal decision: the US dollar would no longer be convertible into gold, marking the end of the gold standard and effectively of the Bretton Woods system as a whole. Nixon's impulsive move stabilised the immediate crisis, but the global monetary order was forever changed. The decision to end the gold standard turned the dollar into a 'fiat' currency, meaning it was no longer backed by a physical commodity but only by its issuing government. From this moment onwards, the value of the US dollar was reliant on US public debt and therefore in large part determined by the ability of the US government (and therefore US taxpayers) to repay such debt over time. In the wake of this, major currencies that had previously been pegged to a fixed exchange rate, such as the British pound (though it had nevertheless undergone two devaluations during this period), moved towards free-floating exchange rates; a shift officially recognised by the Jamaica Accords in 1976. The so-called 'Nixon Shock' marked the beginning of a new chapter in international finance, characterised by fluid currency values determined by market forces rather than the value of gold or the US dollar.

This ushered in a period marked by macroeconomic and social turbulence, compounded by the oil crises of 1973 and 1979. However, one way or another, financial instability was largely kept at bay, thanks in part to a series of brilliant geopolitical manoeuvres on the part of the US.

THE RISE OF THE PETRODOLLAR

Shortly after the end of the Bretton Woods system, the world economy was rocked by its first oil shock after OPEC (Organization of the Petroleum Exporting Countries) decided to hike oil prices in response to the US backing Israel during the Yom Kippur War of 1973. This decision dramatically increased the revenues of oil-producing nations, particularly in the Middle East, and significantly altered global power dynamics.

The Americans did not take this lying down, however. That very same year, the US struck a crucial deal with Saudi Arabia. Under this deal, the two nations agreed to price and trade oil exclusively in US dollars in exchange for the US providing military protection to the Saudi regime, compelling any country purchasing oil from Saudi Arabia to pay for it in US dollars. This was soon extended to other oil-producing nations. The petrodollar system was born: as both developed and developing economies continued to industrialise at a rapid pace in the latter decades of the twentieth century, oil soon became the new gold, spurring a renewed demand for the American currency. Once again, the US had created a system which served its own needs, shoring up the US dollar as the primary global reserve currency and buying itself an advantage with regard to managing its trade deficits and public debt.

The rise of the petrodollar system had profound economic and political consequences for both oil-exporting and oil-importing nations. For oil exporters, their newfound wealth and influence spurred investments across critical infrastructure and defence. Some of these nations channelled their petrodollars into sovereign wealth funds – state-owned investment entities. These funds have since emerged as significant actors in global financial markets, investing in a range of stocks, bonds, real estate and private equity.

The petrodollar system also gave oil-exporting nations a newfound prominence on the global stage. Contrary to all previous expectations, Saudi Arabia, flush with petrodollars, became an indispensable strategic ally of the US as its principal oil supplier, deeply entwining their economic and political interests. Iran and Iraq, meanwhile, took a slightly different tack, pursuing regional ambitions with considerably more force than they could previously afford, thanks to their newfound economic strength, which they translated into military might.

Conversely, oil-importing countries faced both opportunities and challenges. The new system opened up fresh avenues for trade, as oil-exporting nations sought to diversify their economies and enhance their living standards, creating demand for goods and services from developed oil-importing nations. In many Western countries, however, the increased cost of energy intensified inflation and triggered recessions.

The patience of many oil-importing countries soon began to wear thin. Faced with the volatility of oil markets, they invested heavily in other forms of energy, in a push to lessen their reliance on oil. This led to significant advancements in natural gas, nuclear energy and renewable energy sources such as solar and wind power. These are certainly positive developments in and of themselves, but they also speak to a global system that put its stakeholders at the mercy of the market.

THE TRIUMPH OF NEOLIBERALISM

This has never held truer than in the era following the elections of Margaret Thatcher as prime minister of the UK in 1979 and Ronald Reagan as president of the United States in 1980. Their respective tenures have since become synonymous with a revitalised commitment to capitalism and the free-market system. This represented a distinct shift away from the Keynesian economic policies that had dominated the post-war era, which focused on stimulating aggregate demand to drive economic growth. Such policies had fallen out of favour because of the rampant inflation of the 1970s. Thatcher and Reagan championed economic reforms that emphasised the supply side – based on the belief that stimulating production rather than demand would create a healthier, more sustainable economic environment – sometimes referred to as 'Reaganomics'. The US president and the UK prime minister implemented Reaganomics throughout their respective terms in office, with varying results.

During this period, the primary emerging economic power was not China, but Japan. In the years following the Second World War, Japan had undergone a remarkable transformation, emerging as one of the world's most industrialised nations and a leader in technological innovation, buttressed by its innovative production techniques and early adoption of transistor technology in the 1980s. This allowed Japan to make huge strides when it came to producing high-tech products: by the mid-1980s, for example, Japan's impressive automobile industry appeared poised to challenge that of the United States, which had reigned supreme in the Western world up until this point.

The US consequently found itself grappling with a substantial trade deficit with Japan, mirroring the contemporary situation with China. A trade deficit occurs when a country imports more goods and services than it exports, leading to a net outflow of domestic currency to foreign markets. During the 1980s, the significant trade deficit with Japan was often seen as a sign of the US's economic dominance, as Japan heavily relied on the US market for its exports and was deeply integrated into the American financial system. Today, a similar pattern is observed with China, from which the US imports a vast array of goods, contributing to a substantial trade deficit.

A persistent trade deficit raises concerns about the sustainability of a country's economic position. According to economic theory, such a deficit should lead to the depreciation of the country's currency, which means that the value of the country's currency falls relative to other currencies. This depreciation has two primary effects: it makes the country's exports cheaper and more competitive abroad, and it makes imports more expensive for domestic consumers. Over time, these changes help to correct the trade imbalance by increasing exports and reducing imports.

In this case, however, the expected adjustment was not forthcoming. From 1980 to 1985, the US dollar appreciated by about 50 per cent against major currencies like the Japanese yen, German mark, French franc and British pound[10] – the currencies of the largest economies within the G7. This strengthening of the dollar created issues for a number of American industrial sectors, including manufacturing, services and agriculture. However, the Reagan administration was loath to act, given its commitment to free-market capitalism and focus on curbing inflation after the oil shocks of the 1970s.

By 1985, the problem had grown too big to ignore. A broad coalition of influential US companies, spanning everything from grain export to heavy industry and high-tech, had initiated a campaign pushing for economic change. With this movement gaining momentum, the US Congress was forced to consider the adoption of protectionist measures. But Reagan remained apprehensive about the prospect of trade restrictions. In an effort to avert this, he persuaded his international allies to embark on a path of coordinated market intervention, culminating in the Plaza Accord.

This agreement, signed by the United States, Japan, West Germany, France and the United Kingdom on 22 September 1985, aimed to devalue the US dollar relative to the Japanese yen and the German mark, in order to diminish the US trade deficit. It marked the first time that these five nations agreed to jointly recalibrate the exchange rate system, requiring each nation's central bank to actively intervene in the currency markets over a period of two years. By the conclusion of this period, the United States saw its currency devalued by approximately 50 per cent, while the currencies of West Germany, France, the UK and Japan experienced a corresponding appreciation.[11] This was ostensibly a successful outcome, but ultimately became something of an overcorrection, with the values of non-US currencies rising excessively. Accordingly, a new agreement, the Louvre Accord, was signed in 1987, with the objective of stabilising exchange rates at their contemporary levels to prevent further volatility and misalignments.

The long-term effects of these accords remain a contentious topic among economists and policymakers. To be sure, some admire Reagan's boldness in pursuing the Plaza Accord, which rectified global imbalances, restored market confidence and promoted international cooperation. Others, however, argue that it precipitated a stock market crash and recession in the US and abroad.

Indeed, it is difficult to argue against the fact that the accords negatively impacted the other participating countries. Japan in particular, which had been positioned to challenge US dominance within the Western hemisphere, entered a prolonged period of deflation and stagnation. To Reagan this was of little consequence; he was serving American interests, ensuring that Washington retained the levers of power over the global financial system and sidelined its potential rivals.

These historical examples highlight the strong connection between a nation's global dominance and its associated monetary regime. Changes in this regime often signal shifts in the geopolitical landscape. Japan's experience in the 1980s illustrates this point well. The US succeeded in orchestrating a series of international agreements aimed at manipulating the value of the Japanese yen. This artificial manipulation of currency values significantly impacted Japan's export-driven economy, leading to a period of economic stagnation known as the 'Lost Decade' and marking the end of Japan's economic dominance during that era. Japan, and other countries involved in the Plaza Accord, agreed to increase the value of their currencies relative to the US dollar for several reasons. Primarily, these nations faced mounting pressure from the US, which was dealing with a significant trade deficit and believed that the strong dollar was hurting its manufacturing sector. The US argued that the undervalued yen and other currencies were giving foreign exporters an unfair advantage, flooding the American market with cheaper goods and causing job losses in US industries. Faced with the possibility of trade sanctions and deteriorating diplomatic relations, Japan and the other signatories calculated that complying with the US demands was a lesser evil compared to the potential fallout from a trade war with the world's largest economy.

The fear was that losing access to the US market, which was crucial for their export-driven growth, would be far more detrimental than adjusting their currency values. This strategy was meant to appease the US while attempting to manage their own economic interests. In contrast, China today presents a different scenario. Unlike Japan in the 1980s, China has been reluctant to significantly amend its trading policies or currency values. The Chinese government maintains tight control over the yuan's exchange rate to keep its exports competitively priced. This approach has enabled China to run a massive trade surplus, particularly with the United States. China's strategy reflects its broader economic policies, which prioritise maintaining strong economic growth and stability over yielding to external pressures for currency revaluation.

China's refusal to adjust its currency value highlights a significant departure from Japan's approach in the 1980s. By maintaining a trade surplus and a controlled currency, China underscores its determination to sustain its economic momentum and geopolitical influence. This approach has fuelled ongoing tensions between the US and China, with accusations of currency manipulation and unfair trade practices becoming central issues in their economic relations. In short, while Japan in the 1980s acquiesced to US pressure to avoid the potentially devastating consequences of losing access to American markets, China has chosen a path of economic self-reliance and assertiveness.

THE END OF HISTORY, OR THE BEGINNING OF THE US-LED UNIPOLAR WORLD

Reagan was hellbent on victory in the Cold War. Correctly assessing that the Soviet economy couldn't simultaneously sustain robust growth and keep pace with the escalating nuclear arms race, Reagan set out to bankrupt the Soviet Union as a means of inciting a social revolt and instigating regime change.

The American strategy ultimately proved successful. In 1989, the Berlin Wall fell; by 1991, the Soviet Union was no more, effectively bringing the First Cold War to a close.

This marked the end of what the historian Eric Hobsbawm termed 'The Short Century', beginning with the First World War and culminating with the end of the Cold War. In his 1994 book *The Age of Extremes*, Hobsbawm recognised that the world was on the cusp of a new historical epoch;[12] similarly, American political scientist Francis Fukuyama argued in a 1989 article – which later evolved into a book, published in 1992 – that the world was approaching the 'end of history', with mankind's ideological evolution culminating with the ascendancy of Western liberal democracy and market forces.[13] The 1990s did herald a period of relative tranquillity among the superpowers, in stark contrast to the preceding decades of conflict, both overt and covert. This era saw Russia, under the leadership of President Boris Yeltsin, join the ranks of the most industrialised nations, expanding the G7 into the G8. Democracy was on the rise, with even the most enduring dictatorships of the 1980s giving way to liberal democracies.

A prime example of this was observed in Chile. The country had been under the authoritarian rule of Augusto Pinochet since his coup in September 1973; the Pinochet regime was notorious for its human rights abuses, but had found support in Ronald Reagan and Margaret Thatcher, both ardent advocates of free-market capitalism. Yet, in 1988, the population of Chile voted 'No' in a pivotal referendum on whether Pinochet should extend his presidency for another eight years, marking the beginning of the end of the dictator's sixteen-and-a-half-year rule. This watershed moment led to democratic elections in 1989 and the establishment of a new government by 1990.

The landscape of Eastern Europe also transformed dramatically after the fall of the Berlin Wall and the dissolution of the Soviet Union. Nations formerly aligned with the Warsaw Pact – a collective defence treaty established by the Soviet Union and seven other Soviet satellite states in Central and Eastern Europe – embarked on a journey towards democracy. By 2004, this democratic shift culminated in the European Union's expansion to include many of these countries. Despite Russia's objections and discomfort, several of these former Soviet states also became members of NATO.

During this period, the United States stood at the zenith of global influence, unchallenged by any significant geopolitical rivals. This dominance was rooted not only in its military and economic power but also in its ability to shape global political and economic policies. The US successfully reorganised its global alliances and economic practices according to what came to be known as the 'Washington Consensus'.

The Washington Consensus, a term coined in 1989 by economist John Williamson, refers to a set of ten economic policy prescriptions considered the standard reform package promoted for crisis-wracked developing countries by institutions based in Washington, D.C., such as the IMF, World Bank and the US Treasury Department.[14] These policies emphasised liberalisation, deregulation and privatisation. They were designed to open markets, reduce the role of the state in the economy and encourage foreign investment, with the ultimate goal of fostering economic growth and development. Countries like Argentina, Brazil and Mexico adopted these policies, leading to significant economic reforms. Argentina, for instance, undertook massive privatisation of state-owned enterprises and liberalised its trade policies.

Initially, these reforms led to economic growth and increased foreign investment. However, in some cases, they also resulted in social discontent and economic crises. The influence of the Washington Consensus extended beyond Latin America. Eastern European countries transitioning from centrally planned economies to market economies in the post-Cold War era also adopted similar reforms. Poland, for example, implemented rapid privatisation and liberalisation, which helped stabilise its economy and set it on a path of sustained growth, though not without significant short-term social costs. This period of unchallenged influence allowed the US to mould the global economic landscape in a way that promoted its values of free markets and liberal democracy, setting the stage for the globalisation that would define the late twentieth and early twenty-first centuries.

THE ROLE OF THE US MILITARY

Throughout these decades, a critical contributing factor towards the US dollar's status as the global reserve currency that cannot be overlooked – or overstated – was the role of the US military in protecting, controlling and overseeing global supply chains, especially as it emerged victorious through a series of wars and confrontations.

During the Korean War (1950–53) and the Vietnam War (1955–75), the United States maintained military bases throughout Southeast Asia, which played a crucial role in protecting key maritime routes and ensuring regional stability.

In South Korea, the United States established Camp Humphreys, which has since grown to become the largest overseas US military base, crucial not only for the defence of South Korea but also for projecting US military power across the Pacific. American forces provide a deterrent against further aggression from North Korea and other potential adversaries.

In Japan, the US established several significant bases, including those on Okinawa, such as Kadena Air Base and Marine Corps Base Camp Smedley D. Butler. They served as critical hubs for US military operations in the Pacific, allowing for rapid deployment and logistical support for American forces throughout the region.

The stability provided by US forces facilitated the post-war economic recovery and rapid industrialisation of Japan and South Korea, helping to attract foreign investment and spur export-led growth in these countries. By the 1960s, both countries had become key players in the global economy. Japan emerged as the world's second-largest economy, and South Korea experienced an economic miracle, transforming from a war-torn nation into one of the world's leading economies by the 1980s.[15]

The US military presence in Asia also helped secure key maritime routes. The Pacific Ocean is home to some of the world's busiest shipping lanes, including routes through the South China Sea, the East China Sea and the Sea of Japan. These waters are vital for global trade, with significant amounts of oil, natural gas and manufactured goods passing through them. For instance, it is estimated that about one-third of global shipping passes through the South China Sea alone.

These trade routes remain critical to this day. The Asia–Pacific countries accounted for over 68.7 per cent of global GDP growth over the decade to 2023, with much of this economic activity relying on secure and efficient maritime trade routes.[16] The US military's role in safeguarding these routes therefore directly supports the economic prosperity not only of the region but of the world.

The same trends can be seen in Europe, North Africa and the Middle East. The establishment of the North Atlantic Treaty Organization (NATO) in 1949, initially a military alliance between the United States, Canada and several European countries – to counter the threat posed by the Soviet Union and to ensure collective security among its member states – not only enhanced the US military presence in Europe but also provided the safety and stability essential for the growth of international trade and the dominance of the US dollar.

As European economies grew, they increasingly engaged in international trade that was predominantly conducted in US dollars. NATO ensured that Western Europe remained economically aligned with the United States, thereby reinforcing the use of the dollar in international transactions.

A pivotal moment that underscored the United States' ability to protect global supply chains was the Suez Crisis in 1956. The crisis began when Egyptian president Gamal Abdel Nasser nationalised the Suez Canal, a vital waterway for global trade that connects the Mediterranean Sea to the Red Sea, providing the shortest maritime route between Europe and Asia. This action prompted a military response from the United Kingdom, France and Israel, who aimed to regain control of the canal and remove Nasser from power.

The US played a crucial diplomatic role in resolving the crisis. President Dwight D. Eisenhower, recognising the potential for broader conflict and economic disruption, exerted significant pressure on the British, French and Israeli governments to withdraw their forces from Egypt. The US leveraged its influence through various means, including the threat of economic sanctions and the use of diplomatic channels at the United Nations, where it pushed for a ceasefire and the establishment of a UN peacekeeping force to ensure the canal's reopening.

The Suez Canal was, and remains, a critical artery for the global economy. During the 1950s, it was particularly vital for the transportation of oil from the Middle East to Europe. Approximately two-thirds of Europe's oil passed through the canal at the time.[17] The disruption of this route due to the conflict threatened to severely impact global oil supplies and prices. The successful diplomatic intervention by the US ensured that the canal was quickly reopened, thereby preventing a prolonged disruption in the supply of oil and other goods.

The resolution of the Suez Crisis reinforced global trust in the US dollar in several ways. By ensuring the uninterrupted flow of oil and goods, the US helped maintain economic stability in Europe and other regions dependent on Middle Eastern oil. This stability was crucial for the post-war economic recovery and growth in Europe, which was underpinned by the use of the US dollar for international transactions.

The US's effective handling of the crisis demonstrated its capability and willingness to act as a global leader and protector of international trade routes. This leadership reinforced the perception of the US dollar as a reliable reserve currency.

The Gulf War (1990–91) further demonstrated the US military's capability to secure vital oil supply routes in the Persian Gulf. The successful operation to liberate Kuwait from Iraqi occupation ensured the continued flow of oil from the Persian Gulf to global markets. This intervention reinforced the global reliance on the US dollar for oil transactions, as peace in the region assured that oil would continue to be traded in dollars. The Persian Gulf region produces approximately one-third of the world's oil, and the smooth operation of its supply chains is indispensable for the world economy.[18]

Modern US naval operations continue to ensure the sanctity of global shipping lanes. The US Navy's presence in the Strait of Hormuz, the South China Sea and the Bab-el-Mandeb Strait, is crucial for deterring piracy, protecting against potential state-based threats and ensuring the free passage of commercial vessels. For example, the Fifth Fleet, headquartered in Bahrain, oversees operations in the Persian Gulf, the Red Sea and parts of the Indian Ocean, safeguarding the flow of oil and other critical goods. The annual value of maritime trade passing through the Strait of Hormuz alone is estimated to be around $1.2 trillion.[19]

While simplified, these historical events illustrate how the power of the US military has played a crucial role in establishing and maintaining the global reserve status of the US dollar by securing critical supply chains, such that by the end of the First Cold War the US was at the peak of its powers.

CHINA: FRIEND OR FOE?

However, as we've seen, pride comes before a fall. China, though on an upward trajectory, was not regarded as a threat throughout these decades. Instead, the US began to see the Chinese as vital economic partners, given that they supplied a wide range of goods consumed by the American middle class. As such, the US decided to integrate China into the global economic system, driven by the belief that China's inclusion in institutions like the WTO would eventually lead to its democratisation.

This was a clear miscalculation; a hubristic misjudgement. Western nations, overly confident in their own historical narratives, believed that China would follow a trajectory similar to their own: they anticipated that the emergence of a robust Chinese middle class would spark a democratic transformation, akin to the bourgeois revolutions of the seventeenth and eighteenth centuries that paved the way for liberal democracies in countries like the Netherlands, the UK, France and the US.

There was admittedly great cause for confidence in the West. By the end of the twentieth century, the Western powers had successfully navigated a number of challenges after the end of the Bretton Woods system. Throughout the 1990s, markets were stable and globalisation was rapidly accelerating, supporting strong growth. To take the US as an example, according to data from the World Bank, its GDP saw a remarkable increase from $5.9 trillion in 1990 to $9.8 trillion by the end of the decade, making up about 30 per cent of the world's total economic output.[20]

Buoyed by the end of the Cold War, the US's growth seemed unstoppable, especially when paired with its spirit of innovation in new sectors like information technology, biotechnology and aerospace. The World Intellectual Property Organization reported that the US filed over 1.2 million patents during the 1990s, more than any other country, showcasing its role as a hotbed of invention and technological advancement.[21]

What, then, could possibly go wrong? US president Bill Clinton was so confident in the dominance of American financial

architecture during this period that he not only advocated for
China's inclusion in the WTO but also made the crucial decision
to repeal the Glass–Steagall Act of 1933 with the enactment of the
Gramm–Leach–Bliley Act in 1999.[22]

This act effectively dismantled the barriers between commercial
and investment banking that had been established by the Glass–
Steagall Act in the wake of the stock market crash of 1929. To be
sure, by the late 1990s, many considered the Glass–Steagall Act to
be obsolete, as commercial banks and their affiliates had gradually
been allowed to expand their involvement in securities activities
since the 1960s. Nonetheless, the original restrictions imposed by
the Glass–Steagall Act had played a significant role in maintaining
the stability of the US financial system. Its repeal, then, marked
a new era in US financial history, one that would eventually lead
to both high financial innovation and increased vulnerability to
market fluctuations and crises. This decision was a key moment
in the liberalisation of financial services and had far-reaching
implications for the US and major economies across the world.

THE RETURN OF HISTORY: 2000–1

The dawn of the new millennium almost immediately challenged
Fukuyama's notion that history had reached its culmination in the
early 1990s. In August 2000, US equity indices reached their peak,
driven by inflated valuations of technology and internet-related
companies. This led to the bursting of the 'dot-com' bubble, which
was followed by the onset of a prolonged decline. The year 2000
also saw one of the most contentious presidential elections in US
history, with George W. Bush, the son of former president George
H. W. Bush, narrowly defeating Vice President Al Gore.

In September 2001, the terrorist attacks on the Twin Towers
in New York and the Pentagon in Washington, D.C. completely
reconfigured the geopolitical landscape, setting off America's
'Global War on Terrorism' and driving a wedge between the US
and the Middle East.

A new crisis was also brewing at home. The US Federal Reserve had responded to the fallout of the dot-com bubble in 2000 by lowering interest rates to unprecedented levels. This coincided with the deregulation of the financial sector, including the repeal of the Glass–Steagall Act. This combination of low interest rates and relaxed financial regulation proved to be a recipe for disaster, allowing banks as well as individuals to engage in increasingly complex and risky financial transactions, laying the groundwork for the global financial crisis.

THE GLOBAL FINANCIAL CRISIS OF 2007–9

The financial crisis that spanned 2007 to 2009 was one of the most severe liquidity crunches to hit global financial markets since the Great Depression. The crisis was triggered by the collapse of the American housing market, before swiftly escalating to threaten the very fabric of the international financial system. It led to the failure or near collapse of numerous key financial institutions, including major banks, mortgage lenders, insurance companies and more, and ushered in the Great Recession.

In the years leading up to 2007, many of the risky loans in question, including mortgages, had been packaged into intricate financial instruments and sold globally. This process created an intricate web of interconnected risks and exposures, magnifying the impact of the crisis. To add insult to injury, these systemic risks and their potential spillover effects had been grossly underestimated by financial institutions, rating agencies, policymakers and regulators alike. The catastrophe unfolded in stages, each exacerbating the turmoil. In 2007, there was a surge in defaults on subprime mortgages in the United States, leading to a severe liquidity crunch in the US mortgage market. Across the Atlantic, UK mortgage lender Northern Rock collapsed due to its own exposure to subprime mortgages, a lack of risk management and a securitisation strategy that involved packaging up mortgages to sell on to other banks.

This had spilled over into other sectors of the financial system by 2008, engulfing investment banks, insurance companies and money market funds. The most catastrophic events in this year included the collapse of Lehman Brothers, a global financial services firm, which marked the largest bankruptcy in US history, the bailout of American International Group (AIG), then the world's largest insurance company, and the government takeover of Fannie Mae and Freddie Mac, which together guaranteed or owned nearly half of all US mortgages.

By 2009, the crisis morphed into a global disaster, impacting financial markets and institutions across Europe, Asia and beyond. The resulting global credit crunch triggered a sharp decline in economic activity and trade, leading to rising unemployment, dwindling incomes and plummeting consumer and business confidence.

The response to the crisis by policymakers was unprecedented in its breadth and intensity. In the US, the Fed slashed its target federal funds rate – the interest rate at which depository institutions (banks and credit unions) lend reserve balances to other depository institutions overnight – to nearly zero, making borrowing cheaper for banks, which, in turn, could offer lower interest rates to consumers and businesses, and embarked on an array of unconventional monetary policies to infuse liquidity and stability into financial markets. These included purchasing vast quantities of various securities and assets.

In addition, the US government rolled out several fiscal stimulus packages to stimulate aggregate demand and provide relief to households and businesses reeling from the crisis, encompassing everything from tax cuts, extended unemployment benefits and direct payments to citizens.

On the international level, the IMF provided emergency loans to countries grappling with balance-of-payments crises and the World Bank, alongside other multilateral development banks, ramped up its lending efforts to developing countries.

Since the storm had laid bare numerous vulnerabilities within the financial system, a wave of reforms came next. In the US, the 2010 Dodd–Frank Wall Street Reform and Consumer Protection Act led to the creation of new regulatory bodies, including the Consumer

Financial Protection Bureau and the Financial Stability Oversight Council. Internationally, the Basel III framework raised capital and liquidity standards for banks, and the European Banking Union introduced mechanisms for supervisory and resolution processes for banks within the eurozone.

Still, the fallout from the crisis was vast. It led to a massive erosion of wealth for both individuals and businesses, particularly in housing and equity markets. Global wealth plummeted by an estimated $17 trillion between 2007 and 2008 alone.[23] Income inequality and poverty were exacerbated, disproportionately affecting lower-income groups through unemployment, fore-closures, bankruptcies and diminished access to credit and social services.

Public distrust towards the financial sector, as well as government establishments, grew to stratospheric levels, with disillusionment eventually giving rise to populist and 'anti-globalist' movements both in the US and Europe.

The financial crisis of 2007–9 shook global faith in the Washington Consensus – it suddenly appeared that the American Emperor had no clothes. This was the pivotal moment at which China started to move dangerously, establishing itself as a serious threat to the floundering Uncle Sam – and to Western democracies as a whole. At the same time, the advent of Bitcoin and blockchain technology in 2008 – which marked the birth of decentralised finance and represented the separation of money and state – was a direct consequence of the collapsed faith in the legacy financial systems of the twentieth century, characterised by centralisation, greed and hubris.

THE RISE OF THE MULTIPOLAR WORLD

Somewhat ironically, the global financial crisis represented a high point in US–China cooperation, while heralding a change in their dynamic. China cooperated with Western fiscal recovery efforts, but Beijing was acutely aware that US global dominance was on the wane just as its star was rising.

China began to view the US and Europe not just as partners but as 'old clients', whose perceived moral authority had been compromised. Prior to the crisis, Western leaders often lectured their Chinese counterparts on the virtues of democracy and human rights, frequently citing issues like the situation in Tibet. But the economic, social and moral turmoil unleashed by the financial crisis eroded this sense of moral high ground. In the aftermath, Chinese leaders began to assert the strengths of their autocratic regime, emphasising its efficiency and decisiveness with regard to crisis management.

Soon, they were gearing up to make a bid for supremacy, capitalising on the US's perceptibly weakened position to make new geopolitical alliances, especially in the Middle East, Southeast Asia and Latin America.

Most importantly, the Chinese have since boldly signalled that they intend to challenge the primacy of the dollar in ways no other nation has before. And why should they not? The US dollar is no longer backed by gold and no longer guaranteed a privileged position within international oil trade – so, what exactly is preserving the US dollar's reserve currency status? Simply put, the US dollar's position is upheld by the strength and creditworthiness of the US economy and its taxpayers' ability to finance its deficits. For nearly eighty years, the US has not been faced by any economic rivals willing or able to build alternative payment rails that could challenge the network effects that the Bretton Woods agreements have afforded the US dollar.

But times are changing, and, if China has anything to do with it, the baton of world leadership – the '*Weltgeist*' – will soon be moving eastward. For China, the way to achieve this would soon become obvious. Rather than transforming the monetary system, they would instead focus on transforming money itself.

2

The Dragon Awakens – the Rise of China: Historical Pride, State-Driven Enterprise and Technological Prowess

'China is a sleeping giant. Let her sleep, for when she wakes she will move the world.'
NAPOLEON BONAPARTE[1]

Over the last twenty years, new powers have come to the fore, prime among which is China. The era during which the United States stood unchallenged as the sole global superpower – an era that arguably spanned the two decades after the collapse of the Soviet Union – has ended.

The US's control over the world's financial institutions and protocols of global trade, by means of issuing the global reserve currency, is being seriously undermined. Today, we find ourselves in a world where traditional powers – the United States, major European economies and Japan, collectively represented by the G7 – are facing big challenges. This is in part driven by the emergence of rapidly growing economies, such as India, along with a group of revisionist countries like Russia, Iran and Pakistan. These nations are striving to reshape the international economic and security order that was established by Western nations after the Second World War. But one country stands out as the most formidable threat: China.

China is not only poised to overtake the United States as the world's largest economy, but it wields immense military, security and geopolitical ambition. In many ways, China's rapid development and assertive foreign policy are redefining what power – and money – means in the twenty-first century.

To resort helplessly to an overused but appropriate analogy, China's meteoric rise puts one in mind of a dragon awakening after decades of slumber. Having been out of action for a while, China has embarked on a strategic odyssey over the last decade, aiming to rebuild its historic power, overturn old grievances and re-engineer the world order in a manner that is conducive to being controlled – or at the very least heavily influenced – from Beijing. To do this, China must both upgrade the world's hardware and reprogramme its software. Ultimately, it seeks to control the global operating system of the twenty-first century and make the equipment on which it runs.

To grasp the significance of this venture, we must take a look at China's trajectory over the course of the twentieth century and early twenty-first century. In some ways similar to the US, in other ways different, China's story is one of relentless ambition as well as staggering growth. Since its 1978 economic reforms, China's average GDP growth has been over 10 per cent annually; even exceeding 13 per cent some years.[2] Where China differs most markedly from the US is in the fact that this growth has been underpinned by a totally centralised power structure that eschews individual liberties in favour of state authority. This has enabled swift, large-scale policy shifts and infrastructure development, unfettered by the constraints of democratic processes.

From the Western vantage point, this has been difficult to understand. China was previously perceived as a potential convert to liberal democracy, but, contrary to expectations, it has become ever more authoritarian and assertive on the global stage. Accordingly, the relationship between the West and China has been a rollercoaster of engagement and rebuke, encouragement and confrontation, depending on Western nations' varying estimation of China's capabilities and intentions.

And while China was content to occupy a relatively 'safe' role as the world's factory floor in the last decades of the twentieth century, it has now outgrown these parameters. Once only a supplier to key Western markets, China is now in a position to control global supply chains. It dominates the rare metals market, which is crucial for the transition to renewable energy, to name just one. But China has faced one towering obstacle to reaching the global stature of the United States: its persistent dependence on the US dollar. Its solution? To overhaul the very global financial system within which it operates – redefining money in the process.

Around 2,000 years ago, China was – relatively speaking – an economic colossus, commanding approximately 20–25 per cent of global GDP.[3] Another of the twenty-first century's emerging powers, India, was in a similar position at this time – in fact, it slightly surpassed China in its share of the global economy.[4] At this point in history, these two civilisations were economic powerhouses, driving global trade and wealth.

China's proportion of global GDP remained relatively stable for around 1,500 years – that is, until the emergence of European powers and, later, the rise of the United States in the eighteenth and nineteenth centuries, which marked the beginning of a new economic era. Western ascendancy, fuelled by industrialisation and colonial expansion, led to a gradual but significant erosion of China's and India's share of global GDP – by 1950 China and India accounted for just above 5 per cent of the total each.[5]

At this time, China was the world's most populated country with over half a billion people – 21 per cent of the estimated global population of 2.5 billion – followed by India with over 350 million people. In recent decades however, this trend has been reversed: China has seen its portion of the global GDP return towards what it was previously. Today, China accounts for 17 per cent of the global population and roughly 18 per cent of global GDP[6], with India's population accounting for 17.8% of the world's population and 3.37% of global GDP.[7] This puts into sharp relief how much the output of each country has increased in the context of their populations.

The reasons for this are multifaceted, but can be reduced to four main influences, namely, China's economic transformation, the US's engagement with China, the end of the gold standard and the acceleration of globalisation.

CHINA'S ECONOMIC TRANSFORMATION

The end of the nineteenth century and first half of the twentieth century was a hugely tumultuous period in China's history, which saw the end of dynastic imperial rule as well as numerous conflicts with regional and international powers, alongside a bitter civil war, which was eventually won by Mao Zedong, chairman of the Chinese Communist Party (CCP), who founded the People's Republic of China in 1949.

The years that followed were marked by the Chinese Cultural Revolution of 1966 to 1976, which purged any remaining capitalist elements from Chinese society. Above all, Mao wanted to enforce communist dogma and reassert his control within the CCP.

The revolution led to widespread socio-political upheaval and severe disruptions for China's economy. Educational institutions were totally shut down, and millions of people, who had been deemed 'counter-revolutionaries', faced persecution, violence and death. Young people were encouraged to challenge figures of authority, including their own parents, leading to a total breakdown of family values and of the social fabric more broadly.

This period, however, also saw the (somewhat convoluted) rise of a new Chinese leader. Deng Xiaoping, a veteran figure in the CCP, originally fell from grace during the Cultural Revolution. After being accused of taking a 'capitalist road' in 1967, he was stripped of all his positions and sent to work in a tractor factory in Jiangxi province.

Despite these hardships, Deng's political career saw a revival in the early 1970s. With the help of Premier Zhou Enlai, who recognised Deng's skills in administration – skills that the CCP desperately needed – Deng was brought back to a seat of power in 1973. Subsequently, after a brief power struggle following Mao's death in 1976, Deng emerged as the de facto leader of China by 1978.

Deng, who is often called the 'Architect of Modern China', transformed the nation, steadying the ship after the chaos of the Cultural Revolution. He spearheaded the 'Reform and Opening-Up' policy, which made China's economic strategy much more market-oriented and open to the international community, laying the foundation for modern China's economic rise. In a nutshell, Deng drove China forwards, towards modernisation and global integration.

Deng's sweeping economic reforms, which aimed to open China to the world and infuse elements of a capitalist economy into its existing socialist system, clearly worked. Instead of being bound by rigid ideological constraints, which had characterised Mao's tenure, Deng focused on what would effectively spur growth; or, in his own words, he was guided by the philosophy that 'it doesn't matter whether a cat is black or white, as long as it catches mice'.

Under Deng's pragmatic leadership, China experienced a period of robust economic expansion, with growth rates soaring to highs of 15 per cent in the early 1990s and again in the early 2000s.[8] What's more, in the five decades following the early 1970s, over 800 million people in China were lifted out of poverty (defined as living on less than $2 per day).[9] This remarkable reduction in poverty contributed to a significant shift in the global distribution of income and wealth.

RELATIONSHIP WITH THE UNITED STATES: NIXON IN CHINA

While China's opening-up was certainly driven by Deng, a key role was also played by the United States. Across the Pacific, Richard Nixon took office in 1969 and remained in power until 1974. Nixon's presidency is overshadowed by the Watergate scandal, which ultimately led to his resignation, but he also implemented several impactful and far-reaching policies, especially in foreign affairs. Among his most significant strategic manoeuvres was the reframing of the geopolitical dynamics of the Cold War, particularly the relationship between China and the Soviet Union.

At the time, the Soviet Union, under the leadership of figures like Nikita Khrushchev and later Leonid Brezhnev, was the dominant global communist power, exerting significant influence in Eastern Europe and beyond. Meanwhile, China, under Mao Zedong, was emerging as a formidable communist state, though with minimal diplomatic or economic interactions and was largely isolated from the West. In fact, the US had not recognised the People's Republic of China since its establishment in 1949.

But in 1972, Nixon and his Secretary of State, Henry Kissinger, initiated a bold diplomatic pivot. Acknowledging the strategic importance of disrupting the Sino-Soviet alliance, Nixon became the first US president to visit the People's Republic of China in a move that would change the fabric of international diplomacy forever.

By visiting emblematic sites like the Great Wall, the serene city of Hangzhou and the bustling metropolis of Shanghai, and by meeting a number of Chinese political leaders, Nixon inaugurated a new era of reconciliation and mutual understanding between two of the world's most powerful nations. Nixon's reputation as a staunch anti-communist gave him cover against potential domestic criticism that he was engaging with an overt rival. The phrase 'Nixon in China' has since come to refer to the ability of certain politicians to successfully adopt policies that seem contrary to their popular reputations. But Nixon's visit affected much more than relations between the two states: by acknowledging China as a significant actor on the world stage, Nixon reshaped the world's perceptions of and interactions with the Asian giant.

The trip was a masterstroke in the context of Cold War politics. Not only did it weaken the unified communist front represented by the Sino-Soviet alliance but it paved the way for China's gradual integration into the global economy. Moreover, Nixon's rapprochement set a precedent for subsequent US administrations to engage with Beijing.

THE ACCELERATION OF GLOBALISATION

As we've seen, another of Nixon's more memorable moves was to end the gold standard in 1971, effectively terminating the Bretton Woods system and transitioning to a new currency model marked by floating exchange rates. This facilitated greater flexibility in international trade and finance, accelerating global economic integration – arguably, it laid the groundwork for the dynamic and interconnected global economy we see today.

Soon after the end of the Bretton Woods system, global trade and economic integration stepped up a level: the protectionist policies and economic challenges of the mid-twentieth century had created a phase of relative stagnation, but countries began trading much more extensively after 1971. In fact, according to the World Bank, global trade as a percentage of global GDP increased from about 25 per cent in the early 1970s to over 60 per cent by the early twenty-first century.[10]

This all chimed with a wider move towards 'global governance'. From the 1970s, as international trade exploded, multinational corporations rose and capital – along with people and ideas – began to flow more freely across borders, it felt like the world was transitioning to a new, truly global era.

That sentiment reached its peak in the 1990s with the aforementioned 'end of history' and the Washington Consensus, which was seen as unifying previously divided nations and ideologies. The election of Bill Clinton symbolised a generational shift in leadership; moving away from the old guard, epitomised by George H. W. Bush, who had witnessed the ravages of the Second World War and the deep divisions of the Cold War. Clinton's presidency embodied a new perspective and approach to global politics and economics.

With the fall of the Berlin Wall in 1989 and the collapse of the Soviet Union in 1991, formerly closed economies began to open up to global markets. Countries in Eastern Europe, Central Asia and beyond began to integrate into the world economy.

The 1990s also witnessed breakthroughs in telecommunications and information technology, which not only played a critical role in facilitating globalisation but changed life as we know it. The advent of the internet transformed the way people and businesses operated and interacted, shrinking distances and catapulting humanity into new levels of connectedness and heights of innovation. It was in this phase of digitised globalisation that China began to emerge as a global economic powerhouse. Having embraced economic reform under Deng Xiaoping in the late 1970s, which coincided with this period of increasing global integration, China experienced rapid industrialisation and economic growth, which put it in prime position to manufacture for the world of the internet.

However, this had not yet been accompanied by democratic reform. Indeed, in Western countries it had been somewhat hoped that the Tiananmen Square massacre of 1989 – when student-led protests against CCP corruption and calls for freedom of speech were brutally crushed by military forces – would be China's Berlin Wall moment, and serve to catalyse the collapse of the authoritarian regime and initiate a transition to a more democratic government. This did not transpire, but the West still thought that such a transition might be brought about by engaging with China economically.

And so, with the US's support, China joined the WTO in 2001, fully integrating itself into the global economy as a major manufacturing and trade hub and transforming itself into the world's second-largest economy in the process.

This happened for a number of reasons. Joining the WTO required China to lower tariffs and open up its markets to imports from other countries. This increased access encouraged foreign businesses to invest in China. It also helped Chinese products gain easier routes to foreign markets. WTO membership also obliged China to reform its legal and regulatory framework to align with international standards. This included stronger protections for intellectual property rights, a move that encouraged foreign companies to share technology and engage in joint ventures within China.

The reduced tariffs and increased market access helped attract massive amounts of foreign direct investment into China's manufacturing sector. This influx of capital and technology transformed China into a global manufacturing powerhouse.

As a result of its manufacturing capabilities and global market access, China experienced a surge in exports. This not only bolstered its economic growth but solidified its role as a critical node in global supply chains.

CHINA ON THE GLOBAL STAGE

When China started opening up, many Westerners firmly believed that nurturing the country's growth might also serve to plant the seeds of democracy.

Accordingly, many had high hopes for China's accession to the WTO in 2001. The significance of this milestone extended far beyond a mere formal recognition of China as a market economy; it symbolised the international community's confidence in China's potential to interact and compete on equal footing with the world's major economic powers. It also meant that China was, in theory, committed to adhering to international trade norms and practices.

But the liberalisation and democratisation of China did not materialise. While the country became more market-oriented and globally integrated, its political system has remained autocratic, and become increasingly repressive. Nevertheless, China's trajectory on the global economic stage was now well underway. Not even the catastrophic terrorist attacks on the United States in September 2001, which affected border controls and therefore trade flows, could stem China's rapidly burgeoning influence.

In the same vein, China's growth largely continued unabated throughout the global financial crisis of 2007–9. In contrast to the US, UK and Europe, China was a bastion of relative stability and health, bolstered by Beijing's massive fiscal stimulus package, totalling an estimated $586 billion, which not only propped up their own economy but provided a crucial lifeline to global markets during a period of acute uncertainty and instability.

Arguably, the year 2008–9 represented the apotheosis of China's rapid integration into the international community, symbolised by its participation in the inaugural G20 forum held in Washington, D.C. The G20 was established in the aftermath of the financial crash as a platform for the world's largest developed and emerging economies to discuss financial markets and the world economy. The meeting has often been described as Bretton Woods II, given its focus on redrawing the world's financial architecture. China was a driving force from the start, using the forum to shape global economic policy in a way it never could before. Chinese isolationism was a thing of the past, Beijing now wanted power and influence to accompany its economic clout.

THE RISE OF XI JINPING

In March 2013, Xi Jinping rose to become the leader of the CCP. Apparently eager to tackle the widespread corruption that had become endemic within the party, Xi was heralded by the hopeful as a possible reformer. He quickly launched a sweeping anti-graft campaign to purge corrupt officials from the party ranks.

The campaign had a deeper purpose, of course, enabling Xi to dismantle his political opponents and consolidate his power. Xi's rule has quickly come to resemble the centralised and authoritarian style of governance of Mao Zedong. His decision to begin wearing the 'Mao Suit' – a modern Chinese tunic suit famously worn by the CCP founder – at significant Party events was viewed with trepidation across the world. Needless to say, the choice was more symbolic than sartorial.

Xi's tenure has strengthened the party's control over many aspects of Chinese society, including the economy, the military and the media. In contrast to the previous decades of economic and social liberalisation, Xi has sought to reinforce the CCP's role in everyday life across the country, while developing a more assertive foreign policy.

Like Mao, he has taken steps to prolong his rule. In 2018, he put forward a proposal to abolish the presidential term limits that had been a cornerstone of the country's governance framework and had ensured relatively smooth and predictable transitions of power, typically every ten years, between leaders – who were largely placeholder technocrats – ever since Mao's death. Xi had positioned himself to hold power indefinitely.

The new president for life has sought to cement his position at the helm of the CCP by ensuring that the upper ranks of the party are filled with loyalists and sycophants. He has simultaneously moved to eliminate his political rivals. In 2022 he dismissed Premier Li Keqiang in favour of loyalist Li Qiang and memorably had former president Hu Jintao forcibly removed from China's 20th National Congress, likely as an act of deliberate humiliation.

There persists a minority view that Xi could himself be replaced if China were to experience significant economic underperformance in the years to come, of which there have been ominous signs. This might be wishful thinking, but many still hope that Xi could be succeeded by a leader eager to pivot to a more liberalised method of economic growth, in the spirit of Deng Xiaoping. After all, Deng's 'Open Door Policy' catalysed China's economic boom and opened the country up to international markets – an astounding shift, given that it came directly after Mao's years of centralised control. While Xi's current position appears rock-solid, Deng's story highlights the potential for change in Chinese leadership and policy, even in a system that seems set in stone.

'CHRONIC WEAKNESS'

Under Xi's leadership, the Beijing regime has increasingly recognised – and resented – its reliance on the US dollar and the US-backed financial system as a strategic vulnerability and source of 'chronic weakness'.[11]

China's economic rise has been one of the most significant global developments of recent decades. The world's second-largest economy is central to all aspects of international trade and finance. However, its trade is still, for the most part, conducted in US dollars and therefore governed by US economic policy, bestowing significant advantages on the United States.

Despite being the top merchandise exporter in 2023 for the seventh straight year with its share of global exports accounting for 14.2 per cent,[12] China remains at the mercy of fluctuations in the value of the dollar and shifts in US monetary policy, over which it has no direct influence. These fluctuations have major implications: changes in the value of the dollar directly affect China's trade balance and, by extension, its economy. More specifically, when the dollar strengthens, Chinese exports become relatively more expensive and less competitive in the global market, impacting its trade surplus.

China's reliance on the US dollar is increasingly perceived by President Xi as a constraint on the country's economic autonomy and national sovereignty, acting as a crucial bargaining chip for the US in diplomatic and economic negotiations. Indeed, the dollar's dominance allows the US to exert influence not only through direct sanctions but also by influencing global financial standards and practices.

For example, in response to geopolitical tensions or disputes over human rights and territorial sovereignty, the US has imposed sanctions that restrict access to the international banking system. This has been seen in cases involving Iran and North Korea, where US sanctions have significantly limited their ability to engage in global commerce due to their reliance on dollar-denominated transactions. For China, this means that any number of its companies and financial institutions engaging in dollar-denominated transactions could be vulnerable to significant disruption.

Additionally, the US has used the dollar's role in international finance to influence the behaviour of multinational corporations and governments, as seen in cases when penalties were applied to foreign firms dealing with sanctioned entities, even when those dealings were lawful under the jurisdiction of those firms.

The US dollar's continued stranglehold over global trade would make it easier to isolate China economically if it made its long-desired move on Taiwan. In addition to imposing direct sanctions, the US could also limit China's access to international financial markets and cut off its financial institutions from the SWIFT banking communication system, which would severely hamper China's ability to conduct international trade and finance.

This has been underscored during the US–China trade tensions of recent years, where financial sanctions have been used as a threat in the broader geopolitical contest. Being cut off from the dollar-based system would be a disaster for China.

In response, President Xi's government has embarked on a multipronged, comprehensive strategy to elevate the international status of the Chinese yuan.

This started with establishing currency-swap agreements with various countries. These agreements allow trade and investment to take place between the countries in question without the need for conversion into US dollars. In addition, China has been promoting the yuan as a viable reserve currency in the global market; the inclusion of the yuan in the IMF's Special Drawing Rights basket in 2016 was testament to the success of these efforts, representing an endorsement of its international credibility.

However, China's capital controls and the comparative weakness of the yuan in the global financial system have continued to represent major obstacles to challenging the US dollar's global dominion.

Only a technological breakthrough of unprecedented magnitude could change this picture. This moment arrived with the realisation of the opportunity presented by the advent of digital money; money that did not rely on the Washington Consensus; money that relied only on the internet. But how is digital money any different to the money we use today? Isn't money digital already? To answer these questions, we must also ask the most important social, cultural and geopolitical question of our time: what is money?

3

The New Era of Money:
Who Controls the Ledger?

The financial world is presently undergoing a technological revolution from which there is no going back. With the advent of distributed ledger technology such as blockchain, we are entering a new era for money. A revolution that started in the private sector – or rather, on the internet – through Bitcoin and other cryptocurrencies, is now a matter of interest to governments across the world.

There are presently over 134 countries, representing 98 per cent of global GDP, researching or pursuing a Central Bank Digital Currency (CBDC).

What is the significance of this? Digital money enables novel and self-sufficient monetary paradigms to be erected almost overnight. Cryptocurrencies such as Bitcoin, Ethereum and Solana allow people all over the world to trade with each other without the need for any third parties, and have huge market capitalisations and enormous networks. They are monetary systems that have effectively been memed into existence through sophisticated computer engineering.

While it took the United States over half a century to build up the network effects from which the US dollar benefits today, it is not hard to imagine how the network effects enabled by the internet could equal the dollar's reach almost overnight.

It took Facebook less than nine years to reach one billion users. WeChat took seven years, TikTok five. Bitcoin's price has increased over 70,000 per cent since its inception in 2008, and at the time of writing its market capitalisation is over $1.36 trillion, greater than the nominal annual GDP of Indonesia and Saudi Arabia, and just shy of the annual GDP of Spain, the world's fifteenth-largest economy.[1]

So what happens when countries digitise their own money? Or when great powers conscript their allies to digitise their money? And what are the implications of how this digital money is designed, and what properties it takes on, and who is able to use it? What are CBDCs and how might they change our understanding of what money is, or should be? How should we think of them? Are they just instruments for state surveillance and control? Or could they advance financial inclusion for the billions of unbanked across the world? Might they be tools of geopolitical warfare?

The truth is, CBDCs remain an unknown quantity, capable of embodying all or none of the above, depending on how they are designed and implemented. This will, in turn, depend on the conversation society has about them – in those countries where such conversations are allowed to happen.

Digital money represents the greatest monetary paradigm shift since paper money was invented in seventh-century China, and the rise of state-issued digital money signifies the global monetary system becoming truly digital for the first time.

Up until today, we have merely *used* the internet to move money. Governments, financial institutions and individuals can all send and receive money at the click of a finger. But these clicks do not move money. They send instructions to people, asking them to move money. By contrast, digital money moves straight *through* the internet. The click of the finger moves the money directly. In short, monetary and economic value is moving into the digital age in the same way that information did in the early 2000s.

Before we consider the wider implications of this, it is first necessary to delve into the question which this gives immediate rise to, the question that is likely to be the most important of our time: what is money? Who creates it, defines it and controls it? Why is money currently undergoing a technological revolution? In other words, what's wrong – if anything – with existing forms of money?

PROPERTIES OF MONEY

Before looking at how new technologies are revolutionising money, we need to remind ourselves of the properties that define money in the first place. It is broadly agreed that the role and utility of money in commerce and finance is characterised by three key properties:

1. Store of value: the purpose of money is to retain value over time, making it a reliable repository of wealth. For money to be a good store of value, it should not be subject to rapid devaluation or loss of purchasing power. This distinguishes money from perishable goods or volatile assets. For example, if apples were used as money, their value would perish within weeks, which is why metals such as gold and silver, whose intrinsic properties are long-lasting, have been adopted as money.

2. Means of exchange: money serves as an intermediary in the exchange of goods and services, facilitating trade. This function solves the problem of the 'double coincidence of wants' inherent in barter systems, where two parties must have exactly what the other desires. If you want apples but I am only selling pears, we will not enter into voluntary trade. With money as a universal medium, individuals can sell goods or services for money and then use that money to purchase what they need or want from others.

3. Unit of account: a unit of account is something that is divisible, fungible and countable. Money provides a standard measure of value, which simplifies the process of pricing goods and services. This property means that money is a yardstick for measuring the worth of various items, allowing for easy comparison and accounting, as well as to track changes in the value of items over time. If you have $10, and apples cost $2 and oranges $3, we know how many of each you can buy. If their price goes up or

down, the amount you can buy will change. A unit of account is also necessary to enable the formulation of agreements involving debt.

We can add a fourth property to this list: money as a store of information. Every transaction made with money reflects and records an exchange of value, providing data about economic activities, trends and consumer behaviour. The flow of money within an economy can also signal its health and vitality. For instance, increased spending can indicate consumer confidence, while a lack of liquidity can signal economic distress.

GOOD MONEY

The key properties of money beg the question of what constitutes *good* money and differentiates it from bad money. There are a number of factors to consider.

Saleability across space: this refers to money's ability to be easily transported and accepted as a medium of exchange across different geographical locations.

Saleability across time: this property underscores money's capability to hold value over time, making it a reliable store of wealth for future use.

Divisibility: good money should be easily divisible into smaller units to facilitate transactions of varying sizes.

Durability: money must be durable and resistant to physical wear and tear.

Fungibility: good money is fungible, meaning each unit is interchangeable with any other unit of the same value. This property ensures that all units of money are perceived as equal and can be replaced or exchanged without any loss of value.

SOUND MONEY

Further to the properties of good money, some economists attribute additional properties to money which they deem to be *sound*.

The terms 'good money' and 'sound money' are often used interchangeably in economic discussions, but they can have slightly different connotations depending on the context.

Good money generally refers to a form of currency that efficiently serves the primary functions of money in an economy: a medium of exchange, a store of value and a unit of account. Characteristics of good money are those outlined above. Sound money, on the other hand, emphasises the stability and intrinsic value of the currency. It often implies a resistance to inflation and manipulation, and a strong backing by physical assets or a robust monetary policy. Key characteristics include:

1. Limited supply: a controlled or limited supply, often to prevent inflation.
2. Store of value: retains its value over time, making it a reliable means for saving.
3. Trust and confidence: backed by a system that instils trust in its value and stability.
4. Hard to counterfeit: strong security features to prevent counterfeiting.

In essence, while all sound money can be considered good money due to its reliable and stable nature, not all good money may be considered sound, particularly if it lacks a robust backing or is subject to inflationary pressures. Good money focuses more on the practical aspects of currency in facilitating everyday transactions, while sound money emphasises long-term stability and value preservation.

The properties of good and sound fiat money as we know it will be pertinent to our discussion of new forms of money created by new technologies.

THE LEGACY FINANCIAL SYSTEM AND ITS DISCONTENTS

We have seen how the US dollar's 'exorbitant privilege' has been upheld since 1945 by three crucial factors. Firstly, through the unmatched military and economic power of the United States. Secondly, and by virtue of this military and economic power, the *network effects* and *system of dependency* which the US dollar has entrenched over the course of eighty years, first through the establishment of the Bretton Woods system, and latterly through the petrodollar system. Thirdly, because of the lack of viable alternative payment rails – or superior forms of technology – through which international trade and finance can be conducted.

Today, these long-standing advantages are rife for technological disruption. Moreover, the technologies which are disrupting them rely on nothing but the internet to achieve their network effects, and do not require military might to be upheld.

Once economic value can travel through the internet in the same way as information does, we will have entered a new, and unrecognisable, global monetary order. The legacy financial system effectively runs on a structure of antiquated payment rails. On an international level, the majority of banks and financial institutions conduct their transactions through the Society for Worldwide Interbank Financial Telecommunication (SWIFT). It is nothing more than a messaging network, through which participants correspond about where to move money, transmitting information and instructions.

Again, people use the internet to communicate about where to move money. The internet itself is not moving any of the money.

The same is the case with all retail banking. As such, when it comes to payments, especially international transfers, the system shows its age and limitations even more starkly. Traditional methods, such as wire transfers, can be painfully slow, taking several days to clear and settle. They are also costly, with fees that can significantly erode the transfer value – this is especially burdensome for remittances sent by migrant workers back to their home countries, where every dollar counts.

According to the World Bank, the global average cost of sending $200 was around 6.20 per cent in 2023, a substantial expense for low-income workers.[2] But why is it so slow and costly? All transactions require the management of extensive personnel and are subject to a labyrinth of regulatory scrutiny designed to combat fraud and money laundering, adding layers of complexity and delay.

The reliance on physical banking infrastructure – branches, paperwork and traditional person-to-person services – though diminishing, still plays a significant role, especially in less developed or rural areas. This infrastructure is costly to maintain and often inefficient, leading to higher operational costs that can be passed on to consumers in the form of fees.

The payments and banking services industry, despite its central role in the global economy, has been slow to embrace the potential of new financial technologies. This has kept financial transactions stuck in the twentieth century, as most payments continue to rely on manual processes and protocols and fail to reflect the latest technologies.

Today's instant payments and mobile money apps only present a façade of modernity and efficiency, with user-friendly interfaces and the promise of seamless financial transactions. However, beneath the polished exteriors, these services rely on outdated, slow and error-prone mechanisms to move funds, such as transaction pre-funding, where funds are allocated in advance to facilitate the illusion of instantaneous transfers.

Such approaches mask the inherent delays of the system instead of addressing the underlying problems. Additionally, when it comes to foreign exchange transactions, many platforms impose exploitative fees and unfavourable exchange rates, further eroding the value of cross-border remittances which are crucial for millions of families worldwide.

The legacy payments sphere is also plagued by a lack of interoperability. Most mobile money and digital payment apps are designed to operate within their own ecosystems, so to speak, leading to a fragmented landscape where services are often directly incompatible with one another.

For people in developed markets, these problems are rarely encountered, if at all noticeable. Provided an internet connection is present and armed with a PIN code, there is little trouble processing payments. However, the smooth front-end user experience hides a complex and inefficient back-end infrastructure. The cost and delays are hidden within the back-end and take the shape of enormous financial institutions – which are really just storehouses of records of transactions – such as Visa and Mastercard. These systems handle trillions of dollars' worth of transactions, extracting small fees that, when accumulated, represent a significant economic burden.

This reliance on a few dominant players stifles innovation and can lead to vulnerabilities in the financial system by creating single points of failure. For instance, if a major player experiences downtime or security breaches, it can impact millions of transactions globally, as evidenced by occasional outages reported by Visa and Mastercard that temporarily halt transactions across their colossal networks.

In the developing world these problems are exacerbated. For example, in many parts of Africa and Asia, users might need to have multiple apps on their phones to make payments to different merchants or to send money to friends and family using different networks.

This fragmentation is also an obstacle to global financial inclusion, leaving vast regions of the developing world underserved, much as they were a century ago. Despite the astonishing progress that has been made in the tech world in recent decades, from clunky personal computers to ubiquitous smartphones, an estimated 1.4 billion adults worldwide remained unbanked as of 2021, according to the World Bank Group, lacking even basic bank accounts.[3] This financial exclusion has a disproportionate impact on marginalised groups, standing in the way of their personal stability and economic opportunity.

Against this backdrop, it is not surprising that new technologies are poised to disrupt the legacy banking system. As we will see, blockchain and other decentralised technologies can be used to build highly interoperable systems, allowing for seamless transactions across diverse payment platforms without the need for centralised intermediaries. To understand how, we must return to the simple but most important question of all – what is money?

MONEY AS INFORMATION

Today, we live in a world where we can communicate and share information by voice, text, images and video, free of charge in most cases, with anyone, at any time, regardless of their location, their make and model of smartphone, or their mobile network operator. This is our reality because of the exponential evolution of telecommunications technologies and their supporting infrastructure.

Unfortunately, the same cannot be said for the payments and banking services industry, which has been much slower to accept and adopt innovative technologies.

Through social apps like X (formerly Twitter) or WhatsApp, we can send information – like a message – to someone else, anywhere on the globe, and it will arrive near instantly. However, if these apps wanted to enable their users to send money to each other via the legacy financial system, their staff would need to liaise with a wide range of authorities and regulators in different jurisdictions to make it happen. As a result, cross-border transactions today still take several days to settle in the majority of cases and almost always incur a significant cost.

As Elon Musk has said, money is nothing more than an information system. In fact, it is the world's most important information system. It is the means through which we denote, store and transfer value itself. So, in a world in which we can share information at lightning speed through the internet, where is the internet for the world's money?

There are two key reasons why, to this day, the movement of money – of monetary value – lags behind the flow of other forms of information. The first is a lack of inherent trust between transacting parties that might not know each other, and the second is a lack of scalable, cost-effective, regulatory-compliant technology. These two problems are in many ways two sides of the same coin.

MONEY AS A LEDGER

Financial institutions such as retail banks exist in order to play the role of trusted intermediaries in financial transactions. Financial intermediaries need to be trusted to maintain accurate ledgers of accounts, and the trust we place in our transactions being faithfully executed is *centralised* in these institutions. At its base, money is nothing more than a ledger maintained by a trusted authority. As Lyn Alden explains in her book *Broken Money*, people often assume that money 'starts with something like coins or shells, but the story really begins before that. It begins as a ledger', which is 'a summary of transactions and is used to keep track of who owns what.'[4]

Understanding ledgers to be the ultimate definition of money is critical to grasping the transformative potential of new technologies in the realm of digital money. Financial systems hinge on the integrity of ledgers – records that track the movement of money between entities. Trusted financial intermediaries, such as banks, are tasked with maintaining the accuracy and security of these ledgers. Their primary challenge is to prevent the 'double-spend problem', a predicament unique to transactions recorded digitally.

The 'double-spend problem' refers to the risk that currency represented in digital form (not to be confused with a digital currency) can be fraudulently duplicated and spent more than once, unlike physical currency, like paper notes and coins, which inherently avoid this problem by being tangible. For instance, once a $20 bill is handed over in a transaction, it physically leaves the possession of the spender, making it impossible for that same bill to be spent again by them. By contrast, currencies represented as entries in a bank's ledger require rigorous monitoring and verification by financial institutions to ensure that once a dollar is spent, it is unequivocally marked as such, preventing any attempt to reuse the same funds for multiple transactions.

This is why we place significant trust in our financial inter-mediaries. However, this trust comes at a cost, both in terms of the fees charged for these services and the layers of bureaucracy that can slow down transactions.

In parallel, these trusted institutions bear the responsibility of ensuring that all transactions comply with legal standards. This is where Know Your Customer (KYC) protocols, Anti-Money Laundering (AML) regulations and Combating the Financing of Terrorism (CFT) checks come into play. These regulations are designed to prevent financial crimes by requiring banks to verify the identity of their clients, monitor transactions for suspicious activity and report any potentially illicit transactions.

The implementation of these regulations, however, adds layers of complexity and cost to financial transactions. International bank transfers can take several days to clear due to the need for banks to verify transaction details. Unfortunately, this work is highly necessary. The United Nations Office on Drugs and Crime estimates that between 2 per cent and 5 per cent of global GDP, or $800 billion to $2 trillion, is laundered each year, highlighting the scale of the challenge faced by financial institutions in combating financial crimes.[5]

In short, the ledgers that serve as the backbone of the global financial system – arguably the most critical ledgers in existence – remain anchored in outdated models that are cumbersome, analogue and heavily reliant on human trust and manual intervention. Not only does this introduce risks of human error, but it also limits the system's ability to scale and adapt to the demands of economic growth and global commerce, which is mostly conducted digitally. How is it still the case that information can move at the speed of light, but not money?

This brings us to the primary reason why the legacy system is ripe for disruption. Today, new technologies have been developed which are able to dispense with the double-spend problem, enable instant settlement, automatically comply with legal requirements and be interoperable – all without requiring the intervention of myriad financial institutions.

THE SEPARATION OF MONEY AND STATE:
DLT, BITCOIN AND BLOCKCHAIN

Since the dawn of the digital age, we have used computers to keep our monetary ledgers updated. When we open our mobile banking app on our smartphones, our checking and savings accounts show us some figures, displayed digitally. But this is not digital money. This figure represents *physical cash*, recorded on a ledger at our retail bank, whose own reserves are vouched for by a central bank and recorded on its own ledger.

So what is new, different or significant, about so-called distributed ledger technology (DLT)? As the name would imply, DLT enables digital ledgers to be maintained or updated in a distributed or *decentralised* way.

The concept of a distributed ledger is easy enough to understand. We simply have to imagine a set of dispersed computers whose Excel sheets all update at once when an entry is made. The key question to bear in mind is: who is able to make updates? In other words, who *controls* the distributed ledger? After all, someone, or some technology, needs to make sure that the ledger is not subject to invalid entries or changes. This begs the further question, is the ledger centralised or decentralised? If the ledger is centrally controlled, who is the controlling authority? Is it Google, or Meta; is it the Bank of England, or is it the People's Bank of China? And what would it mean for the distributed ledger to be decentralised?

Bitcoin's breakthrough was the invention of the first truly decentralised ledger. If the ledger is decentralised, it is not controlled by any single individual or entity. In a sense, it is controlled, or validated, by *everyone*. Decentralised ledgers are made possible through blockchain technology. Blockchain is a novel form of distributed ledger technology, which was first devised in 2008 by Satoshi Nakamoto, the pseudonymous inventor of Bitcoin, to power his creation.

A blockchain is a distributed, immutable and decentralised ledger across a peer-to-peer network. It consists of a chain of 'blocks', with each block containing a set of data. The blocks are linked together using cryptographic techniques and form a chronological and immutable chain of information. Using this technology, participants can confirm transactions without the need for a central clearing authority. The blockchain also serves as a store of information, including the availability of funds and the fact of transactions occurring, all of which can be verified by simple reference to the information encoded on the blockchain.

The blockchain is not stored in one place; it is distributed across multiple computers and systems within the network. These systems are called nodes. Every node has a copy of the blockchain, and every copy is updated whenever there is a validated change to the blockchain.

This system enables peer-to-peer transactions on a digital platform without the need of financial intermediaries. In doing so, Bitcoin was the first cryptographic invention to successfully overcome the double-spend problem. This means that when someone sends a quantity of bitcoin over the Bitcoin blockchain, the recipient will receive it without the need of a trusted third party. For this reason, Bitcoin is known as a *trustless* monetary system, because it does not require trust in a third party to process transactions. Crucially, the Bitcoin blockchain is 'permissionless', meaning that anyone can join it. By contrast, a permissioned blockchain is a distributed ledger that is not publicly accessible and can only be accessed by users with permission.

But why would someone trust the blockchain, or the people who keep it updated, you might ask? In a sense, such a question represents a sort of misunderstanding or category error. Transactions proceed on the basis of verification through cryptography, rather than human trust. In Bitcoin circles this is encapsulated in the phrase 'don't trust, verify'. In other words, one only needs to trust the laws of mathematics. As such, it is no exaggeration to state that the Bitcoin blockchain represents the separation of money and state by digital means, in the sense that citizens can exchange monetary value through the internet without the need for state-issued fiat money held in retail banks backed by central banks.

The rise of Bitcoin and blockchain technology was the original reason why governments and central banks felt compelled to explore their own digital currencies. As such, it is critical to understand some of its key properties, which serve to explain both its popular appeal as well as its differences and similarities with other cryptocurrencies, stablecoins and CBDCs.

Firstly, Bitcoin is a form of money that allows users the unprecedented ability to take self-custody of their digital assets. This capability empowers individuals to hold and manage their monetary value independently, free from the constraints and controls of the traditional fiat currency system, which is under the jurisdiction of state governments and central banks. This often gives rise to the objection that Bitcoin must primarily be used for illicit or illegal transactions, or that, apart from illegal goods or services, there is nothing that can be bought with Bitcoin that cannot be bought with fiat money.

The novelty of Bitcoin, however, does not reside in its properties as a currency or a means of exchange, but rather as a long-term store of value over which an individual can exercise self-custody. In effect, Bitcoin gives people the ability to hold digital property. As such, Bitcoin also represents a movement towards financial autonomy. Its potential to enable individuals to manage their wealth outside the conventional financial system heralds a new chapter in the story of personal financial sovereignty.

With regards to long-term store of value, one of the defining characteristics of Bitcoin is its inherently limited supply, a feature that sets it apart in the world of finance. The currency is ingeniously programmed to have a maximum cap of 21 million bitcoins, each divisible into 100 million smaller units known as 'satoshis'. This finite supply ensures the currency's base cannot be devalued through inflation. This makes Bitcoin an effective shield against the inflation that happens to fiat currencies, mostly due to central banks diluting their value by increasing their supply, particularly in developing economies where national currencies can experience double or even triple digit inflation. For example, the average inflation rate in Venezuela is predicted to be 150 per cent in 2025 (an improvement on the 9,033 per cent it experienced in the ten years up to 2022).[6] However, over a long enough time period even stable reserve currencies lose significant value. The US dollar has lost 99 per cent of its purchasing power since 1913.[7]

The supply of Bitcoin, however, cannot be increased. As such, it is highly saleable across time. For this reason, it is often promoted as an example of *sound* money. Critics however would argue that it is not *good* money, given that its volatility makes it a poor store of value in the short term, and it has not yet gained significant momentum as a means of exchange.

Since it is money that moves straight through the internet, it enables large amounts of value to be transacted much faster, and at a lower cost, than fiat money or gold. It would not be easy or cheap to move billions of dollars of gold across continents, but billions of dollars of Bitcoin can be moved directly between parties on different continents in a matter of minutes, if not seconds. As such, it is highly saleable across space.

Another notable aspect of the Bitcoin ledger is its self-auditing nature. The ledger undergoes an automatic audit and update every ten minutes. This continuous process of verification and updating adds another layer of security and accuracy to the system, ensuring that the data on the blockchain is always current and reliable.

A combination of these features has led a small number of countries to adopt or recognise Bitcoin as legal tender, including El Salvador and the Central African Republic. In November 2023, Argentina, whose rate of inflation in recent years has hit 142 per cent, elected an overtly pro-Bitcoin president in the form of Javier Milei. President Milei has described Bitcoin as a crucial means to return money and value creation to the private sector, and as a way in which citizens can prevent their money being debased by inflation brought about due to the excessive printing of money by the central bank.[8]

Bitcoin's novel qualities have also garnered newfound attention and respect from Wall Street. Larry Fink, the CEO of BlackRock – the world's largest asset management firm – once a sceptic of Bitcoin, has shifted his stance, now recognising Bitcoin as a 'flight to quality' asset.[9] In January 2024, the US Securities and Exchange Commission approved the incorporation of Bitcoin into exchange-traded funds in the US, enabling vast institutional adoption of the asset in what was widely seen as a watershed moment for digital currencies.

Bitcoin will doubtless play a significant role in the future of money. In the not-too-distant future, it could serve as an off-ramp or alternative option to the world's increasingly polarised and politicised fiat currencies (whether digital or not), a hedge against inflationary pressures, and effectively come to act as the internet's native form of money.

It is not within the scope of this book to discuss the various merits and risks of Bitcoin, and there are many excellent books which do this, such as Lyn Alden's *Broken Money* and *The Bitcoin Standard* by Saifedean Ammous.

However, there is an important reason why Bitcoin and other cryptocurrencies are destined to play a non-trivial role in the digital currency wars to come: precisely because they represent threats to the monopolies that state-issued currencies once held over their citizens, through which states project their economic power. As we will see, it is not just that blockchain technology inspired governments to create their own digital currencies. Governments began to create their own digital currencies because they were worried that decentralised digital assets such as Bitcoin would take the control of money out of their hands.

In an article published in *Foreign Policy* magazine in December 2021, Parag Khanna, the founder and CEO of Climate Alpha, and Balaji S. Srinivasan, an angel investor and entrepreneur, argued that 'The 21st century doesn't belong to China, the United States, or Silicon Valley. It belongs to the internet.'[10] In the essay, titled 'Great Protocol Politics', the pair write: 'We are about to enter an age of global monetary competition, where national currencies must earn their place in someone's wallet portfolio every hour of every day, even among citizens of their own countries.'[11]

In the race for the future of money, governments will not just be competing against the CBDCs of other countries. They will also be competing against Bitcoin and other cryptocurrencies on a global scale.

CRYPTOCURRENCIES

Cryptocurrencies are created using sophisticated encryption algorithms. They are designed to work as a medium of exchange through a computer network, and therefore do not require any central authority, such as a bank or a government, to uphold or maintain them. As digital currencies, they exist solely in electronic form, devoid of any physical counterpart.

They attempt to improve on the shortcomings of the legacy financial system by offering faster transaction times and lower transaction fees, among other features. Like Bitcoin, their supplies can also be algorithmically capped in order to mitigate against price inflation.

Cryptocurrencies, by virtue of their underlying blockchain technology, have the potential to revolutionise the way financial compliance is managed, especially in the domain of KYC, AML and CFT. Typically, traditional banking systems rely on extensive manual processes to enforce regulations. As we've seen, this requires significant human resources, which leads to delays and costs that trickle down to consumers.

By contrast, certain cryptocurrencies and blockchains are exploring the integration of compliance measures directly into their protocols. For instance, a blockchain could be programmed to automatically execute KYC procedures by verifying the identities of parties in a transaction against secure and encrypted user data stored on the blockchain. This could cut down the time needed for identity verification.

But who, you might ask, is doing this work? How are they performing the checks and why should we trust them? Again, such a question would represent a category error. While humans are engineering the blockchains in question, the ongoing implementations of the regulations that are being checked for, are being automatically conducted through the algorithms and cryptography encoded in the blockchain. In other words, a blockchain that conducted KYC, once set in motion, would not require any compliance officers. Blockchains can also be engineered to handle increasing amounts of data, so no more personnel are needed if the number of transactions increases.

The same is the case with AML or CFT measures. Regarding AML measures, cryptocurrencies can be designed to trace the history of transactions. Given that every transaction is recorded on a blockchain, it is possible to track the flow of funds transparently and identify patterns indicative of money laundering.

When it comes to CFT measures, blockchain technology can restrict transactions based on watchlists of individuals and entities that have been flagged for involvement in terrorist activities. Smart contracts, which are self-executing contracts with the terms of the agreement written into code, can be programmed to reject or flag transactions that involve these blacklisted addresses.

An illustrative example of these principles in action is the use of privacy-preserving zero-knowledge proofs, which allow for the verification of certain attributes (such as age or nationality) without revealing the underlying data. This could help ensure that only eligible parties participate in certain transactions without exposing their complete identity, thereby maintaining privacy while still complying with regulation. Although this might be useful for the purchase of age-restricted cinema tickets, some CFT measures might of course require the disclosure of further information about an individual, such as their provenance.

Another example is the development of blockchain-based compliance platforms by companies like Chainalysis and Elliptic, which provide tools for detecting and preventing illegal activities across multiple cryptocurrencies. They analyse blockchain data to help institutions comply with AML regulations, monitor risk and identify illicit transactions.

However, developing such technology is complex and expensive, and made more complicated by the lack of regulatory clarity surrounding cryptocurrencies in many jurisdictions. There is also resistance from those who value the anonymity of cryptocurrencies.

The cryptocurrency market is diverse and each asset has different properties: Bitcoin is known for its decentralised nature and capped supply, Ethereum is notable for its decentralised applications and role in financial services, and Ripple's XRP is recognised for its speed and cost efficiency. Cardano stands out for its decentralised, open-source blockchain, Solana for its smart contract capabilities, and Polkadot for its ability to interconnect various blockchains.

The different variations of cryptocurrency can seem mind-boggling. However, the easiest way to understand the landscape is to bear one question in mind. As with every system of money, every cryptocurrency can be understood as a ledger. So again, the key question to ask is: who controls the ledger?

As we've seen, the Bitcoin ledger is not controlled by any single individual or organisation, but is algorithmically designed to automatically update every ten minutes.

By contrast, some cryptocurrencies can be issued by private parties, such as companies and large corporations, and have their ledgers centrally controlled by those organisations. This would have been the case with the failed 'Diem' experiment undertaken by Meta (then Facebook), which would have consisted of a virtual currency whose ledger was permissioned and therefore controlled by the company.

However, cryptocurrencies can take other forms than either fully centralised or fully decentralised ledgers. To further complicate matters, it is also possible for some cryptocurrencies to be both decentralised and privately issued, as seen in the cases of Cardano's ADA and Ripple's XRP.

This means that while the control over the transaction processing and validation is distributed across a network of decentralised users, the overarching development, governance and policy decisions are in the hands of a private organisation or group that ultimately controls the ledger.

In essence, cryptocurrencies can be programmed as rules-based monetary systems, with the ability to design the specific circulation of currency, the level of their supply cap, the frequency with which their supply is increased (if at all) and the degree to which they are decentralised through multiple 'nodes' that can audit their transaction histories.

With such properties it is not difficult to see how government-issued fiat currencies are being challenged by the private sector.

Cryptocurrencies represent money reimagined through the power of computing. A popular internet meme – recently shared on X by Elon Musk – serves to illustrate the manner in which the properties of legacy fiat money pale in comparison to money that can be digitally engineered:

> These scam coins are just getting crazy. Someone just tried to sell me the following coin:
>
> – 27 trillion in circulation
> – Owes 34 trillion in debt
> – Unlimited supply cap
> – Only 1 node
> – 25% of supply minted in the last 6 months
> – 1% of holders own 30%
>
> Just joking. That's the US dollar.[12]

STABLECOINS

Stablecoins are designed to offer stability in an otherwise volatile cryptocurrency market. Unlike typical cryptocurrencies, which are known for their price fluctuations, stablecoins aim to maintain a consistent value over time.

They achieve this by being backed by a reserve of assets. These assets can range from fiat currencies like the US dollar or the euro, to commodities like gold or even other cryptocurrencies. The idea is to peg the value of the stablecoin to these underlying assets, thereby stabilising its price.

For example, a stablecoin might be designed to maintain a 1:1 value ratio with the US dollar, meaning one unit of the stablecoin should always be worth one US dollar. This linkage is maintained through various mechanisms, including holding reserves of the backing asset or using algorithmic formulas that automatically adjust the supply of the stablecoin in response to changes in its market value.

This stability sets stablecoins apart from traditional crypto-currencies which are not backed by physical assets and whose values are determined by market dynamics. The price of these cryptocurrencies can be highly volatile, which makes them less suitable for everyday transactions like buying goods or services.

Stablecoins offer a middle ground, combining the benefits of cryptocurrencies – such as fast cross-border transactions – with the stability of traditional fiat currencies. This unique combination makes them an attractive option for individuals and businesses looking for an efficient and reliable digital payment method.

The most significant stablecoins by market capitalisation, such as Tether (USDT), USDCoin and Dai, are all pegged to the US dollar. USDT, for instance, has a market capitalisation of $83 billion and USDCoin, the second largest, stands at a $28 billion market cap. In fact, the vast majority of stablecoins in the global market are pegged to the US dollar – over 99 per cent are dollar denominated – so are tied directly or indirectly to a bank in the United States. They are backed by reserve assets, including cash, cash equivalents and, in some cases, short-term US Treasuries.

Dollar-based stablecoins are dominant because of the dollar's global reserve status. The widespread use and trust in the US dollar make it a logical choice for stablecoins aiming for constancy and widespread adoption.

Stablecoins are particularly useful for citizens living in countries with volatile currencies or high inflation, such as Argentina or Venezuela. Any citizen in these countries with a smartphone can access stablecoins – so can effectively harness the internet and blockchains to access the US banking system. However, for this reason, US dollar denominated stablecoins are also highly centralised – since the US government has the power to shut down such a stablecoin at any time by freezing the US dollar assets held by the stablecoin issuer at a commercial bank. In other words, the US banks and the US government still ultimately control the ledger in these cases.

In the broader economic context, stablecoins have the potential to support state-issued currencies in the face of competition from other cryptocurrencies. They can act as a bridge between the traditional financial system and the emerging digital economy, facilitating a smoother transition for users and businesses accustomed to dealing in fiat currencies. This is because stablecoins can be integrated into existing financial infrastructures, providing a digital currency option that aligns with regulatory standards and economic policies. This integration could help central banks and financial authorities to better understand and engage with the digital currency space, allowing them to leverage the benefits of blockchain technology while maintaining control over monetary policy.

A new variation on stablecoins beginning to be discussed in policy circles are 'flatcoins'. These differ from most stablecoins that are ostensibly pegged to one asset. Instead, flatcoins are backed by a basket of different assets that aim to produce returns in line with a goal such as hedging against inflation. Flatcoins reflect the value of their underlying basket of assets. As economist Professor Nouriel Roubini outlined in the *Financial Times* in December 2023, flatcoins are 'programmable securities backed by a portfolio of assets that protect against a variety of risks. These include inflation, currency debasement, and potential de-dollarisation, as well as political and geopolitical instability and climate change.'[13]

Effectively, a flatcoin could do a social good by providing investment in assets that ameliorate or seek to offset the effects of challenges such as climate change, while also hedging against other risks like inflation.

The new era for money represents a new dawn for mankind. Thanks to cryptography, blockchain technology and the power of network effects, we are now in a position to bring money into the twenty-first century by digitally engineering our monetary systems. We can make money move faster and more cheaply, yes. But we can also bring money to life and endow it with new properties, even new dimensions. Digital money can not only be good money, and sound money, it can be *smart* money. So far, this great reimagining has largely been undertaken by the private sector. But what can we expect to happen when governments jump on the bandwagon, and try to turn their national currencies into smart money, too?

4

Smart Money:
Central Bank Digital Currencies

What role cryptocurrencies will play in the future of money remains unclear. However, what is almost certain is that Bitcoin, private cryptocurrencies and stablecoins will not dispense with governments and national currencies.

In July 2021, the *Financial Times*'s chief economic commentator Martin Wolf published an article titled, 'The time to embrace central bank digital currencies is now'.[1] Commenting on Bitcoin, Wolf argued that 'the state cannot and must not abandon its role in ensuring the safety and usability of money. The idea that it should is a libertarian fantasy.' He is right. Bitcoin and other cryptocurrencies are here to stay – but so are nation states, governments and national currencies.

The advent of Bitcoin and blockchain technology awakened governments and central banks around the world to the possibility of digitising their national currencies, and to the manifold technological, economic and geopolitical opportunities – and threats – that would arise from doing so.

Central bank digital currencies are digital equivalents of state-issued physical cash. They are tools and instruments of the state. A digital yuan, pound or dollar would sit in a wallet on your smartphone, much like a digital train ticket or concert ticket.

Rather than representing physical cash sitting in a retail or commercial bank, the digital dollar on your phone would be a direct liability of the central bank (in this case the US Federal Reserve), denoted by a specific and unique code or number, which would be recorded on a ledger controlled by the Fed. Unlike using a debit card, processing a transaction using a CBDC would not kick off a lengthy process of checks and debits through the legacy banking system. It would bypass the banking system entirely. It would be money that passes directly between smartphones in the same way that paper notes pass between hands.

However, there is of course an important difference between the two. By definition, and as the name implies, a CBDC will involve a centralised ledger maintained and controlled by a country's central bank. A decentralised CBDC would of course not only defy its namesake, but run counter to the concept of a central bank. So, whereas cash transactions are anonymous and unbeknownst to the central bank, a transaction using a CBDC – being a direct liability of the central bank – would instantly update the central bank's ledger.

This does not necessarily mean that the central bank would know everything about your transaction – this comes down to policy and design. Cash is known as a bearer instrument, meaning that its issuing party does not have information about its owner. There are means and technologies presently in development through which CBDCs could be made to resemble bearer instruments. For example, while it might not be possible to avoid the ledger being updated with the fact of a transaction having occurred, it could be made such that no further information about the transaction is recorded. In this case, the central bank's record would reflect the fact that some digital money – embodied in a piece of code – had changed hands, but it would not show between whom the transaction had taken place or what had been purchased.

One way of making CBDCs resemble bearer instruments would be by cooperating with retail and commercial banks. It is likely that CBDCs will operate a two-tier distribution system, whereby the central bank issues digital currency to retail and commercial banks, which then distribute it to the public. In this system, private bank-issued stable coins will act as an intermediary, facilitating the use of digital currency by the general public. This means that information about transactions would be the remit of retail and commercial banks, as they are with digital payments today, rather than central banks.

Before diving further into such detail, let's start from the beginning. What are the reasons for central banks wanting to introduce CBDCs in the first place? And what might be the new properties of state-issued digital money, from the mundane to the profound, the sacred and the profane?

THE DECLINE OF CASH

Over the past few decades, the convenience and efficiency of digital payments has surged, thanks to the proliferation of online banking, mobile payment apps and e-commerce platforms. According to the 2022 Federal Reserve Payments Study, between 2018 and 2021, the value of these payments in the United States grew by 9.5 per cent annually, reaching $128.51 trillion.[2]

By 2023, non-cash transaction volumes reached approximately 1.3 trillion transactions worldwide and are projected to increase to 2.3 trillion by 2027, growing at a rate of 15 per cent annually.[3] This growth is largely driven by new digital payment methods such as instant payments, e-money, digital wallets, account-to-account and QR code payments, according to Capgemini.

Moreover, the digital payments landscape is becoming increasingly important in various regions with varied growth rates. For instance, the Asia Pacific region is seeing the fastest growth, with digital payments expected to increase by 19.8 per cent by 2027.[4] In comparison, Europe and North America are experiencing growth rates of 10.7 per cent and 6.5 per cent, respectively.[5]

The advent of cryptocurrencies has further accelerated this trend, appealing to users who value privacy, lower transaction fees and independence from government-controlled monetary systems. As of 2024, the global cryptocurrency market cap had soared to over $2 trillion, underscoring the vast scale of digital currency adoption.[6]

This shift has profound implications for the role of cash in the economy. Cash, as the only direct liability of a central bank, symbolises a physical claim on the reserves of the central bank. In contrast, the balances we see in our bank accounts are essentially promises from retail or commercial banks to pay the equivalent in cash upon demand. However, with the majority of transactions now executed digitally via cards and electronic transfers, the physical money that represents a direct claim on central bank reserves is becoming an increasingly smaller fraction of the total money supply in circulation.

This is one of the more humdrum and practical reasons why the concept of CBDCs have gained traction. As a digital form of a country's fiat currency, issued and regulated by the central bank, they would help central banks retain oversight over more of the money in circulation, while blending the efficiency and convenience of digital transactions with the reliability and regulatory oversight of traditional banking systems.

By introducing CBDCs, central banks see themselves providing a safe, stable alternative to the private banking ecosystem, ensuring that the public has access to a form of money that is a direct liability of the central bank, even as the use of physical cash declines.

INSTANT SETTLEMENT

Some potential benefits of CBDCs, like instant settlement, seem like no-brainers, especially in the realm of cross-border payments. This groundbreaking capability is a sharp departure from the slow and cumbersome process characteristic of the existing international banking system we've looked at.

CBDCs leverage blockchain or other distributed ledger technologies that allow for the instantaneous transfer of value – the direct exchange of digital currency between parties without the need for intermediaries.

For example, if a business in Japan wants to pay a supplier in France, a CBDC system could enable the payment to be transferred directly and instantly, without routing through multiple banks and countries.

Instant settlement of transactions, particularly cross-border ones, offers several benefits. Firstly, it greatly reduces counterparty risk – the risk that one party in the transaction fails to meet their obligations after the other party has already done so. This risk is prevalent in traditional systems due to the time lag between the initiation and completion of transactions.

Additionally, the efficiency of instant settlement can foster better cash-flow management for businesses and individuals. In the legacy banking system, the uncertainty and variability in transaction times can complicate financial planning and liquidity management. The speed and predictability of CBDC transactions can improve financial planning and reduce the need for businesses to hold large cash buffers.

For developing countries or regions with less sophisticated banking infrastructure, CBDCs can be particularly transformative. They offer an opportunity to leapfrog traditional banking systems, providing access to fast and affordable international payment mechanisms.

RETAIL VERSUS WHOLESALE CBDCS

The question of cross-border settlements touches on an important distinction – that between retail and wholesale CBDCs.

Retail CBDCs are designed for use by the general public, encompassing everyday transactions and financial interactions typical for individuals and businesses. They are the digital equivalent of the banknotes and coins in our wallets.

On the other hand, wholesale CBDCs are restricted to financial institutions that hold reserve deposits with a central bank. A wholesale CBDC would be used for large-value interbank transfers and related wholesale financial activities, such as the settlement of interbank payments and financial asset transactions. The focus here is taking advantage of the benefits of instant settlement on a macro-scale.

Retail CBDCs have the potential to fundamentally change how everyday consumers interact with money; possibly even altering the role of traditional banks in the financial system. Wholesale CBDCs, conversely, are more about refining and enhancing existing financial infrastructure, largely invisible to the average consumer but crucial for the stability and efficiency of financial markets.

Digital currencies for consumers could be transformative in promoting financial inclusion. For individuals who are unbanked or underbanked, a retail CBDC provides a gateway to participate in the digital economy. For example, those without access to traditional banking due to geographical barriers or economic constraints could still engage in online transactions, receive direct government benefits and enjoy reduced transaction costs.

In countries like Kenya, digital currency systems like M-Pesa have already revolutionised financial inclusion by enabling mobile phone-based money transfers, showing the potential impact CBDCs could have on a larger scale. Moreover, a retail CBDC system could also feature simplified registration processes adhering to KYC norms, ensuring security while remaining accessible to those without formal identification or credit history.

However, retail CBDCs also pose notable risks, particularly concerning privacy. Being inherently digital and possibly leveraging blockchain technology, CBDCs present a double-edged sword in terms of transaction traceability and transparency. On the one hand, they could be a boon for regulators and law enforcement agencies, helping curb financial crimes like money laundering and fraud.

On the other hand, this transparency raises significant concerns regarding individual privacy. Imagine a scenario where every transaction you make with a CBDC is like leaving a digital footprint, visible to the central bank or government authorities. This isn't just about the big purchases; it's about every coffee, every online subscription, every penny spent or saved. Such pervasive oversight and data collection could paint a detailed picture of a person's financial life, opening the door to financial surveillance. This raises crucial questions about the delicate balance between ensuring security and upholding the right to individual privacy. It's a tightrope walk for policymakers and technologists designing CBDC systems. Technologies are being developed that safeguard the privacy of citizens. These include the implementation of privacy-enhancing technologies that anonymise transactions, or tiered levels of privacy where smaller, routine transactions remain private, while larger transactions are subject to scrutiny. The path forward requires careful consideration and innovative solutions, and will probably involve a fair amount of debate and compromise to ensure that it aligns with the values and expectations of a society increasingly concerned with digital privacy.

COMMERCIAL BANK DISRUPTION

There is also significant concern that retail CBDCs might destabilise the traditional banking sector, particularly the role of commercial banks.

Commercial banks are like the crucial connectors in the economy's circuit board. They gather savings from individuals and businesses, and then channel these funds into loans for those needing capital. This process is the lifeblood of economic growth and credit creation.

Enter CBDCs, and the plot thickens. Retail CBDCs would offer a direct line between consumers and the central bank, bypassing commercial banks. Imagine if people and businesses start preferring to park their funds in digital currency directly with the central bank, because it's perceived as a more stable and safer vault. This shift could trigger a significant movement of capital away from commercial banks, draining their primary source of loanable funds.

Commercial banks could find their lending capacity crippled. Less money to lend would lead to a scarcity of credit, making borrowing more expensive. In this scenario, economic growth could take a hit, as businesses and individuals struggle to access the funds they need to invest, expand and consume.

There is also the risk of a 'digital bank run'. This would be like a traditional bank run, but turbocharged by the speed and ease of digital transactions. In times of economic uncertainty, if people start seeing the central bank as a safer haven for their deposits, even a small scare could trigger a mass exodus of funds from commercial banks to CBDCs. This rapid shift could amplify financial instability, especially during economic downturns.

The key for policymakers is to navigate these waters carefully, ensuring that the role of CBDCs complements rather than upends the existing financial ecosystem.

NEW DIMENSIONS: PROGRAMMABILITY

However, the real elephant in the room when it comes to CBDCs, especially retail CBDCs, is the concept of 'programmability'. This is a catch-all term about the fact that in turning digital, state-issued money does not so much take on new properties, as entirely new dimensions.

Programmability in the context of CBDCs refers to the ability to embed specific software code into the currency, which allows it to execute certain functions automatically. This means that a CBDC can be programmed to carry out transactions based on predefined conditions, effectively enabling smart contracts. For example, CBDCs could be programmed to release or transfer funds at a specific future date, without any manual intervention. Salaries or government benefits could be distributed automatically at set times.

CBDCs could be designed to comply automatically with regulations such as AML rules or tax requirements. For instance, transactions above a certain threshold could be programmed to require additional verification checks or to be reported automatically to relevant authorities.

CBDCs could also be restricted to transact within specific geographical boundaries. This could be useful in regional economic programmes or for controlling capital flows in and out of a country.

For social welfare programmes, CBDCs can ensure that funds are spent only on necessities such as food, housing or education. This could be achieved by programming the currency to be acceptable only for certain types of transactions or by approved vendors.

However, the scope of programmability extends far beyond this, and we are only beginning to apprehend what might be possible. As with the creation of the iPhone, it was not initially clear what range of applications would eventually evolve to work on it. The same is the case with CBDCs, but we can start to make some educated guesses. We might divide this outlook between 'micro-programmability' – for transactions between users of retail CBDCs such as consumers and businesses – and 'macro-programmability' – for transactions between financial institutions and governments and central banks.

MICRO-PROGRAMMABILITY

Programmability allows for fascinating as well as potentially terrifying applications. However, it is the latter that have captured the imagination of many in the West and caused retail CBDCs to become a bogeyman in the public imagination.

Undeniably, the programmability of CBDCs opens doors to concerning possibilities. In theory, governments could programme currencies to control spending, effectively dictating where, when and how individuals can spend their money, leading to significant intrusions into personal freedom.

Another alarming prospect is that of real-time taxation, mirroring real-time information apps on iPhones. Imagine a scenario where taxes are instantly deducted at the point of every transaction. While efficient, this would represent an invasive overreach, with the government having immediate access to a portion of every financial transaction.

The most unsettling possibility, perhaps, is the use of CBDCs in a social credit system. This could mirror the functionality of social rating apps but with far more dystopian consequences. Financial rewards or penalties could be automatically applied based on a person's behaviour as judged by the state, tying financial freedom to government-approved behaviour.

For example, a person's score could determine their eligibility for certain financial services, like low-interest loans or high-yield savings accounts, basing economic opportunities on state-determined criteria. Scores might affect a person's ability to rent a flat, find a job, run for public office, work in sensitive or governmental positions, or participate in state-funded programmes, linking political and social trustworthiness with economic capability. Those with higher social credit scores might be granted priority in public housing, educational opportunities or even healthcare services, creating a tiered system of access based on government-assessed behaviours.

Fears of such Kafkaesque outcomes dominate the present conversation about CBDCs, while the potentially beneficial aspects of programmability have either remained undocumented or been confined to enthusiastic reports consumed only by central bankers and management consultants.

In terms of practical, pragmatic benefits, programmability allows for the automation of payments upon the fulfilment of certain conditions. For example, in a business contract, payment can be programmed to be released only when the goods are delivered, or a service is completed. This automatic execution reduces the need for intermediaries, simplifies transaction processes, and minimises the risk of non-payment.

Programmable CBDCs can also play a crucial role in enhancing financial inclusion. By simplifying the process of distributing funds, especially to unbanked or underbanked populations, CBDCs can provide easier access to financial resources and government assistance programmes.

MACRO-PROGRAMMABILITY

But how might the programmable – or 'smart' – features of CBDCs play out on an international scale?

For a start, programmable CBDCs could revolutionise how aid, development and investment funds are distributed and used. Donor and investor countries could issue funds that are programmed to be spent only on specific projects, such as infrastructure development, education or healthcare initiatives. For example, in July 2024, Kazakhstan announced the launch of a pilot project to pay for the construction of a rail line to China using its programmable CBDC, the digital teng. By 'marking' various steps along the supply chain, the Kazakhs can ensure that the money is only disbursed upon completion of the work, and only allocated to the intended recipients, serving to guard against potential corruption and embezzlement.[7]

On a deeper level, CBDCs could offer a revolutionary tool for governments to micromanage and direct the flow of international trade and finance with an unprecedented level of precision, for both good and ill.

By creating CBDCs with built-in rules and conditions for their use, states can directly influence which goods and services are traded, and with whom, enhancing their ability to enforce trade agreements and strategic economic policies.

For example, the European Union, with its Green Deal, could leverage a programmable euro to facilitate trade in green technologies among member states and approved partners, ensuring that certain trades using the digital euro directly support the EU's climate goals. A specific bucket of digital euros (or 'green euros') could also be set aside for climate objectives and programmed to ensure they can only be spent on specific green projects. This approach could boost the bloc's transition to a sustainable economy while promoting intra-bloc trade.

However, the strategic use of programmable CBDCs could serve to break up global supply chains. By favouring trade with certain countries through the programmable features of a CBDC, governments could reinforce insulated economic blocs.

This could further entrench distinct economic and geopolitical spheres, each with its own preferred trading partners and financial systems. The long-term effects could mirror the First Cold War era's economic divisions, where trade was heavily influenced by political alliances rather than market dynamics or efficiency.

For instance, if major economies like the United States, China and the European Union each developed their own programmable

CBDCs with different sets of rules and trading preferences, global companies would need to navigate a complex web of currency systems and regulations. This would hugely complicate international business operations, increase costs and slow down the globalisation process that has characterised the world economy over the past few decades.

On the plus side, smart contracts embedded in CBDC transactions can act as automated compliance checks for international trade. A practical example might be the cobalt mining industry in the Democratic Republic of Congo, which accounts for more than 60 per cent of the world's cobalt supply, a metal essential for lithium-ion batteries.[8] Reports of child labour and unsafe working conditions have marred the cobalt supply chain. A programmable CBDC could ensure that payments for cobalt are released only when mining operations are certified to be free of child labour and meet safety standards, providing a direct financial incentive for ethical mining practices.

Conversely, this could also open up ways through which to ring-fence supply chains and exacerbate monopolies over critical natural resources. By utilising programmable CBDCs, countries with abundant natural resources have a unique opportunity to not only streamline and secure their supply chains but also to exert a greater degree of strategic influence over global commodity markets.

Lithium, often referred to as 'white gold' due to its importance in the production of electric vehicle (EV) batteries, presents a case in point. With countries like Australia, Chile and Argentina leading in lithium production, the establishment of a CBDC network could enable these nations to offer preferential trade terms to allies. Given the projected increase in demand for lithium, which is expected to grow by over 40 per cent in the next few years according to Benchmark Mineral Intelligence,[9] such strategic use of programmable CBDCs could significantly impact the global EV market.

While such practices are possible to promote with existing paper fiat currency, digital money would increase the likelihood that trade practices were baked into the algorithms of the currency being used, rather than relying on human trust.

Programmable CBDCs could also be weaponised as tools of geopolitical leverage. Consider the hypothetical scenario where Country A issues a programmable CBDC for purchasing its critical exports, such as oil or rare minerals. The CBDC could be programmed to be non-transferable to certain jurisdictions, effectively allowing Country A to control which economies have access to its critical exports. Similarly, during a geopolitical dispute, Country B could programme its CBDC used for international aid to be unusable for purchasing goods or services from Country C, in order to exert economic pressure.

On the sanctions front, programmable CBDCs could act as a powerful tool for geopolitical strategy. By programming a CBDC to automatically block transactions with entities or countries on sanction lists, governments can ensure immediate compliance with international sanctions without relying on the traditional banking system's slower, more cumbersome processes. The question is, which countries will have this ability?

When money becomes digital – when it becomes *smart* – it takes on new properties, even new dimensions. Money is no longer merely a store of value, a means of exchange and a unit of account. In the hands of the state, digital money can become a tool of surveillance, a method of control and a weapon of geopolitical warfare. However, it might also become an instrument for the enhancement of financial inclusion or a means through which to enforce ethical trading practices.

These will be determined by design and policy decisions. But more importantly, they will be determined by the answer to the question we started with. Who is going to control the ledger?

THE DIGITAL YUAN: CHINA STARTS THE RACE
FOR THE FUTURE OF MONEY

Beijing has long been frustrated by the stark contrast between China's robust contribution to global GDP and the relatively modest role of the yuan on the world stage, in terms of international trade and foreign reserves. This discrepancy has hindered China's ambition to project its economic influence overseas, making Beijing feel it is punching under its weight.

Remarkably, China exceeds the United States in its contribution to GDP expressed as purchasing power parity – the exchange rate at which the yuan would be converted into the dollar to purchase the same basket of goods – standing at about 19 per cent compared to 15.5 per cent, according to the IMF.[10] This suggests that China's economy can produce and consume more goods and services compared to the US, taking into account the cost of living and price levels in both countries.

However, the dominance of the US dollar in global trade means that China is not realising this newly accrued influence in practical terms. The Chinese yuan is used for just 5.8 per cent of global payments, whereas the US dollar is involved in 88–90 per cent of foreign exchange transactions.[11] Three-quarters of Asia–Pacific trade is denominated in US dollars, according to the Bank for International Settlements.[12] Moreover, the dollar makes up a staggering 59 per cent of global foreign exchange reserves. By contrast, the Chinese yuan represents just 2.69 per cent.[13]

Even in highly developed markets with strong currencies such as the UK, a significant portion of the country's foreign exchange transactions are carried out in dollars due to its stability and widespread acceptance.

The Chinese government has been forced to recognise that the yuan is unlikely to challenge the dominance of the US dollar in the current global financial system unless China completely removes its capital controls. However, this would be a hugely risky move, potentially triggering a substantial outflow of capital, which could have serious repercussions for China's economic stability.

The CCP knows that it cannot beat the US dollar at its own game, namely by flooding international capital markets with the yuan and running large current account deficits. To challenge the dollar, China would have to play an entirely new game, with new sets of rules.

The invention of Bitcoin represented a threat to governments around the world. By eliminating the need for financial inter-mediaries and centralised issuers, Bitcoin effectively facilitated the separation of money and state, undermining and potentially removing the role of governments in monetary affairs.

However, as we've seen, the advent of money which exists solely in digital form also awakened governments to the possibility of harnessing new technologies to bring their national currencies into the digital era. China was the first major power to apprehend the potential magnitude of this development, and started working on a digital version of its national currency in 2014.

The CCP intuited that this was the answer to its struggles against the US dollar. If money existed in a purely digital form, as opposed to paper, then money would move straight *through* the internet, directly between transacting parties, removing the need for the intervention of myriad financial institutions which remained at the mercy of the US government. With digital money, China could entirely circumvent the financial protocols and institutions through which the dollar maintained its status as the undisputed global reserve currency, and build entirely new ones.

Money could be moved directly between transacting parties – such as from the Chinese central bank to the Nigerian central bank, or from a Chinese chip manufacturer to a Congolese rare metals company – without having to worry about the approval of the SWIFT messaging system, the consent of an international commercial bank or international sanctions enforced through the legacy banking system. Indeed, if it won the race for the future of digital money, China could be the one imposing the sanctions.

The advent of digital money didn't just signify a new chapter in global finance; it meant an entirely new book – one in which China could not only participate but actually set the rules, if it acted swiftly.

China grasped that the race to define the future of money wasn't just about making technological upgrades; it was a geopolitical battleground with monumental stakes. Winning this race would mean seizing the baton of global dominance – indeed, the *Weltgeist* – from the United States.

NON-OVERLAPPING MAGISTERIA

As we've seen, most people consider the money on their mobile apps or the devices which we use to pay for items by tapping a card or punching numbers into websites, to constitute 'digital' money. But it isn't really. Truly digital money – money which *is* digital, rather than paper money that is digitally represented – is an entirely different beast. It is money that exists as computer code.

The payment rails on which digital money runs will therefore be entirely different to the payment rails of paper money. Indeed, the old and new payment rails do not need to overlap at all, becoming 'non-overlapping magisteria', to borrow a term from palaeontologist Stephen J. Gould.[14]

Gould used this concept to talk about the spheres of science and religion, but we can apply this analogy to the situation at hand: the institutional, dollar-based payment rails of the twentieth century represent the old 'religion', which is currently being disrupted by the new 'science' of digital money that runs straight through the internet.

China bet that the world would eventually move on to digital money, and that this would require new payment rails; digital payment rails. Beijing realised that if it built the world's digital payment rails, it could exercise a great degree of control over the future of money. For the past decade, Beijing has been figuring out how to do this, starting with the development of its own digital currency.

GENESIS

The digital yuan, also known as the electronic Chinese yuan, e-CNY, digital renminbi or digital RMB, is the result of these efforts: a CBDC issued by the People's Bank of China (PBOC).[15]

The story of its digital genesis is certainly not straightforward. The Chinese have invested a gargantuan amount of time, energy and money to get to this point – almost ten years of research and development, trial and error.

The origins of the digital yuan date from 2014, when PBOC Governor Zhou Xiaochuan assigned a team of 996 personnel to the project. In its initial research phase, the PBOC delved into the mechanics of digitising the national currency.

In 2016, the project was taken to the next level with the establishment of the Digital Currency Institute within the PBOC, tasked with developing a proof of concept. This meant demonstrating how the digital yuan would integrate into existing financial infrastructure while navigating a labyrinth of technical complexities and security concerns.

In 2017, the State Council, the chief administrative authority of China, formally endorsed the development of the digital yuan, giving the PBOC the greenlight to tackle the actual design and development of the currency.

The PBOC formed partnerships with retail and commercial banks, technology firms and companies from the gig economy, such as ride-hailing services and food delivery platforms. These collaborations were crucial in assessing the digital yuan's functionality in a wide range of transactions, from large-scale commercial dealings to everyday consumer purchases. User feedback provided a wealth of data which was used to fine-tune the digital yuan to suit different technical contexts and test user preferences.

Finally, the digital yuan was tested in a series of pilots rolled out across selected regions in China, providing real-world insights into its use, performance and acceptance by the general public. The first trial was launched in April 2020 in four strategically chosen cities, Shenzhen, Suzhou, Xiong'an and Chengdu, whose varied demographics, technological infrastructure and economic significance made them useful testbeds. The PBOC encouraged user engagement via invitations and cash incentives.

The pilots quickly witnessed impressive uptake. By August 2021, the digital yuan had been rolled out to more than twenty-eight cities and national areas, including major economic and political centres like Shanghai, Beijing, Guangzhou and Tianjin. By October 2021, 123 million individual wallets and 9.2 million corporate wallets had been opened with a total transaction value of 56 billion yuan – equivalent to approximately $8.8 billion.[16]

Though adoption rates have since been relatively low, at least in the context of the country's population, the digital yuan is still by far the largest CBDC pilot in the world by both the amount of currency in circulation (13.61 billion yuan) and the number of users (260 million wallets), according to 2024 Atlantic Council estimates.[17]

The decade of research and development that led to this point was arduous, but progress was made quickly, thanks to an almost unlimited flow of funding, the most advanced technological infrastructure known to man, a world-beating group of technologists and the unrelenting determination of the autocratic state, which didn't need to debate the merits of its mission in parliament or compel the public to agree with the project of digital money.

CHALLENGES

To study China's journey is to realise how far behind the United States and the West have fallen in the race for the future of money. A huge amount of capital – economic, human and intellectual – is required to pull off this kind of project and, as things stand, it doesn't appear that the West is willing or able to make a similar level of investment.

Integrating a state-of-the-art digital currency into the world's second-largest economy did not happen overnight. The decade-long odyssey to develop China's digital yuan was marked by a series of intricate technological challenges.

Constructing robust and scalable digital infrastructure capable of handling the immense volume and variety of transactions across China took a Herculean effort. Given the size of China's population and economy, the system needed to be able to process a colossal number of transactions quickly and without failure.

According to some estimates, transactions amounting to 1.8 trillion of digital yuan ($250 billion) were conducted in just the first six months of 2023, which represents an eighteen-fold increase from the roughly 100 billion yuan that passed through the system between the digital currency's launch in 2019 and August 2022.[18]

The digital yuan also had to be made robust against cyber-attacks, fraud and counterfeiting, while remaining compatible with existing financial and banking systems, both domestically and internationally. The system had to be able to coexist with existing payment methods, including mobile payment platforms that are already deeply entrenched in the Chinese economy, such as Alipay and WeChat Pay.

The PBOC was also tasked with crafting a system that could facilitate not only domestic transactions in a vast and diverse population but also play a leading role in international trade and finance. Accordingly, the team had to consider currency exchange, cross-border transaction protocols and international financial regulations and standards.

In essence, the development of the digital yuan involved breakneck speed innovation across the spheres of electronic payment technology, cybersecurity, system interoperability, user interface design and international financial integration. Each of these aspects had to be meticulously planned and executed to bring the digital yuan from concept to functional reality. The cost of developing the digital yuan has not been publicly disclosed by the Chinese government. Suffice to say that the years of research, advanced technological infrastructure, extensive pilot programmes and collaboration with various stakeholders in the financial and commercial sectors will not have come cheap.

FUNCTIONALITY

It's important to clarify what the digital yuan is and what it is not. The digital yuan does not operate on a blockchain network. A blockchain-based service network does exist in China – an initiative to develop state-supported infrastructure for blockchain – but the digital yuan presently operates independently from this. As we'll see in Part II, blockchain technology only comes into use in the context of the internationalisation of the digital yuan and the creation of multi-CBDC bridges.

The digital yuan functions as a digital currency/electronic payment (DC/EP) system. From a user's perspective, it operates in a similar way to other popular digital payment systems in China, such as Alipay and WeChat Pay: users can download digital wallets which store their funds and register using a phone number or ID number. The wallet generates a QR code that can be scanned by payment terminals in shops. A conventional bank account is not needed to use the digital yuan. This approach lowers the barrier to entry, making the digital yuan accessible to a broader segment of the population. Similar technologies are utilised by Western companies such as Venmo and PayPal Mobile Cash, but these are private payment platforms that liaise with retail banks to streamline payments.

The digital yuan is distributed through a two-tiered model. It is of course backed and issued by the PBOC, which maintains regulatory and monetary control over the digital yuan, aligning with the broader financial policies of the Chinese government and steering its overarching operations. Digital wallets are set up through secondary entities, including the six primary state-owned banks along with two digital banks, WeBank and MYBank, and can be done online or in person.

After initiating their digital yuan wallet, users gain access to an expansive suite of services. These offerings are not limited to the originating bank; they extend across a network of service providers and other banking institutions, and include both payment solutions and other services. For example, some platforms offer financial management tools, discounts at partnered retailers or even investment services tailored to use with digital yuan funds.

Businesses collaborate with secondary institutions to integrate digital yuan payments, for both digital and physical point-of-sale environments. Most e-commerce platforms have updated their checkout processes to accept digital yuan, and businesses have integrated loyalty and reward programmes directly into the digital yuan payment process, enhancing customer engagement and retention.

Beyond simple payments, the digital yuan can be used by the government for direct disbursement of social benefits and subsidies, and to execute smart contracts. The digital yuan can also facilitate micropayments for digital content consumption, such as paying small amounts to access individual articles on news sites or buying single episodes of television series, without the need for subscriptions.

Tourists can use the digital yuan to pay for entry tickets to museums, historical sites and cultural events directly through their phones.

It can also be used for offline payments, which is a critical feature in areas where internet connectivity is poor or non-existent, or in situations where there is a power outage. The devices of both parties involved in the transaction – such as smartphones or specialised payment terminals – need to be equipped with Near Field Communication (NFC) technology. After the transaction is completed offline, the details are stored within the device. Once connectivity is re-established, the transaction data are synced with the central system to update account balances and transaction histories.

Like cash, the digital yuan does not accrue interest nor does it impose transaction fees on its users. While the digital yuan is presently being marketed as a complementary option to paper yuan and other electronic payment methods, it's clear that the CCP is pushing this as the future of all money – with the ambition to gradually phase out all cash.

DOMESTIC MOTIVATIONS

China's domestic motivations for introducing the digital yuan are both pragmatic and political. By introducing the digital yuan, the CCP is able to make strides towards a number of domestic goals, from staving off private sector competition in the payments landscape to widening access to digital money for more segments of the population. In a nation where digital transactions are rapidly increasing – with the number of mobile payment transactions in China amounting to 185 billion in 2023, up from 158 billion in the previous year[19] – the digital yuan is poised to be a catalyst for further digitisation across the Chinese economy. By providing a state-backed digital currency, the CCP is not just digitising money; it's laying the groundwork for a more integrated digital economy, ensuring transactions are faster and more accessible.

Despite China's rapid economic growth, a significant proportion of the population remains unbanked or underbanked, particularly in rural areas. The digital yuan, easily accessible via smartphones, could help promote financial inclusion. Wallets could offer savings accounts with interest benefits to these people. But wallets can also include more complex financial services like micro-loans, insurance products and even investment opportunities, like government bonds or securities, which could be bought and managed directly through digital wallets.

Small loans for personal or small business use are especially beneficial where traditional banking infrastructure is limited. These loans can be managed entirely through a digital yuan wallet, with repayment conditions that are automatically managed and tracked.

However, the digital yuan is most emphatically a tool to reinforce the CCP's control over China's population as well as its payments landscape. With the rise of dominant private payment platforms like Alipay and WeChat Pay – and in an era where cryptocurrencies and decentralised finance are gaining traction globally – the digital yuan serves to promote the CCP's broader goal to increase its oversight over the economy and centralise control of the monetary system.

The digital yuan enables the monitoring and analysis of financial transactions on an unprecedented scale. It is likely that the data gathered from digital yuan transactions will ultimately feed into China's evolving social credit system, which aims to rate citizens based on their social and economic conduct.

Good financial behaviour, such as timely payment of bills and taxes or spending on community-supporting activities, could be rewarded with lower interest rates on loans, discounts on utilities or priority service in government transactions. Conversely, negative behaviours such as fraudulent transactions, late payments or financial mismanagement could lead to penalties, such as higher interest rates for loans, restrictions on certain types of purchases or even limitations on the ability to travel.

This integration could extend beyond financial transactions to influence broader social behaviours. For example, purchasing items deemed positive by the state (like eco-friendly products) might improve one's score, while indulging in behaviours seen as wasteful or unethical (like excessive gambling) could harm it.

Such practices inevitably bring to mind an Orwellian surveillance state in which financial and social data are not only intertwined but leveraged by the state to restrict individual liberties.

China's ambitions for the digital yuan are not just domestic of course. Beijing launched its digital currency with the aim of promoting the yuan's presence on the global stage. This will naturally start within China's closest spheres of influence. In May 2024, Hong Kong launched a pilot programme enabling digital yuan payments through major Chinese banks, the first example of Beijing's digital currency being launched beyond the mainland. However, China's ambitions are much grander – and more strategic – than this. Beijing does not simply aim to export its own digital currency. It is seeking to build the digital payment rails on which the rest of the world's digital money will run, starting with developing nations. This is where the Belt and Road Initiative and the Digital Silk Road come in.

5

The Fault-lines of De-dollarisation: The Belt and Road Initiative and the Digital Silk Road

Much has been written about China's ambitious Belt and Road Initiative (BRI), the largest international infrastructure project the world has ever seen. But only with the benefit of hindsight are we able to view it through the prism of the development of smart money. Viewed through this lens, the significance of the BRI is thrown into sharp relief.

As we've seen, a critical factor in maintaining the US dollar's reserve currency status has been the establishment and protection of global supply routes by the US military. China knew that if it wanted to compete with the US, it too would have to target the arteries of the world economy – its supply chains.

While China has made an impressive resurgence on the global stage, Beijing has remained keenly aware of the comparative advantages held by its strategic rivals, particularly when it comes to geography and economics. Unlike the United States, which is flanked by two oceans, China is constrained by a number of less than friendly neighbours, including South Korea, Japan, the Philippines and, most notably, Taiwan. China also has issues with Japan around the East China Sea. This contrasts with the United States, which has much more open seaboards, and generally friendly relations with its neighbours Canada and Mexico (though not Cuba).

So, while the US Navy can patrol international waters with relative ease, much like the British Royal Navy did from the mid-eighteenth century until the Second World War, China has to navigate a complex regional landscape – putting paid to many of its maritime aspirations and limiting its control over critical supply routes.

To add insult to injury, tensions in the region have been exacerbated by the 'island chains' containment plan, originally devised by American foreign policy strategist John Foster Dulles during the Korean War. This plan aimed to encircle the Soviet Union and China with a network of US naval bases in the Western Pacific, thereby extending US military power and limiting their Cold War rivals' access to the sea. The legacy of this strategy continues to influence the geopolitical dynamics of the region.

To break this maritime encirclement, in 2013 China launched the One Belt One Road project, now known as the Belt and Road Initiative. This mammoth infrastructure project aims to develop a 'maritime road' connecting an extensive network of ports across South Asia, East Africa, the Middle East and Europe, alongside a vast system of overland routes. By facilitating more exports, these land and sea routes are designed to enable China's continued economic expansion while increasing its military presence across the network. China is even building artificial islands in the South China Sea, a point of contention with Southeast Asian nations, including the Philippines and Vietnam, both of whom also claim territorial rights in the area.

The BRI is the key to China expanding its influence beyond the Asian continent: it is boldly seeking to establish a Chinese stake in crucial areas across the globe. By targeting countries that are currently aligned with the United States and NATO, the BRI could tilt not only the economic balance of the Eurasian landmass in China's favour but also the balance of power.

With so much at stake, it is crucial to understand the BRI – its political background, key components, targets and the role of resources – and the part it plays in China's broader strategy for global economic dominance; because, to control the world's money, one must first control its supply chains. To succeed in that aim, China will need to incentivise vast swathes of the world to use its payment infrastructure.

This is where the BRI comes in. China's flagship international development project is scheduled to pump trillions of dollars' worth of investment into infrastructure-related projects in over seventy countries spanning across Central Asia and Africa. The investment avenues mapped out by the BRI provide the perfect sphere of influence through which China can enlist developing countries to move onto digital payment rails and, critically, to help immunise China's business along the BRI against US sanctions.

China is already increasing international (paper) yuan circulation via the BRI by promoting its use for cross-border trade. At the Belt and Road Forum held in Beijing in October 2023, Chinese banks signed a swathe of yuan-denominated loan contracts with foreign lenders.[1]

China is the largest trade partner to around twenty-five countries along the BRI and has struck currency swap agreements with more than twenty BRI nations. To help finance the BRI, the People's Bank of China and China Construction Bank have also issued offshore yuan-denominated bonds and foreign currency bonds.

As author and former IBM executive Richard Turrin argues in *Cashless: China's Digital Currency Revolution*:

> While the BRI's main focus is on infrastructure, stated goals also include 'unimpeded trade' and 'currency circulation', making China's use of DC/EP [digital yuan] compelling. ... As most BRI countries are developing, more than a few may welcome the stability that the RMB brings as a currency.[2]

Since assuming the mantle of general secretary of the CCP in November 2012 – before then taking on the role of president of the republic in March 2013 – Xi Jinping has unequivocally signalled that he wants to usher in a new era for China, both within its borders and on the global stage. Having solidified his position at the helm of the party, Xi has set out to elevate China from the world's manufacturing hub to a global economic powerhouse – a country that is not content with simply exporting its products to other countries but wants to shape the very rules of commerce, and in turn shape the economic incentives of the countries it is exporting to. Shaping the future of money is a critical part of this plan.

CORE COMPONENTS

Though its primary aim is to invest in countries in the so-called Global South – which broadly refers to emerging economies in Africa, Latin America and the Caribbean, Asia and Oceania – by August 2023, 155 out of the 193 countries recognised by the UN, or approximately 80 per cent of the world's countries, had signed on to the BRI in some capacity.[3] As such, the participating nations encompass nearly three-quarters of the global population and account for over half of the world's GDP.

The question is, how has China managed this? What does the BRI actually consist of?

The plan was first unveiled during a visit to Kazakhstan in September 2013, where President Xi talked about a modern reincarnation of the ancient Silk Road – the 'Silk Road Economic Belt'.[4] The following month, in Indonesia, he announced plans for a complementary 'Maritime Silk Road'.[5]

The Economic Belt revives the ancient Silk Road trade routes that connected China to Europe through Central Asia; it aims to build a network of railways, roads, pipelines and streamlined border crossings, both westward – through the mountainous former Soviet republics – and southward, to Pakistan, India and the rest of Southeast Asia. The objective of this overland network is to facilitate trade, improve access to foreign markets and promote economic integration across a diverse range of countries.

The Maritime Road, on the other hand, is designed to create a network of ports and maritime routes that link China to the countries of Southeast Asia, the Gulf countries, North Africa and Europe via the South China Sea, the South Pacific Ocean, the wider Indian Ocean and the Mediterranean Sea. This side of the initiative focuses on infrastructure development, including the construction and expansion of ports and logistics hubs to enhance maritime trade and connectivity, supporting China's quest to broaden its maritime influence.

Through the BRI China invests across various sectors beyond infrastructure, including energy, telecommunications and technology, building power plants, pipelines, cell towers and more.

It also creates economic corridors to open up new market opportunities and spur economic development in participating countries. Financial integration goes hand in hand with this: the BRI has established institutions like the Silk Road Fund and the New Development Bank (both in 2014) and the Asian Infrastructure Investment Bank (in 2016). These multilateral development banks play a key role in funding infrastructure and development projects across the BRI.

While China's self-interested motivations are clear, BRI partner countries get tangible benefits from these projects. This contrasts with US engagement in the developing world, which has notably failed to invest in infrastructure, preferring instead to focus on promoting governance reforms, humanitarian assistance and direct financial aid. For example, the US Agency for International Development has implemented initiatives such as health programmes in Sub-Saharan Africa and education support in South Asia, but has invested less directly in large-scale infrastructure projects like those seen in the BRI.

Cultural and academic exchange is also a major part of the BRI, with various endeavours aimed at fostering greater understanding and collaboration between China and the countries along its route through educational programmes and joint research projects.

In essence, the BRI internationalises China's integration into the global economy, a process which formally began with its entry into the WTO in December 2001. No longer content with being the world's factory floor, China seeks to remap and reroute the developing world's supply chains and build its critical infrastructure.

The BRI was initially perceived as a positive development by the West, even by the United States, as it opened up avenues for cheap imports from China while providing opportunities to export products and services to the burgeoning Chinese market. However, over time, it has become increasingly apparent that China intends to fence in the developing countries participating in the BRI – many of which lack the political and financial capital to break free.

COMPREHENSIVE OFFERS AND DEBT TRAP DIPLOMACY

Crucially, China's BRI strategy involves making 'comprehensive offers' that are hard to resist and subsequently hard to leave. These offers do not just involve the construction of physical infrastructure like roads, bridges and ports – they also extend to digital infrastructure, including the development of payment systems.

Many of the countries participating most heavily in the BRI lack the necessary financial resources to fund such projects independently. It is in this context that China steps in, offering financial support in the form of loans. However, these loans come with strings attached in the form of stringent covenants or conditions.

This financing model has raised concerns about the long-term implications for the participating countries. In effect, China is spinning an intricate web of geopolitical influence and financial dependency in which a wide range of countries will find themselves trapped.

It is generally accepted that China's approach to international lending operates outside the traditional framework of the Paris Club, an informal group of creditor nations set up to regulate challenges faced by debtor countries struggling with repayment. Guided by a set of core principles related to debt relief and restructuring, Paris Club members include major economies such as the United States, Japan, Germany and the United Kingdom – but not China.

Accordingly, China is not bound by the Paris Club's values of fairness, sustainability, solidarity and clarity. Where the Club's members seek to implement proportionate, equitable measures for all creditors – for example, by assessing each debtor country's circumstances individually and endeavouring to ensure that any debt repayment measures do not compromise the country's long-term financial stability or economic development prospects – China implements rather more draconian debt recovery policies.

This is compounded by the Paris Club's principle of acknowledging a non-member creditor as the 'preferred creditor', should it decide to assume the debt of a nation engaged in debt restructuring negotiations within the Club. This status of preferred creditor ensures that the debt owed to the crediting country is repaid first, before debts owed to Paris Club members. So, if China stepped in to provide credit to an indebted nation, China would get repaid first.

Thanks to its extensive lending for projects under the BRI, China often attains this preferred creditor status. This in turn gives China substantial leverage over the public finances of the recipient countries, often placing them in a precarious position.

As of 2023, China remains the world's single largest official source of development finance, out-funding any single G7 developed economy as well as multilateral lenders.[6] Research from AidData, a university research lab at the College of William & Mary in Virginia, also found that nearly 80 per cent of China's lending portfolio in the developing world is currently supporting countries in financial distress. Developing countries now owe Chinese lenders at least $1.1 trillion.[7]

Contracts between China and the governments it deals with are often shrouded in mystery, with the terms and conditions not disclosed. All we know for sure is that China's provisions for infrastructure development come with rigid conditions, which the Chinese authorities are not afraid to enforce.

Several countries engaged in these agreements with China have already encountered challenges in regaining their monetary and fiscal independence – falling into debt traps and compromising their sovereignty over essential national infrastructure.

Sri Lanka is an exemplary case study. In 2017, having borrowed heavily from China to finance the Hambantota Port project (as well as involving the Chinese in its construction), the Sri Lankan government found itself facing a default, with China being its largest bilateral creditor. China did not meet Sri Lanka's financial challenges with leniency, meaning that the Sri Lankan authorities had no choice but to cede control of this strategic port to a Chinese state-owned company, entering into a ninety-nine-year lease agreement.

A similar situation has unfolded in Montenegro, where the construction of the Bar–Boljare highway – a colossal Chinese-backed infrastructural venture – is saddled with huge financial obligations that Montenegro is unlikely to meet, and which the small Balkan nation will therefore likely have to cede control over.

China's international lending practices effectively entice developing countries to remortgage their national sovereignty with Beijing.

What's more, when it comes to China's targets for BRI investment, there is reason to believe that some developing countries are more equal than others.

In his book *China's Chance to Lead*, Professor Richard Carney delves into the relationship between the BRI and the political regimes of participating countries, positing that authoritarian governments are more likely to engage with BRI projects than democracies.[8]

Carney argues that 'electoral autocracies' are particularly inclined to receive Chinese funding. These are regimes where elections do take place, but they are not, generally speaking, free and fair – the electoral process is usually marred by significant irregularities, state control over media and repression of opposition. The ruling party or leader often uses state resources for electoral advantage, and the separation of powers is weak.

In Carney's view, all of the above makes electoral autocracies particularly open to accepting Chinese terms and conditions. These regimes typically make decisions centrally, bypassing the lengthy deliberations, democratic checks or public scrutiny found in more liberal democracies. This is especially advantageous when it comes to large-scale infrastructure projects, which involve multi-year financial and geopolitical entanglements and enormous contracts for the companies involved – and which tend to involve rife debate in democratic countries for these very reasons.

THE TECH WAR

Today, technological prowess is synonymous with global leadership. The country with the most advanced technology not only shapes the world's digital landscape but also has a substantial military advantage.

The role of technology in the conduct of trade also cannot be overstated. On a global scale, the total value of *daily* transactions that rely on a standardised and secure global information and communications technology (ICT) framework is staggering – estimated to be nearly $9 trillion per day. For comparison, this is nine times the *annual* value of bilateral trade in goods and services between the US and China, making the annual global ICT trade over 3,000 times larger than annual US–China bilateral trade, according to the International Institute for Strategic Studies.[9]

Tech plays an immense role in today's highly digitised economy. It's not just about who has the latest gadgets or the fastest internet. It's about controlling the backbone of global trade and international security. A fast-emerging tech war is where the real battle for global supremacy is taking place, with implications that ripple across every aspect of modern life, from our transport networks to our smartphones.

This tech war is a defining feature of the emerging New Cold War between the United States and China. China is pushing to develop the technology of tomorrow across a wide array of industries, including aerospace, advanced manufacturing, robotics and artificial intelligence (AI). Central to this ambition is the 'Made in China 2025' plan, or 'Agenda 2025', announced in 2015. This sets a target for China to drastically increase domestic production of the core materials in key technologies. Specifically, China aims to ensure that 70 per cent of the technological components in its products are domestically produced by 2025.[10]

But China's ambitions go far beyond this drive towards self-reliance. More importantly, it aims to export and embed its technological infrastructure across the globe, especially throughout the developing economies of the Global South and its key BRI partners. Bit by bit, China is becoming the most significant builder – and owner – of digital infrastructure in these economies.

And so, an increasing number of countries, many of which are set to become some of the world's largest economies, now depend on China to participate in a global economy that runs on digital infrastructure. This trend is only going in one direction, with increasing momentum: we will soon find ourselves in a world in which a significant portion – perhaps even a majority – of global trade is conducted via infrastructure built by China.

This extends beyond the equipment required to transact in today's digital economy, and includes the infrastructure needed to operate the smart money of tomorrow.

THE DIGITAL SILK ROAD

To support this vision, China has developed a less visible but equally – if not more – significant counterpart to the BRI: the Digital Silk Road (DSR). Launched in 2015 as a digital cousin to the BRI, the DSR initially focused on incorporating cutting-edge technology into existing infrastructure initiatives by, for example, combating cybercrime along the BRI's network of telecommunications hubs, before evolving into a linchpin of China's strategy for global digital dominance.

Today, the DSR is a technological juggernaut, luring China's partners into implementing its advanced telecommunications, 5G networks, sprawling data centres and satellite technologies across their lands. The DSR integrates surveillance systems, smart city initiatives, burgeoning e-commerce and e-government platforms and financial technology (fintech) solutions. It also promotes academic collaboration and knowledge transfer programmes, designed to import the best ideas from abroad while exporting its own technological blueprints.

The scope of the DSR is vast, with sprawling terrestrial as well as submarine cables being installed across the globe to power critical communications infrastructure and cloud computing capability.

The charge is being led by China's corporate powerhouses. Huawei and ZTE head up telecommunications tech; China Satellite Communications the satellite tech; State Grid Corporation of China contributes to electrical grids; while Baidu leads on internet services and AI.

The DSR is designed to expand China's digital footprint by exporting its technological standards and cultivating digital alliances. Under Xi Jinping's stewardship, the DSR has become a vital component of China's foreign policy and will play a pivotal role in shaping the future of global digital governance. In essence, the DSR is a blueprint for a digital future where China holds the reins, influencing everything from technology standards to digital trade routes, setting the stage for a new era of digital geopolitics.

It has catapulted China ahead of the United States in several key domains, across both hardware and software. On the hardware front, China is less encumbered by health and safety requirements in its domestic research and development. While US companies like Tesla and Uber have been dogged by high-profile safety incidents, incurring the ire of regulators, China can develop its electric driverless vehicles without such impediments. China's new EV sales increased by 82 per cent in 2022, accounting for nearly 60 per cent of global EV purchases, while China's BYD overtook Tesla as the top-selling electric car manufacturer in January 2024.[11]

China's leap forward in the fintech sector has been even more meteoric. Traditional banking systems, once the unquestioned default for financial transactions, have been swept away by China's digital payment platforms. Applications like Alipay and WeChat Pay have become known as 'everything apps' because of their wide range of functions beyond payments, from messaging and video conferencing to video games and photograph sharing. So ubiquitous have these apps become that China is likely to become the world's first cashless society, where even street vendors as well as beggars have started accepting payments through everything apps.

What makes the DSR particularly noteworthy is its 'franchise' model, according to which both public and private Chinese tech companies can leverage state funding, political support and the China 'brand' to win bids for significant tech projects across the developing world, which dovetail with the BRI.

Huawei is an infamous example of this trend, having successfully lobbied to build 5G networks across Africa and Latin America. Huawei technology is being integrated into a growing network of BRI trade hubs, known as smart ports or digital free trade zones (DFTZ) – physical regions promising benefits to digital trade partners. The China–Malaysia DFTZ was launched in March 2017, and it was supposed to help small and medium enterprises grow by streamlining their e-commerce capabilities. However, these regions now serve as platforms for China to deploy its AI, facial recognition and surveillance systems.

For example, Huawei's involvement in Kenya's 5G network has enabled the implementation of advanced surveillance systems in Nairobi, enhancing urban security but also raising privacy concerns. Similarly, in Brazil, Huawei's 5G infrastructure supports extensive data collection and monitoring, which critics argue could be used for state surveillance.

Huawei reportedly controls 70 per cent of the African 4G market, which positions it strategically to dominate the 5G market as well.[12]

Smart ports such as the one in Djibouti, equipped with Huawei's technology, illustrate how digital and physical trade operations are becoming increasingly intertwined. These ports utilise AI and big data analytics to optimise logistics and customs processes, making them more efficient but also embedding Chinese technology deeply into global trade networks.

THE 'SPLINTERNET'

One of the most significant but under-reported aspects of the DSR is China's bid to roll out cybersecurity systems modelled on the famed 'Great Firewall of China', an internet filtering system that China employs domestically. This has already been done in Nigeria, where the Chinese have built a national internet firewall that gives the Nigerian government control over popular social media platforms.

In China, the firewall enables the CCP to block out negative content about the Beijing government as well as to curtail the influence of Western culture and values within its borders. By extending this to countries in its sphere of influence, China not only amplifies its technological footprint but also establishes cultural and political influence over their digital landscape, leading to what's known as the 'splinternet', the fragmentation of the World Wide Web into distinct regional or national digital realms, potentially leading to a future where these are no longer interconnected.

Imagine a world where the global internet as we know it splinters into separate zones – one used by China and its allies, and another by the United States and its allies. In this world, online information and communication would look totally different, depending on your country's geopolitical alliances. Each bloc would inhabit a segmented, disjointed digital world, with connection and community defined along these fault-lines.

The splinternet will be accelerated by splintering payment systems. The war in Ukraine illustrated how this can unfold. Following the invasion, US tech companies including Microsoft and Oracle stopped selling software to Russia. After payment companies like Visa and Mastercard also discontinued operations, Russians could no longer pay for the private networking apps they previously used to overcome government censorship of social media sites like Facebook and X. In other words, sanctions against Russia had the unintended consequence of helping the Kremlin prevent Russian citizens from learning the truth about the war.

On top of this, the Russian government has been cracking down on online access in order to curb free speech and dissent against the war. Many '.ru' websites have only been online intermittently since the start of the invasion. Consequently, the internet has become unrecognisable from what it previously looked like for much of the Russian population. A 'digital iron curtain' has effectively been erected around the country.

Splintering the internet across geopolitical spheres would have profound implications for how information is shared, accessed and controlled across the world, and shatter the foundational principle of the internet as a unified, global platform for communication and information exchange. But the implications of the splinternet extend beyond the realms of information and propaganda. It paves the way for the creation of parallel financial systems and economic paradigms, which is where CBDCs come in. The exchange of monetary value relies on systems that exchange information. And as the information ecosystem of China and its allies splinters away from that of the West, so too will its sphere of economic influence.

This is something China has been preparing for over a long period of time. In the early stages of the DSR, China was already taking steps to reshape payment infrastructure by laying the groundwork for an expansive network of yuan-centric payment systems and security protocols in BRI partner countries.

One of the first steps in this mission was the launch of the Cross-Border Interbank Payment System (CIPS) in October 2015. CIPS is a specialised settlement, payment and clearing mechanism, which is tailored to transactions involving the Chinese yuan and is vigilantly supervised by China's central bank. Since its launch, the network has rapidly grown in stature and significance. As of 2023, CIPS processed approximately 25,900 transactions daily, totalling around 482.6 billion yuan ($67 billion), while the system has expanded to include 1,371 indirect participants across 114 jurisdictions globally.[13]

The Chinese are aiming to position CIPS as a potential challenger to the long-established SWIFT network, the international payment communication system over which the US has significant influence. Despite its impressive growth, CIPS is still dwarfed by SWIFT, which boasts a network of over 11,000 members across 200 countries and handles more than 42 million transactions daily.[14] Nonetheless, CIPS is carving out a niche in the market over time. For example, it offers a lifeline to countries currently under US and allied sanctions, enabling them to conduct international transactions with greater financial autonomy and thereby reduce their reliance on the US-dominated system. As such, CIPS has become a geopolitical instrument as well as a financial tool, rendering US sanctions less effective, particularly in cases like Russia.

But the reach of CIPS has remained limited. When it comes to reshaping the international monetary order, the real significance of the DSR is the role it is playing in the deployment of the digital infrastructure that will underpin the future CBDC ecosystem of the developing world.

THE BRAVE NEW WORLD OF DIGITAL PAYMENT RAILS

China doesn't merely want to develop the first CBDC, but aims to be the chief architect of all trade conducted in state-issued digital currencies, firstly by building the physical and digital infrastructure required for this transition, and secondly by setting the technological standards – the rules – by which they are governed.

In essence, China aims to build the new digital payment rails – the train tracks – for the future of money. Using this metaphor, the digital currencies are the trains, carrying freight consisting of troves of big data. To enable these trains to run, you need highly sophisticated tracks in the form of advanced semiconductor chips, cloud computing power, 5G networks and, later, AI and even quantum computing capabilities. Finally, in order to protect the tracks – the network – you need guardrails in the form of cyber defence. Whoever builds these tracks first will hold significant sway over the trains that run on them.

As we've seen, the most crucial question to consider when thinking about money is: who *controls* the ledger. In the world of digital money, however, there is an additional factor to consider: the question of who controls the infrastructure on which the ledger runs. On a macro level, this has huge implications. In *Broken Money* Lyn Alden states that in the age of telecommunications, control over the ledger on a global scale is likely to belong to the nation state with the greatest 'economic and military prowess ... until there is a better solution ... The mightiest country's ledger serves as the independent third-party unit of account for international transactions.'[15]

This is correct – as we've seen, until now the 'mightiest' country in this respect has been the United States. However, digital money is also changing what it means to be the mightiest country. In a world transitioning to digital money, the mightiest country is the one who builds and controls the digital payment rails, which is not necessarily the country with the biggest economy or most powerful military, but rather the country with the appropriate technology and a decisive strategy for deploying it. To paraphrase Bill Clinton's political advisor James Carville – who famously said that when it came to the deciding factor in elections, 'It's the economy, stupid' – when it comes to the race for the future of money, *It's the infrastructure, stupid.*

If China were to construct the digital payment rails for its BRI partner countries, it would significantly tighten its control over the financial systems of these countries, with profound implications for their economic sovereignty and trading patterns. By providing the technological backbone for CBDCs, China could establish a monopoly over the financial infrastructure of BRI countries. This would make these nations reliant on Chinese technology and standards for virtually all of their trade.

What's more, with CBDC infrastructure rooted in Chinese technology, which is indelibly linked to the Chinese state, China would potentially gain systemic access to the financial transactions within these countries, including back-end controls to manage, oversee and intervene in the operation of CBDC systems. As such, China could have the power to freeze transactions at both individual and state levels – which could be used to enforce economic sanctions or threaten others during political disputes.

Even without this, building the digital payment rails could allow the Chinese to collect vast amounts of economic data from BRI countries, providing Beijing with valuable insights into their economic activities, as well as potentially sensitive information that could be leveraged in trade and diplomatic negotiations.

So the design and operation of CBDC systems could ultimately allow China to influence the monetary policies of BRI countries. Through technical and operational guidelines embedded in the CBDC infrastructure, China could monitor and control transactions, as well as sway decisions on money supply, interest rates and other financial policy decisions – and, as such, it would actually be *China* controlling both the infrastructure and, in some ways, the monetary ledgers of these countries.

And so, while the US controlled the financial market infrastructure of the twentieth century, China plans to control the digital financial market infrastructure (DFMI) of the twenty-first. As we've seen, the two will be 'non-overlapping magisteria'.

For this approach to succeed, speed is of the essence. As Richard Carney writes in *China's Chance to Lead*:

> China is aggressively pursuing the de facto adoption of its
> technical standards ... by directly incorporating them into
> its infrastructure projects ... whereby a recipient country's
> adoption of numerous technology products effectively locks in
> Chinese standards...[16]

This is precisely how China plans to win the race for the future of money. Not only is the digital yuan being embedded in a vast array of infrastructure projects through the BRI and DSR, but the currency's technological standards could soon become the default in emerging economy financial systems – and, as Carney states, it will become increasingly difficult for these countries to move away from Chinese standards.

Countries like Pakistan and Cambodia are using the digital yuan for cross-border transactions, reducing reliance on the US dollar and facilitating smoother trade within BRI projects. For the Gwadar

Port in Pakistan and various smart city initiatives across Africa, the digital yuan is being used to streamline financial transactions. In energy infrastructure projects, like the China–Pakistan Economic Corridor, the digital yuan is used for investment and operational transactions. As more countries within the BRI network and beyond become reliant on Chinese digital financial technologies, the balance of power in global finance will steadily begin shifting towards Beijing.

The key battlefields in the tech war for the future of money are fivefold:

1. Big data and cloud computing
2. 5G networks
3. Semiconductor chips
4. AI and quantum computing
5. Cybersecurity

Each component has a role to play in building the digital payment rails of the future. What's more, in most of these domains, China is ahead of the US – and rapidly accelerating. After all, the Chinese have been steadily developing their capabilities for the past decade, ensuring that they retain control of the key building blocks of the new era for money. Here's a breakdown of each block in turn.

BIG DATA AND CLOUD COMPUTING

First and foremost, in order to successfully deploy and operate a CBDC, you need to harness and filter vast amounts of data.

In this realm, the private sector has the edge over the public sector in the US, China and Europe alike, which makes close public–private collaborations necessary to build CBDCs. US tech giants – Meta, Amazon, Apple, Netflix and Google – have been amassing user data for decades. However, China's tech powerhouses, especially Baidu, Alibaba and Tencent, are rapidly gaining ground. Approximately 800 million people use the internet daily in China, a figure that surpasses the combined internet user base of the US and

India.[17] As such, Chinese tech firms may have access to between ten and fifteen times more data than their US counterparts. Moreover, unlike in the US, Chinese companies can and will be strong-armed into cooperation with their government.

In addition, China has access to a wealth of international data, notably through its involvement in the development of smart cities across BRI countries. For instance, in Pakistan, the Safe City Project in Islamabad has been developed with Chinese collaboration, featuring extensive surveillance systems aimed at enhancing security.

Similarly, in Nairobi, Kenya, Chinese companies have been instrumental in integrating advanced technologies to improve urban management and safety, such as installing smart traffic systems designed to mitigate the city's chronic congestion issues.

These projects feature big data and internet of things (IoT) technologies to improve urban management and services, and, as a result, they collect vast amounts of data which can then be processed and analysed to help inform and refine payment technologies.

By comparison, Europe trails far behind. The US, at least, is a homogenous market which generates an abundance of data, but Europe's diverse demographics and tighter regulations leave it facing a relative scarcity of data and needing to learn to do more with less.

The General Data Protection Regulation (GDPR) in Europe imposes strict privacy and data protection requirements which, while safeguarding individual rights, might potentially hinder the region's ability to compete in the global digital economy. Unlike the United States, which benefits from a more unified regulatory environment that facilitates easier data collection and sharing across states, Europe's approach to data regulation is more fragmented due to varying national implementations of GDPR. This fragmentation, combined with the intrinsic diversity of the European market – where language, culture and legal systems vary significantly from country to country – compounds the challenges businesses face in harnessing big data.

For example, a tech company operating across Europe must navigate different interpretations of GDPR in Germany, France and Spain, each with its own nuances in enforcement and compliance. This not only increases operational costs but also restricts the ability of companies to seamlessly analyse and utilise data across borders.

Furthermore, the stringent consent requirements under GDPR mean that companies must secure explicit permission to process personal data, limiting the volume and variety of data that can be legally collected compared to less restrictive regimes. For instance, while a US company might freely analyse customer behaviour data to enhance user experiences and develop new services, a European counterpart would require explicit consent for each type of data processing activity, potentially reducing the richness of the data pool available for innovation.

However, the trust that GDPR builds among consumers can be a significant strategic asset. Consumers might be more willing to share their data with entities they trust to handle their information responsibly. This could ultimately enhance customer loyalty and facilitate the development of data-driven, consumer-centric business models that are compliant with privacy laws.

Cloud computing provides the technological backbone needed to support this big data. So-called data 'clouds' are not as intangible as they sound. In order to store huge amounts of data, you need substantial physical infrastructure – large servers and mainframes housed in extensive warehouses. Variations in the given cloud's scalability, cost-effectiveness and security will make all the difference in the CBDC world.

China, once again, has thought two steps ahead here, establishing cloud computing services and data centres in a range of BRI countries. Chinese companies have expanded their services into Asia, Africa and Europe, offering cloud storage, big data processing and AI capabilities. Alibaba Cloud, for example, has launched data centres in Dubai, Malaysia and Indonesia, facilitating local businesses' access to big data analytics and cloud computing.

5G NETWORKS

In telecommunications, 5G is the fifth-generation technology standard for cellular networks, which can be up to a hundred times faster than its predecessor, 4G. The deployment of 5G technology will be pivotal for the operational success of CBDCs. Both China and the US are actively rolling out 5G networks – but their approaches and international deployment strategies reveal contrasting priorities and ambitions.

China has clearly pulled ahead in the 5G race. Chinese telco giants like Huawei and ZTE are instrumental to this, both within China's borders and beyond, providing 5G infrastructure to support speeds up to 10 Gbps, facilitating real-time data processing and transactions that will be essential for CBDC operations. China had reached 851 million domestic 5G mobile subscribers by February 2024, according to *China Daily*.[18]

China's 5G deployment, with its emphasis on national coverage and international expansion through the BRI, has put it in a strong position to set global standards for 5G. Significant concerns have been raised internationally about the security implications of using Chinese 5G infrastructure, with many countries worried about threats to data privacy and infiltration of critical national infrastructure.

In 2020, the UK debated whether to allow Huawei to build the country's own 5G network. The UK badly wanted 5G, and only Huawei was equipped to build it, but the US insisted that the UK didn't use them. In the end, Huawei were prevented from doing the work, with a ban instituted in July 2020 which stipulated that all existing Huawei equipment must be fully removed from 5G networks by the end of 2027. However, this was done at the cost of the UK having a poorer network and hurt business opportunities for domestic companies. Local carrier BT said the ban cost them a total of £500 million ($612 million).[19] So why would any country that is not aligned with the US ever incur such an opportunity cost?

SEMICONDUCTOR CHIPS

Semiconductor chips represent a critical battlefield of the tech war in their own right, as chronicled in Chris Miller's recent book, *Chip War*.[20] Predominantly manufactured in Asia, with Taiwan the top producer, semiconductors are integral to all aspects of the technology industry, but especially AI.

They will also be vital for the technological foundation of a CBDC ecosystem: they facilitate the high-performance computing and scalability that are essential to support blockchain and encryption technologies at scale.

Despite being at the forefront of AI research and application, China's reliance on foreign semiconductor technology, especially from its historic opponent Taiwan, makes its supply chain vulnerable – and also represents a huge incentive for China to pursue an invasion of Taiwan.

The US has made successful efforts to build strong connections with Taiwan in this sphere, serving to rebuff China's influence on the island's supply chains and make Beijing's move on the territory all the more forbidding. In April 2024, the world's biggest chipmaker, Taiwan Semiconductor Manufacturing Company (TSMC), agreed to make its most advanced products in Arizona from 2028, in a major boost to White House efforts to bring semiconductor production onto home soil.

The US has also used its technological and political leverage, alongside strategic domestic restrictions, to curb China's access to key AI-related technology. Moreover, chips are advancing so quickly that China is struggling to catch up, and the US has aimed to maintain its lead by insisting that domestic companies do not supply them with the latest versions.

In response, American companies like Nvidia have developed specialised semiconductor chips that comply with these regulations, allowing for continued engagement with the Chinese market, albeit at a potentially reduced capacity.

China is certainly not going to take such measures lying down. In May 2024, it announced the launch of the 'Big Fund' to support its semiconductor industry, raising an astonishing 344 billion yuan ($47 billion) to support President Xi's drive for self-sufficiency in the face of American attempts to cut off its access to the latest technology.[21] The 'National Integrated Circuit Industry Investment Fund Phase III' is the third round of the fund and the largest ever raised by Beijing. The fund will invest in emerging companies and technologies in the semiconductor space, in efforts to overcome critical chokepoints in its chip industry.

AI AND QUANTUM COMPUTING

The ability of AI to process extensive datasets, identify patterns and automate complex decision-making processes will make it crucial to the long-term future of CBDCs. The convergence of these technologies could redefine economic structures on both the micro and macro levels, enabling real-time payments and providing insights for policymaking.

As things stand, the US arguably dominates this field – the diffusion of AI technologies like OpenAI's ChatGPT, now integrated into Microsoft's Edge browser, highlights how American AI-driven companies have steamed ahead.

China, on the other hand, has been aggressively pursuing AI as part of its national strategy – and various Chinese companies have released their own AI platforms, such as Baidu's Ernie. Chinese AI development benefits from the country's more lenient data privacy regulations, allowing for the collection and analysis of massive datasets to train AI models. This could ultimately give China the edge with regard to AI-enhanced CBDCs, enabling real-time economic analysis and policy adjustments. Furthermore, China could use AI to streamline CBDC transaction processes, making digital yuan transactions more efficient and secure.

The competition between China and the US in the field of quantum information science (QIS) is another hard-fought battle with the potential to revolutionise numerous industries, including payments and CBDCs. QIS, which harnesses the principles of quantum mechanics, could dramatically alter fields that depend on speed and processing power, ranging from aerospace and cars to finance and pharmaceuticals. The nation that leads the way in quantum technology will have the capacity to compromise its adversaries' corporate, military and government information systems at a pace that outstrips any current defence mechanisms.

Quantum technology is a groundbreaking shift in computing that drastically enhances data processing speeds and enables complex problems to be solved at unprecedented speeds. While a classical computer performs calculations one at a time, a quantum computer can process vast numbers of calculations simultaneously, thanks to quantum bits, or qubits, that can exist in multiple states at once.

Given these advancements, it's crucial that systems for CBDCs adapt to be 'quantum-aware' and prepared. A CBDC system not optimised for quantum technology could be vulnerable to security breaches once quantum computing becomes commonplace. For example, a quantum computer could potentially decrypt existing encryption methods used in traditional banking systems, exposing financial data to theft or manipulation.

Consequently, the market value of quantum technologies, particularly quantum computing, is anticipated to soar, with some predictions putting the global market value at $1.3 trillion by 2035.[22]

China currently leads the field of quantum communications and holds the highest total number of quantum technology patents. In a notable development, Chinese tech giant Baidu unveiled its first quantum computer in August 2022.

This swift progress has understandably given rise to concern in the West, pithily dubbed 'Encryptogeddon' by the *Financial Times*, expressing the fear that quantum computing could spell the end of existing encryption methods.[23] At present, encrypted codes rely on the fact that conventional computers would need centuries to crack them, but with stable and reliable quantum technology, the same computational tasks could be completed in mere seconds.

CYBERSECURITY

Cyber defence is a critical aspect of the US–China tech war, which is one component of the wider New Cold War. China has made enormous investments in cybersecurity as part of its broader strategy to become a global technology leader – including with regard to the development and deployment of CBDC infrastructure.

China has also sought to export its cybersecurity solutions by integrating them into its digital infrastructure projects abroad. In short, by offering not just technology but also security as part of its packages, China incentivises countries to align with its digital and financial systems, potentially increasing the use and international acceptance of its CBDC, while influencing the design of other CBDCs.

The security systems embedded within Chinese technologies can make them appealing for countries looking to protect their digital and financial systems. However, this does not eliminate the possibility that Beijing may retain the capability to access or control these systems.

Chinese technology exports often have backdoors or other mechanisms that allow CCP authorities access to data or control over the platforms in question, even if these systems are secure against other external threats. For example, laws in China, such as the National Intelligence Law of 2017, mandate that organisations and citizens must 'support, assist, and cooperate with the state intelligence work', which can be used to compel Chinese companies to provide access to foreign data handled or stored by Chinese technology companies.

China's cybersecurity legislation underscores the government's commitment to securing its digital space, but also provides a framework for CBDC security protocols, not just domestically but in BRI partner countries. China thereby encourages other countries to align with its own digital and financial market infrastructure with the promise of facilitating smoother cross-border transactions with lower risks of cyber threats.

To be sure, the US is also leveraging its cybersecurity alliances to influence global standards, but it doesn't directly invest in digital financial infrastructure abroad as China does, which leaves it lagging behind in terms of cybersecurity integration.

All of this puts China in the strongest of positions to run away with the race for the future of money – its trains, tracks, engines and guardrails are all primed and ready for action. Arguably, the train has already left the station.

In the new era of money, who controls the ledger? Simply put, whoever controls the infrastructure. For the last decade, the West has been impervious to China's broader monetary project along the BRI and DSR, and consistently missed the forest for the trees.

6

The Lost Decade:
Western Vacillation and Volte-Face

THE PIVOT EAST, AND BACK...

In the eyes of China, for the better part of the last ten years, the West – and the United States in particular – must have appeared remarkably confused and short-sighted. Beijing looks at Washington, and the West more broadly, and sees a set of economies who dominated the twentieth century, but do not seem sure where they fit into the twenty-first century or how to deal with rising powers. The West seems to lack a grand strategy and vision for its place in the world.

During the Obama administration, the vision was for the US to open up to the world and strike a series of multilateral trade deals. Most notably, the priority was to pivot east – or more accurately, west from America's standpoint – and counter China's rising influence in its own backyard, around the Pacific Rim.

Key to this vision was the Trans-Pacific Partnership (TPP), negotiations for which started back in 2008. The TPP aimed to create a single market for the US and eleven other Pacific Rim economies: Australia, Brunei, Canada, Chile, Japan, Malaysia, Mexico, New Zealand, Peru, Singapore, Vietnam – but not China.

The idea was to make goods flow more freely and cheaply between all partners – who together represented one third of global trading. Specifically, the TPP's largest goal was to maintain US trade dominance in Asia, bringing the various trading partners under America's wing as a way to ward off China's growing economic footprint.

Supporters said the net effect of this would stimulate the economy and, therefore, lead to jobs and better wages for all. According to research by the Peterson Institute cited by Obama's White House, the deal would have increased US exports by $123 billion and helped create 650,000 additional jobs in the US.[1]

The deal was almost ten years in the making, but America's Pacific pivot came to an abrupt end. Anti-globalisation sentiment was on the rise at home, and critics argued the deal was more beneficial for multinational corporations at the expense of blue-collar workers.

In 2016, Donald Trump won the presidency and tore up the TPP on his first day in office. 'Great thing for the American worker, what we just did,' he told the press corps after signing, as his chief adviser Steve Bannon looked on contentedly.

In response, the remaining countries negotiated a new agreement, resulting in the formation of the Comprehensive and Progressive Agreement for Trans-Pacific Partnership (CPTPP), which incorporated most provisions of the original deal. The CPTPP officially came into effect on 30 December 2018. The United Kingdom acceded in 2021, and China applied to join in 2021.

The United States' decision to withdraw from TPP enabled China to further consolidate its influence across Asia, and Beijing is hoping to expand its reach by signing up to the rejigged agreement, unencumbered by American input into the new deal.

China has since sought to expand and deepen its ties across the Pacific region. A pivotal component of this strategy is the Regional Comprehensive Economic Partnership, signed in November 2020. This landmark free trade agreement unites some of Asia's largest economies, including China, Indonesia, Japan and South Korea, with Asia–Pacific nations such as Australia, Brunei, Cambodia, Laos, Malaysia, Myanmar, New Zealand, the Philippines, Singapore, Thailand and Vietnam.

The scope of the partnership is monumental: its fifteen member countries collectively represent approximately 30 per cent of the world's population (roughly 2.2 billion people) and account for about 30 per cent of global GDP (totalling around $29.7 trillion).[2] This makes it the largest trade bloc in history, marking a significant milestone in regional economic integration.

While President Trump's combative stance towards China's international trade practices have become bipartisan consensus in Washington, the US's volte-face on the TPP nevertheless made the US look in turn rash, unreliable and indecisive, signalling to Beijing that the democratic superpower of the twentieth century lacked a clear strategy for the twenty-first. The CCP would have been forgiven for thinking that the dollar's exorbitant privilege was on thin ice.

THE TRADE WAR

Since the election of President Trump in 2016, the US has been engaged in a prolonged trade war with China, to the economic detriment of both countries.

The intensifying dispute was initiated by the US citing China's unfair trade practices, notably the theft of intellectual property and underpriced dumping – making US industries less competitive. In 2018, the United States took a decisive step, imposing stringent tariffs and trade barriers on a substantial volume of Chinese imports. This saw the introduction of a 25 per cent tariff on $250 billion worth of Chinese goods. This unprecedented move targeted a range of products, but focused on those integral to China's key industrial sectors, such as technology and manufacturing.

The imposition of these tariffs was grounded in longstanding grievances. The US accused China of engaging in practices that undermined the competitive landscape. Reports suggested that the US economy suffered significant annual losses, estimated in hundreds of billions, due to intellectual property theft, affecting sectors ranging from tech to entertainment.

China did not remain passive. The Chinese government imposed its own set of tariffs, targeting over $110 billion worth of US imports. This primarily affected the agricultural sector of the US, particularly soybean exports, which saw a substantial drop in demand from the Chinese market. This led to a surplus of soybeans in the US market, causing prices to plummet and putting financial strain on farmers. Conversely, in China, manufacturers who relied on US raw materials and components found their costs unpredictably increasing, which forced them to seek alternative suppliers outside the United States.

The effects of this tit-for-tat escalation of tariffs between the world's two economic giants rippled across the global economy. Supply chains across the world experienced disruptions, while industries in both countries, as well as international businesses, faced uncertainty and increased costs. This was reflected in market volatility, with investors and companies struggling to adapt to an unpredictable trade environment.

The technology sector acutely felt the squeeze. US companies like Apple saw their production costs rise as tariffs made Chinese-manufactured components more expensive. Similarly, Chinese technology firms like Huawei faced restrictions and bans in the US market, limiting their access to crucial US technology and software, such as Google's Android services.

The automobile industry, which relies on a complex and geographically dispersed supply chain, also suffered. Tariffs on steel and aluminium not only increased production costs but also affected global prices and the availability of these essential materials. Automakers around the world, from Germany to Japan, found themselves caught in the crossfire, facing rising operational costs and compelled to reconsider their long-term manufacturing and assembly strategies.

The broader economic implications were significant. The IMF projected that if the trade tensions persisted, the global economy could suffer substantial GDP losses. This forecast was not just a reflection of decreased trade volumes between the US and China but also spoke to reduced business confidence and investment worldwide. Companies hesitated to commit to new projects and expenditures amid uncertainties about future tariff policies and trade norms.

Additionally, the trade war highlighted the difficulty in decoupling economies that are deeply integrated. Many global corporations found it challenging to reconfigure their supply chains quickly. Diversification efforts, such as shifting manufacturing bases to countries like Vietnam and Mexico, were not immediate solutions due to considerations like infrastructure, workforce skills and political stability.

DIGITAL AUTHORITARIANISM

The primary concern, however, has been about China's technological footprint. The US and several other Western countries have questioned whether Huawei might use the DSR as a way to force recipient countries to adopt China's model of technology-enabled authoritarianism, impacting personal freedoms and sovereignty.

This is all compounded by China's National Intelligence Law. While Chinese technology companies are nominally private, they have close links to the Chinese state, and are required to store data on Chinese servers and submit to checks from the authorities. This situation creates a huge risk of surveillance, which could be leveraged for political coercion. In response, the US has aimed to limit China's influence across a number of critical technology sectors. However, the scope of these measures is constrained by the complex interdependence of US and Chinese tech firms, which has turned policy in this sphere into an economic and diplomatic minefield.

The whole web of global technology is intertwined, but the relationships between American and Chinese entities stand out for being strongly linked. To be sure, they compete intensely for global market capture, but their supply chains are heavily interdependent and they also cooperate across innovation and research.

A number of American tech giants have a long-standing physical presence in China, encompassing research labs and manufacturing facilities, as well as partnerships with Chinese companies and academic institutions. Apple in particular has cultivated an extensive manufacturing base in China, while IBM, Nvidia and Qualcomm, to name just a few significant US players, have established collaborative initiatives with Chinese firms across the mainland – all of these examples testify to the fact that the US and China are caught between cooperation and competition.

Still, in a bid to push back against Beijing's international progress, the US has focused on shutting out Chinese firms from the tech market in recent years – with some degree of success.

China has perennially limited, or else banned, major US internet companies such as Google, Meta, X and Amazon from operating within its borders. This move isn't just about censorship or control; it's also about fostering homegrown tech giants, which has proved successful. China's own digital powerhouses, like Alibaba, Baidu and Tencent, dominate its territory, creating a parallel tech universe within its borders.

Until recently, these Chinese tech titans have faced no formal restrictions in the United States and their (modest) presence and operations in the US have been largely tolerated. But there has been a noticeable shift over the course of the Trump and Biden administrations; despite their political differences, both administrations have implemented the principle of 'reciprocity' – according to this logic, if China barred US tech giants from its market, then Chinese tech companies ought to face similar restrictions in the US.

Accordingly, the US has cracked down on a number of Chinese tech firms, including, most notably, Huawei and ZTE. In April 2018, the US Department of Commerce banned American companies from selling equipment to Chinese telecom giant ZTE due to allegations that it violated US sanctions against Iran.

This was notable for being a case of 'extraterritoriality' in sanctions. The US usually only extends its legal jurisdiction beyond its borders in this way to compel foreign financial institutions to comply with sanctions against countries like Iran and Russia. But the ZTE ban – a ban against a foreign telecommunications company for dealing with a third country (Iran) – signals that the US is unafraid to apply extraterritoriality across the tech industry, ushering in a new era of digital diplomacy. While the ZTE ban was later lifted, such heavy-handed actions by the US helped to make it clear to China that it needed to develop a digital currency to conduct international trade on its own terms.

Huawei has faced restrictions in the United States market since 2012, starting with a prohibition on selling its network equipment to American telecom companies, motivated by concerns over national security. The company's attempts to enter the US smartphone market via collaborations with AT&T and Verizon have also been unsuccessful, largely due to political scrutiny. The situation escalated in 2019, when the US Department of Commerce imposed stringent export restrictions on Huawei following thorough investigations which raised concerns about potential access to sensitive data by the Chinese government through Huawei's channels.

As we've seen, the US government has also exerted pressure on its allies to steer clear of Huawei's 5G technology. Washington has made it increasingly clear that any countries wishing to deal closely with the US should distance themselves from Chinese telecoms solutions, leaving a host of countries stuck between a rock and a hard place.

This equipment is often more affordable than alternatives. For developing countries, or those with limited budgets for infrastructure projects, the cost-effective nature of Chinese technology can be particularly appealing. Opting for more expensive Western equivalents could strain national budgets and delay the rollout of crucial infrastructure, such as 5G networks.

Additionally, many countries have already integrated Chinese technology deeply into their existing telecommunications infrastructure. The hardware and software from Chinese companies are often designed to be interoperable with each other but not necessarily with systems from other providers. This makes the process of switching to different technology not only complex and resource intensive but also risky in terms of potential network disruptions.

The global telecom equipment market is dominated by a few key players, with Chinese firms like Huawei and ZTE holding substantial shares. Finding alternative suppliers who can provide the same scale of products and services immediately is challenging. Companies like Ericsson and Nokia, while capable, have more limited production capacity and would be more expensive.

This signifies the US–China tech rivalry entering a new phase, escalating from a straightforward bilateral trade war into a geopolitical battle involving other countries, as both sides seek to build alliances to uphold and enforce their respective technology standards.

This defensive stance is also embodied in the Foreign Investment Risk Review Modernization Act of 2018. This legislation lends the Committee on Foreign Investment in the United States enhanced authority to scrutinise and potentially block foreign investments, particularly those from China. The impact of this legislation has been swift and significant, with a marked decline in Chinese acquisitions of US tech firms and other businesses. For example, the committee was instrumental in obstructing the sale of US money transfer firm MoneyGram to China's Ant Financial and the proposed sale of American semiconductor producer Lattice Semiconductor to Canyon Bridge Partners, a Chinese-backed private equity firm.

Looking across the Atlantic, the European Union has similarly tightened its cybersecurity measures, with the EU Commission prohibiting its staff from using TikTok, the video-based social media app – owned by ByteDance Ltd, a Chinese company – widely suspected of being a tool for Chinese state surveillance.

In the UK, Defence Secretary Gavin Williamson was sacked (having refused to resign) in May 2019 over allegations, which he denied, that he had leaked information from a National Security Council meeting pertaining to the adoption of Huawei technology.

All of this reflects growing concerns about Chinese companies and data privacy and security across the West, which is serving to further split the technological landscape between those countries accepting Chinese tech and those refusing.

FRIENDSHORING AND RESHORING

As trade tensions between the United States and China have continued to escalate, global supply chains have become increasingly balkanised as both superpowers resort to strategies of 'friendshoring' and 'reshoring'.

'Friendshoring' means turning solely to geopolitical allies for manufacturing needs. A classic example is the United States' increased reliance on countries like Canada, Mexico and Japan for microchip manufacturing – by focusing on these alliances, the US is able to ensure supply chain security, especially in critical sectors like technology and defence.

On the other hand, 'reshoring' is about bringing manufacturing operations back to the company's home country. For instance, Intel's announcement that it would invest several billion dollars in new chip plants in Arizona reflects this trend. Similarly, the objective of reshoring is to mitigate risks associated with foreign manufacturing, spurred by factors like intellectual property concerns, supply chain uncertainties and cybersecurity.

This has in part been a direct response to Beijing's 'Made in China 2025' plan. As we've seen, the state-led industrial policy seeks to make China dominant in high-tech manufacturing, using government subsidies, mobilising state-owned enterprises and pursuing intellectual property acquisition to catch up with and eventually surpass Western technological prowess in advanced industries.

For the US and China, these trends are leading to the development of shorter, more resilient supply chains that can better withstand economic disruptions. But, overall, this new landscape poses a significant challenge for many countries and regions caught in the crossfire of this strategic rivalry. Nations across the globe often find themselves compelled to align with either the US or China, despite their preference to maintain strong economic ties with both.

As a result, countries are increasingly faced with difficult choices regarding their supply chain partnerships. Nations like Vietnam, Mexico and Malaysia have benefited significantly from trade with both countries, often serving as intermediaries in larger supply chains. The pressure to choose sides threatens these beneficial arrangements.

Developing independent supply chains requires substantial investment in infrastructure, technology and skills training. Countries in Africa and parts of Latin America, for example, may struggle with the high costs and logistical complexities of diversifying their supply chains away from Chinese or American dominance. The lack of local industrial capacity makes it difficult to replace established supply networks quickly.

Advanced technology products, particularly those involving the semiconductor and telecommunications sectors, exemplify industries where US and Chinese dominance is the greatest. Countries seeking to develop autonomous capabilities in these areas face significant technological and financial barriers. For instance, the semiconductor industry requires billions of dollars in investment for fabrication plants, along with a high level of technical expertise. Nations such as South Korea and Taiwan have managed to establish significant capabilities, but most other countries find it prohibitive.

Brazil, as a major exporter of soybeans and iron ore, has traditionally relied on trade with China. Yet, its strategic ties with the US are also crucial, especially in terms of foreign direct investment and military cooperation. The Brazilian government has to carefully navigate these relationships to avoid economic losses or diplomatic frictions.

Germany faces a similar conundrum in balancing its auto industry's reliance on the Chinese market with its technological and security ties with the US. The German automotive sector, including giants like Volkswagen and BMW, finds the Chinese market indispensable for growth, but it also needs to maintain access to US technology and investment.

Consequently, several US allies, such as Germany, along with other European Union member states, as well as Japan, South Korea and Australia, have ended up trading more extensively with China than with the US. While the US has applied pressure on these nations to reverse and realign their trade agreements, most countries are likely to keep prioritising cost-effective commerce. As trade routes become increasingly embattled, however, there will soon come a time when either Washington or Beijing will seek to force their hand.

This moment is likely to come with the stark choices that nations will soon need to face with regards to trade in smart money.

THE PHASE ONE TRADE DEAL

Both sides eventually recognised that the trade war was unsustainable, and attempted to negotiate a new trade deal, which was signed and took effect on 14 February 2020.

Officially titled the 'Economic and Trade Agreement Between the United States of America and the People's Republic of China: Phase One', the deal outlined a set of requirements for China with regard to structural reforms in areas such as intellectual property, technology transfer, financial services and currency and foreign exchange practices. The deal tried to address some of the core issues at the heart of US–China trade tensions, and included:

1. A commitment from the Chinese to purchase $200 billion of certain US goods and services over a two-year period from 1 January 2020 through to 31 December 2021.
2. Stronger enforcement of IP rights, matched by a simultaneous loosening of the requirement that joint ventures with Chinese firms by foreign investors must be majority-controlled by the Chinese partners (which were often marked by 'forced' technology transfers).
3. A significant reduction of non-tariff barriers to trade, especially in the agricultural sector.
4. The opening-up of a variety of sectors to foreign direct investment, starting with financial services and other services sectors, plus the opening-up of government procurement processes.

5. Currency stabilisation and a more transparent process for monitoring foreign exchange reserves.

6. Mutual enforcement of the trade agreement and the establishment of a new dispute-resolution agreement that would bypass the WTO process.[3]

While these ambitious targets would certainly have made significant steps to bridging the gap between China and the US, they were generally seen to be aspirational rather than realistically attainable. In reality, over the two-year period covered by the Phase One deal, which also saw a change in US leadership with the election of Joe Biden, China's actual purchases fell very short of its commitments – the country only bought about 58 per cent of the total US goods and services it had agreed to.[4] Of course, this shortfall was significantly influenced by the unforeseen Covid-19 pandemic, which erupted globally just weeks after the deal was signed, bringing global trade to a near standstill for several months.

But China's commitment to the deal was also seen to wane over time, in part due to its focus on other things, including but not limited to its stringent zero-Covid policy. As such, the Phase One trade deal was broadly deemed a failure, as well as a perfect encapsulation of the United States' confused and cack-handed dealings with China's growing presence on the world stage.

Beyond the disruptions caused by Covid, China's focus shifted towards other domestic and international priorities that conflicted with the objectives of the Phase One deal. Domestically, China intensified efforts to promote self-reliance in technology and reduce dependency on foreign entities. China's investment in domestic technology sectors saw a substantial increase, with the semiconductor industry alone receiving hundreds of billions in funding to reduce dependency on US imports. Internationally, China redoubled its efforts to control trade routes along the BRI, which often placed it in direct competition with American geopolitical interests. These shifts demonstrated that adhering to the Phase One trade deal was not seen as a high priority for China.

The targets set by the Phase One deal were always overly ambitious. Economists and trade experts agreed that the specified $200 billion increase in Chinese purchases of US goods was not feasible within the set timeframe, especially considering the existing global economic slowdown exacerbated by the pandemic. Moreover, the deal was negotiated under significant political pressure, primarily from the US side, to secure a quick win. This rush led to a lack of comprehensive engagement with broader issues such as state subsidies for Chinese industries, which remained a sore point in US–China economic relations.

The deal was symptomatic of the US's approach to China for much of the previous decade. From 2012 to 2022, the US has been unsure what it's doing, from reversing major trade initiatives with regional partners to taking wild shots at Chinese tech firms due to narrow concerns about data privacy and intellectual property theft – with no broader strategy in view. America's allies have in many cases been forced to compromise their own trade interests as a result. Meanwhile, the bigger picture surrounding China's ambitions to utilise the BRI and DSR as a way of pushing its long-term agenda for de-dollarisation never seems to have come into view or made it onto Western policy agendas.

In February 2022, this all changed overnight.

7

Weeks When Decades Happen

'There are decades where nothing happens, and there are
weeks when decades happen.'
VLADIMIR ILLYICH LENIN[1]

Following almost ten years of blindsided vacillation from the West
in the face of increasing Chinese assertiveness on the global stage,
the broader threat facing the United States and its allies suddenly
crystallised. In 2022, eight decades of monetary continuity – and
US homogeneity – effectively went up in smoke over the course of
several weeks. This was the year that the geopolitical dimension of
CBDCs became self-evident – or should have become self-evident.

Certain dates etch themselves into history as pivotal moments for
world affairs. The 4th of July and 9/11 are such examples, marking
clear paradigm shifts in global power dynamics and international
relations. Often the full impact of these moments is only realised
in retrospect. We would suggest that 4 February 2022 might end
up being one of these understated yet crucial junctures; a date that
future historians will pinpoint as the dawn of a new era.

It was on this day that Xi Jinping and Vladimir Putin convened
in Beijing to kick off the Winter Olympics. The Olympics have
traditionally symbolised a time of global peace, which even Putin
seemingly respected, despite having been orchestrating the invasion
of Ukraine for months, likely years. But it would have been

foolhardy for the Russians to have invaded before the Olympics, since Russia was seeking to forge a strategic alliance with the host nation. Putin sought to ensure that China's leader was supportive of the war, or at least not opposed to it.

The meetings clearly went to plan. On the day of the Olympics' opening ceremony, Xi and Putin released a 'Joint Statement of the Russian Federation and the People's Republic of China'. The document, ambitiously subtitled 'A New Era for International Relations and Global Sustainable Development', was a significant declaration of intent. Its most astonishing excerpt declared that 'friendship between the two States has no limits, there are no "forbidden" areas of cooperation'.[2] The agreement between the world's two most powerful autocracies was a direct challenge to the United States' global stature, NATO's position as a pillar of international security and the Western concept of liberal democracy. The announcement was clearly meant to herald a new chapter in world politics in which the world's autocracies were openly challenging the democratic order. The meaning of the Olympic spirit, it seems, was also being redefined.

To be sure, there have been previous agreements between Moscow and Beijing, including the Treaty of Friendship of 2001, which was also laden with lofty, if vague, rhetoric that has since faded into the footnotes of history. This new and detailed 5,000-word agreement, however, was not just a collection of the usual tropes. Although the agreement falls short of a formal alliance, Robert Daly, Director of the Kissinger Institute on China and the United States at the Wilson Center in Washington, argues that it reflects a more elaborate show of solidarity than any moment in the past. In his words: 'This is a pledge to stand shoulder to shoulder against America and the West, ideologically as well as militarily … This statement might be looked back on as the beginning of Cold War Two,' he told *The New Yorker*.[3]

A key component of the pact was Russia's reaffirmation of the One China principle, which recognises Taiwan as an integral part of China. In a reciprocal gesture, China expressed its staunch opposition to movements like Ukraine's Orange Revolution of

2004–5 and each committed to resist any 'external interference' in one another's affairs. This was effectively President Xi's way of endorsing the impending invasion of Ukraine, which commenced less than three weeks later.

This was underscored by the following statement:

> The sides reaffirm their strong mutual support for the protection of their core interests, state sovereignty and territorial integrity, and oppose interference by external forces in their internal affairs …
>
> The sides oppose further enlargement of NATO and call on the North Atlantic Alliance to abandon its ideologized cold war approaches, to respect the sovereignty, security and interests of other countries, the diversity of their civilizational, cultural and historical backgrounds, and to exercise a fair and objective attitude towards the peaceful development of other States.[4]

In other words, the pact presented a united front against what Putin and Xi perceived to be Western meddling in each other's territorial and political ambitions.

Beyond security, the declaration also promised collaboration on space, climate change, the internet and AI. As Alexander Vershbow, a former US ambassador to Russia, put it to *The New Yorker*, the document 'shows that they're very much aligned in their vision of the world order in the twenty-first century'.[5] Putin described the partnership as 'unprecedented'. Xi, for his part, said that their joint strategy would have a 'far-reaching influence on China, Russia and the world'.[6]

With this proclamation in place, Russia moved forward with its invasion of Ukraine. When Putin's tanks crossed the border on 24 February 2022, eight years after his annexation of Crimea, the geopolitical equilibrium that had largely prevailed since the Second World War was effectively destroyed, marking what Francis Fukuyama might term a 'return of history'.

The pact did not happen in a vacuum, and neither was its timing a coincidence. The Winter Olympics of February 2022 saw another symbolic event: the official launch of the digital yuan. Throughout the games, Beijing had made it clear that it wasn't just competing for medals, it was setting out its stall in the race for the future of money.

China's new digital currency was everywhere. Visitors to the Beijing Games were given the opportunity to download a digital yuan wallet app, to store the digital money on a physical card or else get hold of wristbands, which could be swiped to make transactions.

The digital yuan's debut during the Winter Olympics followed more than a year of pilot runs in a dozen regions across the country. China now wanted to signal to the world that, while its new digital currency might still be in its infancy, it had grand ambitions for its future.

And so, if the pact of limitless cooperation made no mention of the global monetary order that had prevailed for the previous half-century, it's not because this had gone unnoticed by Beijing and Moscow. The timing of the pact and of the launch of the digital yuan went hand in hand, and symbolised the birth of a new world order.

THE INVASION OF UKRAINE: THE END OF THE WASHINGTON CONSENSUS

Soon after Russia's invasion, Moscow was hit by a set of unprecedented financial sanctions.

Starting on the first day of the invasion, the Ukrainian government asked the US and international community for Russia to be banned from using the SWIFT messaging system. As we've seen, this largely US-controlled system is used by thousands of financial institutions in more than 200 countries to facilitate cross-border money transfers. Several EU member states were initially reluctant, likely in fear of reprisals, since European lenders held around $30 billion in foreign banks with links to Russia.

But on Monday 28 February, four days into the war, the US Treasury Department announced its own moves to cut off Russia from the global economy – freezing Russian central bank assets held in the United States and imposing sanctions on the Russian Direct Investment Fund, the country's sovereign wealth fund.

This marked a pivotal shift in the norms and expectations governing the global financial system. Traditionally, central bank reserves – mostly held in US dollars, as the global reserve currency – are considered sovereign assets, immune from confiscation or political interference. This norm is based on the principles of sovereign immunity and the sanctity of central bank reserves, which underpin the stability and predictability of the international monetary system.

By freezing approximately $300 billion of Russia's foreign reserves, the West challenged this long-standing principle. This action demonstrated that reserves could be compromised or seized under certain political circumstances, thereby altering the perceived security of holding assets in foreign jurisdictions.

All of this was meant to curb Russia's ability to use its war chest of international reserves; Putin had been bolstering Russia's defences against sanctions over the course of decades by amassing $643 billion in foreign currency reserves from the country's oil and gas revenues, among other things.[7] By immobilising some of these assets, not only was the US Treasury defaulting on its foreign obligations, but the US was effectively weaponising what remained of the Washington Consensus and the US dollar's status as the world's reserve currency.

The use of the US dollar as the world's primary reserve currency has long been based partly on trust in the stability, reliability and neutrality of the US financial system, despite potential drawbacks, such as exposure to US policy decisions. Economist Eswar Prasad calls this the 'dollar trap'.[8]

The move against Russia's reserves is reminiscent of past instances in which a country's assets were frozen, such as those of Iran by the US during the 1979 hostage crisis. However, the scope and direct targeting of foreign reserves in this case were unprecedented, affecting the foundational trust that countries place in US-led financial architecture.

Then, on 1 March, the European Union, United Kingdom, Canada and the United States finally agreed to remove seven Russian banks from the SWIFT messaging system.

In a matter of weeks, the West had made an unexpected, unprecedented and coordinated decision to isolate Russia from the Western financial system, marking a major break in the international monetary order.

All this effectively created a *de facto* new world order in which foreign reserves were now worth only as much as the United States and its allies wanted them to be. The dollar trap at once became the 'euro-dollar trap'.

Crucially, these moves also signalled to China that the West was no longer abiding by its own protocols, and served to harden Beijing's resolve to create a parallel global financial order based on new digital payment rails.

Russia immediately drew on China's CIPS, alongside various cryptocurrency channels, as an alternative to the SWIFT system for its cross-border payments.

THE SIGNIFICANCE OF THE SINO-RUSSIAN ALLIANCE

To understand the significance of the China–Russia partnership, it helps to understand what is broadly the greatest fear of each nation, which explains the mutual benefits of their union.

Russian history is marked by a deep-seated fear of foreign invasions. Unlike other major nations shielded by natural barriers, such as the UK with its surrounding seas, and Italy and France with their long coastlines and mountainous borders, Russia lacks significant natural defences along its vast Western border. This vulnerability is not theoretical but has been brutally tested over the centuries, notably by Napoleon's invasion in 1812 and Hitler's attempt to capture Moscow in 1941, both aimed at decapitating the Russian or Soviet empires.

In response to these existential threats, Russia, under various regimes – from Tsarist and Soviet to the present-day Russian Federation – has consistently sought to create what analysts refer to as 'geopolitical depth'. This strategy involves establishing buffer states between Russia and the major European powers, primarily Germany and France. Historically, these buffer regions have included countries such as Belarus, Ukraine, the Baltic states, Poland and even Finland. By ensuring these nations lie between itself and potential aggressors, Russia aims to secure a strategic cushion; a protective layer to guard against possible invasions.

To achieve and maintain this geopolitical depth, Russia has resorted to direct military interventions, deeming indirect control and influence over neighbouring countries as inadequate. This ideology underpinned Soviet actions during the Cold War, leading to forceful interventions in neighbouring countries to maintain influence and control, such as the invasions of Hungary in 1956 and Czechoslovakia in 1968. The latter saw Russian tanks rolling into Prague, an iconic and chilling illustration of this doctrine in action.

Russia continues to view neighbouring territories as strategic buffers and extensions of its own security apparatus, rather than as sovereign nations. This historical backdrop is crucial to understanding Russia's underlying anxieties and current geopolitical strategies.

With regards to China's greatest fear, as we've seen, the BRI is designed to transcend its geographical limitations and to leverage its potential as a global economic powerhouse.

China's drive for global prominence is about more than economics, however. It is fuelled by a deep-seated desire to redress a period known as the 'century of humiliation'. Its greatest fear is the failure to rectify what it perceives as historical failures and injustices. This era, stretching from around the mid-nineteenth to the mid-twentieth century, represents a dark chapter in China's history, characterised by foreign domination, territorial concessions and profound internal strife.

During this century, China faced a series of defeats and interventions by Western powers and Japan, leading to significant territorial losses and the imposition of unequal treaties. These events began with the Opium Wars – in which China fought and lost wars against Great Britain from 1839–1842, and both Great Britain and France from 1856–1860 – and included incidents like the Boxer Rebellion and the humiliating terms of the Treaty of Versailles in 1919. The period also saw the loss of Hong Kong and Macau to European powers.

The memories of subjugation and exploitation have left an indelible mark on the Chinese national psyche, fostering a collective resolve to restore the nation's dignity and status on the world stage. The 'century of humiliation' not only motivates China's economic expansion but also informs its diplomatic and military policies, which are aimed at ensuring that the nation never again experiences such subordination.

Today, China is determined to restore its status as a pre-eminent global power, economically and technologically. Breaking away from the dollar-denominated financial system is a key component of this vision, together with advancements in emerging technologies.

So, what is the US's greatest fear? With its foundations in liberal democracy, established by the Founding Fathers who sought to escape European monarchism, America is inherently wary of any authoritarian regime that could challenge its global supremacy. This concern is particularly acute if the regime in question is both resource rich and technologically advanced.

In the 1920s and 1930s, the United States was alert to the rise of two such regimes: the resource-abundant Soviet Union under Stalin and the technologically sophisticated German dictatorship under Hitler. Initially, these developments were concerning but did not instil a deep fear for the US's own destiny. However, this changed dramatically when these two regimes, despite their ideological differences, decided to collaborate.

On 23 August 1939, just before the outbreak of the Second World War, Russia and Germany signed the Molotov-Von Ribbentrop Pact, a treaty of mutual non-aggression that effectively led to the division of Eastern Europe, including the erasure of Poland from geographical maps.

The alliance between Nazi Germany and the Communist Soviet Union – unofficially referred to as the Hitler–Stalin Pact and the

Nazi–Soviet Pact, and sometimes referred to as the 'midnight of the century' – represented Washington's worst geopolitical nightmare.

It signified the unification of Russia's vast natural resources with Germany's industrial prowess. This alliance was particularly disturbing as it brought together two diametrically opposed dictatorships in a unified front against the liberal-democratic principles of the United States. Its formation made the Second World War inevitable. The US's subsequent involvement in the war was driven by the need to dismantle this alliance, which posed an existential threat to the liberal democratic order it championed.

The obvious parallel here is with Presidents Xi and Putin's 'pact of limitless cooperation', which unites Russia's oil and gas reserves with China's formidable tech and manufacturing capabilities, adding a foreboding new dimension to the New Cold War.

THE WESTERN RESPONSE: THE US, UK AND EU SET OUT THEIR STALLS

Following the China–Russia pact of limitless cooperation, the launch of the digital yuan and Russia's subsequent invasion of Ukraine, the US saw that swift action was necessary. On 9 March 2022, two weeks into the conflict, President Joe Biden issued an executive order. This is a directive that can only be issued by the president of the United States. Executive orders are a big deal, and tend to be reserved for dealing with national emergencies, waging wars and initiating policy pivots requiring the direct and immediate intervention of the president. Presidential executive orders, once issued, remain in force until they are cancelled, revoked, adjudicated unlawful or expire on their terms.

In short, they signify national priorities. Amidst the unfolding of a major global conflict involving a key geopolitical adversary – a conflict which signalled the disruption of the post-Cold War equilibria over which the United States had presided for three decades – one might have expected the order to deal with further sanctions, military aid or perhaps even the deployment of troops.

Instead, the national priority being unveiled that day was an 'Executive Order on Ensuring Responsible Development of Digital Assets'. To anyone unfamiliar with the backdrop against which Russia's invasion had occurred, the timing of the order must have seemed puzzling. In the same month, the United Nations General Assembly passed a resolution condemning the invasion and demanding a full Russian withdrawal. The International Court of Justice ordered Russia to suspend military operations and the Council of Europe expelled Russia. But the president of the United States was ordering his government to look into 'digital assets' as a matter of urgent priority.[9]

Why? Finally, it seemed, the penny had dropped. The US was waking up to the geopolitical dimension of digital assets, and of CBDCs in particular. The White House's wordsmiths did their best not to make the connection too overt. The order opened with a generic reference to 'advances in digital and distributed ledger technology for financial services' which were having 'profound implications for the protection of consumers, investors, and businesses'.[10]

But in the paragraphs that immediately followed it cut to the chase, acknowledging that the US was leaving itself vulnerable to having the dollar's 'exorbitant privilege' undermined by alternative payment rails, stating that:

> Monetary authorities globally are also exploring, and in some
> cases introducing, central bank digital currencies (CBDCs).
> While many activities involving digital assets are within
> the scope of existing domestic laws and regulations, an area
> where the United States has been a global leader, growing
> development and adoption of digital assets and related
> innovations, as well as inconsistent controls to defend against
> certain key risks, necessitate an evolution and alignment of the
> United States Government approach to digital assets.[11]

In other words, the US was falling behind, didn't quite know what was going on in this space and needed to catch up. It had become evident that Russia was utilising alternative payment systems like CIPS, cryptocurrencies and digital currencies to sidestep the West's stringent sanctions. Therefore, regulating the realm of digital assets, particularly the evolving landscape of CBDCs, was crucial.

More importantly, however, the order went on to assert that it was high time the US thought seriously about developing its own digital currency:

> We must reinforce United States leadership in the global financial system and in technological and economic competitiveness, including through the responsible development of payment innovations and digital assets … My Administration sees merit in showcasing United States leadership and participation in international fora related to CBDCs and in multi-country conversations and pilot projects involving CBDCs … Any future dollar payment system should be designed in a way that is consistent with United States priorities and democratic values, including privacy protections, and that ensures the global financial system has appropriate transparency, connectivity, and platform and architecture interoperability or transferability, as appropriate … A United States CBDC that is interoperable with CBDCs issued by other monetary authorities could facilitate faster and lower-cost cross-border payments and potentially boost economic growth, support the continued centrality of the United States within the international financial system, and help to protect the unique role that the dollar plays in global finance.[12]

Almost overnight, the United States had awakened from its complacent slumber, and was gearing up to understand the simultaneous threats, opportunities and indeed responsibilities represented by the development of state-issued digital money. The order gave the US Department of the Treasury 180 days to report back on the desirability of developing a CBDC.

On 16 September 2022, the Treasury published three reports in response to Biden's executive order. Their first recommendation was to 'advance work on a possible U.S. CBDC, in case one is determined to be in the national interest'.[13] The Treasury Department was to lead an inter-agency working group (the 'CBDC Working Group') to support the Federal Reserve's efforts and to advance further work on a possible US CBDC, the reports stated. The CBDC Working Group would 'continue to assess the merits of a CBDC' and 'coordinate and consider implications of adoption of a U.S. CBDC for policy objectives such as national security, democratic values, the smooth functioning of the international financial system, financial inclusion, and privacy'.[14]

For a moment, the US appeared intent on leading again. Digital money was coming, and it was going to have far-reaching implications for the role of the dollar on the world stage. It just wasn't clear to Washington exactly how yet. The new Working Group certainly had a formidable task on its hands, and would need to ask and answer some critical questions in a very short space of time. Would the issuance of a CBDC help project or undermine American influence on the global stage? Could a CBDC be designed in a way that was compatible with liberal democracy?

However, there are other questions the US should be asking itself. If China started its work ten years ago and is presently running away with the race for the future of money, is there any point coming in second place? In other words, is it too late for the US to catch up, let alone to lead, even if it wanted to?

If the president's order deliberately omitted mention of the wider geopolitical context, it was left to other members of congress to say the quiet part out loud. On the same day as Biden's directive was issued, US Republican senators Bill Cassidy (Louisiana) and Marsha Blackburn (Tennessee) introduced a bill 'to crack down on China's digital currency'.[15] Titled 'Say No to the Silk Road Act', the bill proposed to 'set new regulations and guidelines on the Chinese Communist Party's (CCP) Digital Yuan'.

The bill warned that 'the Chinese Central Bank introduced the digital currency which could allow countries such as Russia to bypass global financial systems like SWIFT and empower the CCP to collect personal data on users.'

'China's Digital Yuan allows the CCP to collect personal data on their own citizens and foreign users alike,' said Dr Cassidy. 'This bill holds China accountable as they introduce their new digital currency.'

'Under Joe Biden's failed leadership, the new Axis of Evil is thriving,' said Senator Blackburn. 'If left unchecked, technologies including China's Digital Yuan will empower Russia to evade global sanctions on systems such as SWIFT and enable the CCP to further surveil and threaten their citizens. This legislation provides the United States with more information about the Digital Yuan to hold the new Axis of Evil to account.'

Across the Atlantic, the government of the United Kingdom was taking note and embarked on a similar reassessment of its stance on CBDCs.

Prior to Russia's invasion, the prevailing sentiment in UK political circles was largely that of scepticism dosed with a pinch of 'why bother?' This was aptly epitomised by a report published by the House of Lords Economic Affairs Committee in January 2022 that dismissed CBDCs as 'a solution in search of a problem'.[16] The report concluded that, while a CBDC might offer certain benefits, such as faster settlement speeds, it didn't really seem worth the hassle.

Following the outbreak of the war, however, it was growing increasingly apparent on both sides of the Atlantic that 'a problem' was perhaps at play after all when it came to digital money.

HM Treasury and the Bank of England soon began to overcome this initial scepticism, recognising the potential – as well as the inevitability – of CBDCs, in part influenced by the US president's executive order.

On 4 April 2022, four short weeks after President Biden's directive, Rishi Sunak, then the UK's Chancellor, announced the Treasury's official plans to 'make the UK a global crypto asset technology hub'.[17]

Like the Americans' announcement, the Treasury's press release sought to downplay the broader context – opting to entirely omit any overt reference to a CBDC. Instead, it eagerly played up opportunities for the private sector. But the plans made one thing clear, the UK was to become the global epicentre for digital assets, effectively promising to create a regulatory environment conducive to innovation and investment in the sphere of digital money. It was time to catch up with China.

The buried subtext of the announcement alluded to something more specific however. The Treasury's press release harked back to Sunak's Mansion House speech from July 2021 in which he set out his 'plan to ensure that the UK remains at the forefront of technology and innovation' in financial services.[18] Here, the Chancellor had boldly affirmed that, 'just as the UK pioneered paper banknotes in the seventeenth century, the first regulated stock exchange in the nineteenth, and the first ATM in the twentieth … our vision puts the UK at the forefront of technology and innovation in the twenty-first century. To promote the adoption of cutting-edge technologies we're … exploring the case for a central bank digital currency with the Bank of England.'

However, little had happened or been heard about on this front for the previous nine months. Now it was all happening at once. The UK would 'proactively explore the potentially transformative benefits of Distributed Ledger Technology (DLT)'.[19] The plan was supported by a series of groundbreaking proposals, all unveiled in April 2022, including the launch of a 'financial market infrastructure sandbox', the regulation of stablecoins and the establishment of a 'Cryptoasset Engagement Group'.[20] Soon enough these policies transitioned into actions. By June 2022, the UK Treasury granted the Bank of England the power to intervene in the regulation of stablecoins, as part of a broader legislative effort to safeguard against future disruptions in the cryptoasset market.[21]

Just twelve weeks after the House of Lords report, two months after Russia's invasion of Ukraine and a matter of weeks after President Biden's executive order, the UK government was unambiguously putting digital assets – and a CBDC – back on top of the policy agenda.

In April 2022, just as the UK was making a policy shift towards embracing digital assets, the EU made its own stance clear. Fabio

Panetta, then a member of the executive board of the ECB and the lead on the ECB's CBDC project, delivered a speech at Columbia University, in which he characterised the privately issued digital asset landscape as the 'Wild West'.[22] His overriding message was clear. While the cryptosphere is full of risk and uncertainty, digital money is here to stay, and the world's major powers had to act quickly if they wanted to stay ahead of the curve.

Panetta soon emerged as one of the leading advocates for the introduction of a digital euro, a stance that has been taken up by his successor on the ECB board, Piero Cipollone. Under their stewardship, the ECB and the eurozone more broadly has begun to look seriously at the issue of a Eurozone CBDC.

In a matter of weeks in 2022, the global monetary order was turned on its head. Both Russia and China were made to recognise that the United States would weaponise the global reserve currency at a moment's notice, and crystallised their resolve to move on to digital payment rails.

In turn, the West recognised the geopolitical significance of these payment rails and, almost overnight, the theme of digital assets underwent a transformation from a niche, lightly regulated frontier into a domain of immense strategic importance.

Following a lost decade of policy vacillation, there was a sense that the West was finally beginning to apprehend the bigger picture, which President Xi had been painting ever since he took power in 2013.

In June 2022, the alliance of liberal-democratic states set about reverse engineering the BRI. At the G7 Summit in Germany, President Biden announced the Partnership for Global Infrastructure and Investment (PGII), committing $600 billion to developing countries, aligning the investments with the Blue Dot Network principles, founded by the US, Japan and Australia. In an initiative clearly positioned as a liberal, transparent alternative to the BRI, the Blue Dot Network evaluates global infrastructure projects on criteria like financial transparency and environmental sustainability. Almost a decade after the launch of China's BRI and DSR, Western leaders were finally attempting to devise a grand strategy to rival China's influence over the infrastructure of developing countries in the Global South.

MOSCOW, 2023: RUSSIA AND CHINA RENEW THEIR WEDDING VOWS

In the immediate aftermath of Russia's invasion of Ukraine, some observers were eager to play down the connection between – and significance of – the pact of limitless cooperation and the launch of the digital yuan.

Writing in the *Financial Times* on 16 March 2022, Arthur Kroeber, a non-resident fellow at the Brookings Institute and founding partner of Gavekal Dragonomics, a China-focused economic research firm, stressed that the West need not worry, because the digital yuan was not yet ready to help Russia evade sanctions:

> It is reasonable to ask whether China's digital currency paves the way for a new, *dollar-free global monetary system* that would enable countries to evade American sanctions. *In the short run*, the answer is clearly no . . . the e-CNY is not even close to ready for large-scale international use, and has a negligible place even in domestic payments. Chinese policymakers have been clear from the outset that their *main goals for the digital yuan are domestic*: improving payments efficiency, serving the unbanked and fighting corruption.[23] [Authors' italics]

Kroeber's statement helpfully highlights three clear misconceptions that continue to be held in the minds of commentators and policymakers in the West.

The first is the strange insinuation that Vladimir Putin and Xi Jinping might either be short-sighted or short-termist.

The second and more bizarre idea is that the word of 'Chinese policymakers' should be taken at face value, in spite of the mountains of evidence that what Beijing's ruling party *says* does not always neatly equate with what it *does*.

The third is the idea that the internationalisation of the digital yuan would need to be the first step, rather than the last step, in the process of building a 'dollar-free global monetary system'.

Here is an alternative theory of how such a system might be built.

The first step would necessarily consist of building alliances. After all, what use is an internationally interoperable digital currency if one has no allies with whom to transact?

The second step would consist of encouraging one's allies to begin the steady process of denominating their trade in currencies other than the dollar. Perhaps, say, in good old-fashioned – as yet undigitised – Chinese yuan. After all, wouldn't the process of moving transactions to the digital yuan be made more seamless if one were already transacting and holding reserves in yuan rather than dollars?

The third and final step would be to convert – or make interchangeable – the yuan held in the foreign reserve accounts of those countries with a digital yuan, or a digital currency pegged to the yuan, or even a digital currency pegged to a basket of currencies that included the yuan. Or, as we will see, to move trade onto multi-CBDC bridges.

In the time that has elapsed since Russia's invasion of Ukraine, all three steps in this process have been blasted into motion – and in that order.

In March 2023, to mark the one-year anniversary since the pact of limitless cooperation was signed, President Xi made a two-day 'journey of friendship, co-operation and peace' to President Putin in Moscow.[24] The visit shredded any remaining doubts that their pact was either trivial or merely symbolic.

At the very least, the trip affirmed the central place of Russia in China's long-term foreign policy strategy. Mr Xi was the first major global leader to visit Moscow since Putin's invasion of Ukraine, bestowing his trip with undeniable diplomatic significance. Despite China's insistence of neutrality in that conflict, the visit confirmed that China should realistically be seen as Russia-leaning – a stance that has undermined China's relationship with the US and Europe.

From start to finish, the event was an unrelenting theatre. On the opening day's ceremony, the two leaders emerged next to each other through the vast golden doors of the Kremlin's grandest hall, before meeting beneath two flags – one Russian, one Chinese – whose full height the cameras of the world's press were unable to capture in shot.

President Xi, with his measured steps and confident demeanour, symbolised China's rising global influence, while President Putin, renowned – to himself at least – for his strategic finesse, exuded a seasoned and enigmatic aura.

The backdrop was adorned with intricate tapestries depicting the rich histories of their respective nations, serving as a reminder of their deep-rooted ties. It remains an image that many observers still find hard to believe. As former US Defense Secretary James Mattis put it in 2018, Moscow and Beijing have a 'natural nonconvergence of interests'.[25] Geography, history, culture, economics – all the factors that students of international relations focus on – give both nations many reasons to be adversaries.

Significant portions of what was once Chinese territory in earlier centuries now lie within the borders of Russia. Among these areas is Vladivostok, Moscow's crucial naval base in the Pacific – which retains its Chinese name, Haishenwai, on Chinese military maps. The 2,500-mile border separating the two nations has been a site of recurrent violent clashes, with the most recent occurring in 1969.

Russia played a prominent role as an adversary during China's 'century of humiliation'. It allied with Western imperialist powers to quash the Boxer Rebellion and coerced China into signing eight 'unequal treaties' in the latter half of the nineteenth century. In recent decades, the shifting dynamics resulting from Russia's decline as the second superpower in a bipolar world, coupled with China's rapid ascent, are likely to cause consternation for a leader as status-conscious as Putin. The reversal of positions on the global stage must be a matter of concern for him.

But as Harvard historian Graham Alison says, 'while history deals the hands, human beings play the cards', and so here were President Xi and President Putin, hosting a spectacle designed to mark 'a new era for strategic partnership', or what Xi called 'a new model of major-country relations'.[26] The pair wore matching purple ties.

In fact, Xi had set the stage for the announcement of a multipolar world before the first act had even begun. A month prior to the meeting, on 24 February 2023, the Chinese leader released a twelve-point statement aimed at positioning his country as a mediator in the Ukraine conflict.[27]

While the statement was coldly received by both Ukraine and Western countries – and though a Chinese-backed solution to the war remains a dim prospect – the speculative plan made symbolically clear that Xi was in Moscow to resume his negotiations with Putin about the shape of the new world order.

Among the areas of firm agreement was the need to recast the role of the US dollar. Claiming that around two-thirds of trade between Russia and China already took place in yuan, President Putin announced Russia's adoption of the yuan as one of the main currencies for its international reserves, overseas trade and even some personal banking services.[28]

He did not stop there. Putin made clear that he was not only interested in strengthening bilateral ties with China. True to the spirit of the previous year's pact, the Chinese–Russian axis was to serve as the linchpin of the new world order. Putin called for the outright internationalisation of the Chinese yuan and emphasised that Russia was strongly in favour of using the yuan in its settlements with the countries of Asia, Africa and Latin America.

By the end of that month – March 2023 – the yuan had become the most widely used currency for cross-border transactions in Russia, overtaking the dollar for the first time.[29]

As of May 2023, the yuan's share of international payments remained small at 2.54 per cent, according to SWIFT.[30] However, by April 2024 the yuan was approaching 5% of global payments, with the greenback accounting for 47% and the euro 22%.[31]

In the twelve months that elapsed since the pact of limitless cooperation was signed, China dramatically increased its use of the yuan to buy Russian commodities – roughly $88 billion worth – with nearly all of its purchases of oil, coal and some metals from its neighbour being settled in the Chinese currency instead of dollars.[32]

As for Kroeber's reassurance that, when it comes to the digital yuan, 'Chinese policymakers have been clear from the outset that their main goals [are] domestic', we have already seen the manner in which the BRI and DSR are preparing not only for the rollout of China's digital currency but also the very digital payment rails for 'the dollar-free global monetary system'.[33] In Part II, we'll further explore the multi-CBDC bridges through which this system is being built.

The first priority on the Chinese–Russian agenda, however, is to move away from dollars. Accordingly, on 5 July 2023, during his first appearance at an international event after a failed mutiny by the Wagner mercenary group, President Putin again highlighted Russia's trade with China – which he said is now primarily settled in the Chinese yuan and ruble – to tout the use of local currencies for trade on a global scale.

But where does Russia fit into all of this? As things stand, the relationship with China is evidently not one of equals. Russia is now the second-most dependent country on China for imports (next to North Korea) and is increasingly reliant on yuan. The share of yuan in payments for Russian exports has already grown from 0.5 per cent in 2021 to 16 per cent at the beginning of 2023.[34]

Putin's determination for Russia to transition to yuan for much of its international trade is undoubtedly a win for China, which in turn creates multiple vulnerabilities for Russia. The yuan is tightly controlled, giving Beijing power to alter Russia's trade revenues to its own advantage at any given moment. For example, shortly after Russia invaded Ukraine in 2022, China relaxed yuan controls to allow the already depreciating ruble to fall even faster in order to insulate Beijing from economic sanctions on Russia. Beijing could make similar moves in the future in order to boost the price of Chinese imports and decrease the cost of Russian exports to China.

The potential ramifications of this imbalance will not have been lost on Vladimir Putin. So, what is the Russian leader's endgame? The only rational inference that can be drawn is that Putin – like Xi – understands that denominating trade in yuan rather than dollars is not an end in itself. It represents only the first of several steps towards a bipolar monetary order that will serve Russia and China in equal measure. Neither the Russians nor the Chinese are thinking in terms of years or even decades. They are thinking in terms of centuries.

As the summit drew to a close on 22 March 2023, President Xi stood at the door of the Kremlin to bid the Russian leader farewell. Their parting was filmed, with translators speaking for both men. 'Right now, there are changes – the likes of which we haven't seen for a hundred years – and we are the ones driving these changes together,' Xi told Putin. The Russian president responded: 'I agree.'[35]

The challenge to the Western liberal-democratic order that has prevailed since the end of the First Cold War could not have been laid out in more stark terms.

Part II

Smart Money in a Bipolar World

8

What's at Stake?
The New Clash of Civilisations

The chief support of an autocracy is a standing army. The
chief support of a democracy is an educated people.
LOTUS D. COFFMAN[1]

In 2023, the group of G7 liberal democracies was being chaired
by Japan. On 12 April, three weeks after the leaders of China
and Russia had reconvened in Moscow, Japan's vice minister of
finance and international affairs – effectively the country's top
currency diplomat – Masato Kanda, was addressing a seminar in
Washington, D.C.

'As a priority of this year, the G7 will consider how best to help
developing countries introduce CBDC consistent with appropriate
standards, including the G7 public policy principle for retail
CBDC,' he said. This would be a key priority of G7 discussions
throughout the year, he added, emphasising that it was incumbent
on the G7 to 'address risks from the development of CBDC by
ensuring factors such as appropriate transparency and sound
governance'.[2]

The G7 was waking up and beginning to apprehend China's
broader plan. The democratic world's agenda was being reset, and
digital currencies were taking centre stage.

The twenty-first century is set to become a battle for influence over the developing world, and the fault lines of this New Cold War between the United States and China are being drawn around critical infrastructure, *digital* infrastructure – and digital money. Both sides have their allies and proxies. On the one side, there is the G7 group of liberal democracies, and on the other, a loosely assembled but fast consolidating BRICS+ group, made up of a mixture of powerful, technologically advanced and resource-rich autocracies – China, Russia, Saudi Arabia, the United Arab Emirates (UAE), Iran – and fast-growing democracies such as India and Brazil.

What makes this split all the more significant is that we are fast approaching a tipping point: many of the world's natural resources are rapidly depleting, and access to them is becoming more expensive, which means that economic growth (fuelled by these resources) will also be difficult to sustain. The very nature of geopolitical power is changing as a result. In the twenty-first century, great powers will be defined by their ability to access cheap energy, rather than their economic output and military might. After all, the latter is dependent on the former.

How, you might ask, is this connected to smart money? Simply put, the rise of a new monetary paradigm that will run on digital payment rails controlled – or heavily influenced – by China represents a secret weapon for the world's resource-rich autocracies.

Historically, the US and its allies have been able to access the cheap energy they need thanks to the exorbitant privilege of the US dollar. As we've seen, since oil is priced in dollars, countries need to hold substantial reserves of US dollars to participate in the oil market. This ensures sustained global demand for the US dollar, strengthening the currency relative to others. A strong dollar reduces the cost of imports for the US and its allies, effectively making energy cheaper for them.

Additionally, oil-exporting countries selling their oil in dollars tend to invest their profits in dollar-denominated assets, particularly US government bonds, through a system called petrodollar recycling. This keeps global interest rates low and helps maintain the stable economic conditions required for steady oil production and relatively low energy costs.

But this set of favourable circumstances for the US can no longer be taken as a given. As the world splits in two, many liberal democracies – predominantly service- and manufacturing-based economies – could soon find themselves in a position of dependency on resource-rich countries outside their sphere of influence, causing energy prices to skyrocket.

So, in the bipolar monetary order, there is much more at stake than money. In Part II, we will look at how smart money will shape – and be shaped by – competing ideologies, help determine the allocation of critical resources and influence new dimensions of warfare in cyberspace. If the West does not confront the geopolitical ramifications of CBDCs, it could soon be facing a catastrophic collapse in living standards. In other words, the West needs to wake up to the brave new world of smart money, or else risk its own extinction.

I. IDEOLOGY: DEMOCRACY VERSUS AUTOCRACY

Like the First Cold War, today's battlefields are not just about territories but ideologies. But where capitalism and communism defined the conflict between the United States and the Soviet Union in the twentieth century, the current stand-off is about democracy versus autocracy. The Western concept of democracy is under threat from autocracies like China and Russia, which are seeking to dilute and redefine the essence of liberal democracy, as it has traditionally been understood in the West.

As we've seen, the summit that took place in Beijing on 4 February 2022 between Xi Jinping and Vladimir Putin was intended to mark the beginning of a rival world order to that of the West. While committing to 'limitless cooperation' – which led almost immediately to Russia's invasion of Ukraine – the two powers sought to redefine the very nature of democracy. The opening sentences of their joint statement read:

The sides share the understanding that democracy is a universal human value, rather than a privilege of a limited number of States, and that its promotion and protection is a common responsibility of the entire world community.

The sides believe that democracy is a means of citizens' participation in the government of their country with the view to improving the well-being of population [sic] and implementing the principle of popular government ... There is no one-size-fits-all template to guide countries in establishing democracy. A nation can choose such forms and methods of implementing democracy that would best suit its particular state, based on its social and political system, its historical background, traditions and unique cultural characteristics. It is only up to the people of the country to decide whether their State is a democratic one ... The sides note that Russia and China as world powers with rich cultural and historical heritage have long-standing traditions of democracy, which rely on thousand-years of experience of development [sic], broad popular support and consideration of the needs and interests of citizens.[3]

It is indeed curious to witness two autocratic leaders commence a public declaration with an ostensible endorsement of democracy. Yet, the democracy they extol starkly contrasts with the version cherished by Western nations. In the West, democracy is fundamentally a mechanism through which citizens elect their leaders. For Russia and China, however, democracy is framed as the government's role in enhancing the well-being of its citizens through participatory governance. This divergence presents a profound challenge to the West's historical and contemporary understanding – and embodiment – of democracy.

The Western democratic model is anchored in the belief that democratic elections ensure leaders are accountable to their citizens and make decisions aligned with the public's interests. In stark contrast, Russia and China's interpretation of democracy places little emphasis on the electoral process. Both regimes profess to act in their citizens' best interests by prioritising the outcomes of governance: the provision of essential public services, defence against external threats, and fostering a positive economic environment to maintain social stability.

This reframing of democracy serves as a potent rhetorical tool, enabling Russia and China to challenge the moral high ground frequently claimed by the US, Europe and their allies. By emphasising actions and results, they seek to portray the West's vaunted commitment to democratic elections as superficial. Furthermore, by destabilising this traditional democratic narrative and eroding the West's perceived moral authority, China and Russia create a pretext for pursuing their territorial ambitions. According to their logic, the ends justify the means, legitimising even violent attempts to reclaim or annex territories under the guise of reuniting historic motherlands.

In 2023, to mark the tenth anniversary of the BRI, President Xi Jinping unveiled three ambitious new ventures: the Global Development Initiative (GDI), the Global Security Initiative (GSI), and the Global Civilization Initiative (GCI). These initiatives, much like the BRI, ostensibly aim to support developing nations but are, in reality, instruments of China's grand expansionist strategy.

In practice, these schemes are attempts to curry favour and consolidate power in countries crucial to China's global aspirations. The development initiative is an obvious extension of the BRI, through which China has bolstered its infrastructure investments and development aid to key African and Latin American nations. This strategy not only strengthens trade ties but also secures access to vital natural resources and emerging markets.

The security initiative seeks to forge alliances in strategically significant regions such as Central Asia and the Middle East through cooperation in cybersecurity, counterterrorism and military training. This ensures stability in areas critical to China's energy interests. Though somewhat nebulous in its articulation, the initiative is increasingly referenced in diplomatic dialogues and bilateral agreements.

The GSI also serves as Beijing's framework for positioning itself as a mediator in regional conflicts, including the ongoing Russia–Ukraine war. The underlying ambition is clear: to erect a global security architecture capable of rivalling the US-led system of treaties, alliances and institutions.

Meanwhile, the civilisation initiative promotes cultural exchange and dialogue, particularly in Southeast Asia and Central Europe. Its goal is to disseminate favourable narratives about China's governance model and counter Western influence, thereby enhancing China's soft power and cultivating political environments sympathetic to its values and geopolitical objectives.

AUTOCRACY ON THE RISE

The twentieth century witnessed the monumental defeat of fascism and Nazism in the Second World War and the eventual collapse of the communist Soviet Union, which were heralded as significant victories for democratic regimes. These pivotal events fostered a widespread belief that the world would inexorably gravitate towards liberal, capitalist democracy.

However, the twenty-first century presents a more intricate and uncertain landscape. The once prevailing assumption that democracy would triumph globally has been challenged by a resurgence of autocratic governance models and the erosion of democratic norms even within established democracies. The 2023 Democracy Index by the Economist Intelligence Unit reveals that this shift transcends regional boundaries, emerging as a global phenomenon affecting nations with diverse cultural and economic backgrounds.[4] The optimistic narrative of democracy's inevitable ascendancy now contends with a reality far more complex and disconcerting.

What is most alarming is the increasingly blurred distinction between democratic and autocratic governance. Countries that are nominally democratic, such as Hungary and Turkey, have experienced a creeping authoritarianism where elected leaders subvert checks and balances, co-opt the media and erode civil liberties, resulting in what some scholars call 'illiberal democracies' (or 'electoral democracies', as opposed to 'liberal democracies', such as the US and most European countries). Conversely, some autocracies adopt the veneer of democracy by holding elections and establishing pseudo-democratic institutions, all while eschewing genuine democratic principles to legitimise their rule.

Moreover, autocratic leaders often garner support by promising stability, economic development and national rejuvenation – contrasting sharply with the political gridlock and economic stagnation that can plague democratic systems. The allure of the autocratic model in certain contexts reveals deeper societal divisions and a crisis of confidence in democratic institutions, which autocrats deftly exploit to consolidate power.

These shifts in governance styles and the ideological tug of war they signify reflect a world in flux. The very definition of democracy is being contested and redefined, both by those who seek to undermine it from within and by those who outright reject it. This raises critical questions about the future of governance, international cooperation and the global order. The twenty-first century will undoubtedly be marked by an implicit and explicit battle between democratic and autocratic regimes. Just as the future of democracy is under debate, so too is the future of money. Digital state-issued currency is on the horizon, and the pressing question is: will it be shaped and governed by the world's liberal or illiberal states?

II. GEOPOLITICS: ANARCHY AND THE RETURN OF ALLIANCES

The geopolitical stage is currently undergoing a major reshuffle, as it divides once again into two principal power blocs. And as the world order begins to bifurcate, so will the global monetary order. As Professor Nouriel Roubini stated in the *Financial Times* in February 2023:

> Sceptics argue that the global share of the US dollar as unit of account, means of payment and store of value hasn't fallen much, despite all the chatter about a terminal decline ... nuanced arguments point out that there are economies of scale and network that lead to a relative monopoly in reserve currency status, and that the Chinese renminbi cannot become a real reserve currency unless capital controls are phased out and the exchange rate made more flexible ... such sceptics argue that all attempts to create a multipolar reserve currency regime – even an IMF Special Drawing Right basket that includes the renminbi – have so far failed to replace the dollar.
>
> These points may once have had some validity, but in a world that will be increasingly divided into two geopolitical spheres of influence – namely those surrounding the US and China – it is likely that a bipolar, rather than a multipolar, currency regime will eventually replace the unipolar one.[5]

The G7 group of liberal democracies is facing challenges from the Sino-Russian axis and the BRICS+ nations, which include significant players like India, Saudi Arabia, and the UAE – nations whose allegiances remain fluid. The G7 harbours concerns that the synergy of China's technological prowess and Russia's vast natural resources will draw many into the Sino-Russian orbit.

The New Cold War and the advent of smart money are phenomena that mutually reinforce each other. It is not merely the development of digital currencies that will divide the world; rather, the existing geopolitical rift will be deepened and accelerated by the rise of digital currencies. This development will expedite the emergence of a bipolar monetary world, intensify its conflicts and exacerbate their consequences. In essence, while the dawn of a bipolar geopolitical landscape has catalysed the rise of smart money, the proliferation of smart money will, in turn, solidify the contours of a bipolar world.

GLOBAL ANARCHY

To comprehend the key battlegrounds shaping the twenty-first century, one must first grasp the current state of international relations. Today's global political landscape can aptly be described by the concept of anarchy – not in the sense of chaos, but in its original meaning as articulated by political scientist John Mearsheimer: the absence of a centralised global authority or 'ultimate arbiter' capable of governing states or resolving conflicts.[6] This concept underscores the lack of a supranational power that can enforce order and adjudicate disputes among nations.

In such a scenario, global governance institutions are indispensable. However, the current international bodies designed for this purpose are either underperforming or facing significant challenges. The United Nations Security Council (UNSC), ostensibly the highest authority on global security issues, exemplifies this dysfunction. Frequently, the UNSC finds itself in a state of paralysis, as the five permanent members (the United States, the United Kingdom, France, China and Russia) often splinter into opposing factions. Typically, France and the UK align with the US, while Russia and China form the countervailing bloc. This ideological schism mirrors the broader polarisation of the world and severely impedes the UNSC's ability to make unanimous and effective decisions on critical global matters.

Other international fora, such as the G20, which convenes the world's major economies to tackle pressing global economic issues, suffer from similar afflictions. Members frequently align themselves with either the US or China, creating a rupture that hinders consensus and meaningful action.

This division within major international bodies is a microcosm of broader geopolitical tensions, where the major powers are often starkly opposed. Such a fragmented landscape is hardly conducive to multilateral cooperation. In the absence of a unifying global authority, the international arena remains mired in rivalry and a perpetual struggle for dominance.

The G20 summit held in New Delhi in September 2023 epitomised the current geopolitical malaise. The gathered world leaders struggled to find enough consensus to produce a final communiqué, and the eventual joint statement was notable for its lack of substance. Most conspicuously, it entirely omitted any mention of Russia's invasion of Ukraine, opting instead for insipid language that weakly proclaimed: 'all states must refrain from the threat or use of force to seek territorial acquisition against the territorial integrity and sovereignty or political independence of any state'.[7]

Yet, amidst this diplomatic inertia, two significant Western-led initiatives emerged. Firstly, the summit saw the establishment of the India–Middle East–Europe Economic Corridor (IMEC), a topic we shall explore in greater detail later in this chapter.

Secondly, under the stewardship of Prime Minister Giorgia Meloni, Italy decided not to renew its participation in the BRI, marking a notable pivot in its foreign policy towards Western allies, particularly the United States. Italy, under the leadership of Giuseppe Conte, had signed a memorandum of understanding with China in 2019, hoping to benefit from China's burgeoning international investments and its expanding domestic market.

These developments indicate that Western countries are becoming more self-aware and assertive in their engagements with China. Nevertheless, in the grand contest, they represent only modest achievements.

THE RETURN OF ALLIANCES: THE G7 VERSUS BRICS+

The G7 consortium, established in 1975, once enjoyed unchallenged dominance over the global economy. In 1990, the G7 nations collectively accounted for approximately 70 per cent of the world's economic output. However, the economic landscape has undergone a seismic shift over the past three decades. Today, the G7's share of the global economy has dwindled to about 43 per cent.[8] Notably, within the G7, the United States has seen its relative economic influence surge. In 1990, the US constituted

40 per cent of the G7's GDP; by 2024, this figure had climbed to around 58 per cent.[9]

In recent years, a potentially formidable power bloc has emerged, centred around the BRICS group – Brazil, Russia, India, China and South Africa – formally established in 2009. This coalition now presents a substantial challenge to the once unquestioned hegemony of the G7 nations, a threat that has been perilously underestimated.

China's meteoric economic rise has been particularly striking. As we have observed, China is swiftly nearing the United States in terms of its share of global GDP. By 2018, the BRICS countries had surpassed the G7 in their share of the world's total GDP when measured by purchasing power parity.[10] These adjusted GDP metrics underscore the group's rapid economic growth, largely propelled by China and India, where lower domestic costs and expanding consumer markets have led to higher adjusted GDP levels.[11]

The BRICS group has recently undergone a momentous expansion. At a summit in Johannesburg in August 2023, the group extended invitations to six additional countries: Saudi Arabia, Iran, Ethiopia, the UAE, Egypt and Argentina. By January 2024, five of these nations had joined, with Argentina opting out following the election of President Milei in October 2023, who had campaigned on aligning the country's foreign policy more closely with the West.

This enlargement significantly amplifies the group's global influence. The bloc now accounts for approximately 37.5 per cent of global GDP (rising from 26.3 per cent prior to the expansion), 46 per cent of the world's population, 43 per cent of global oil production and 25 per cent of global goods exports.[12] The G7 group accounts for approximately 43 per cent of the world's GDP, 10 per cent of the world's population, 30 per cent of global oil production and 31.5 per cent of global goods exports.[13] However, with populations in sub-Saharan Africa, Latin America, India and Southeast Asia projected to grow – contrasting sharply with stagnating or declining birth rates in the US and Europe – this shift in economic and demographic power is poised to continue, if not accelerate.

China harbours grand ambitions for the expanded BRICS+ coalition, evidenced by its deepening trade relationships with member nations. It aspires to position this group as a formidable counterbalance to the Western-centric G7. In the absence of a global platform for conflict resolution, fora like the G7 and BRICS+ have begun to assume mediation roles. However, it is worth noting that decisions made within these groups lack the binding global authority of those from the UNSC.

As these dynamics unfold, the world seems increasingly vulnerable to conflicts and instability. Over the past decade, the geopolitical landscape has shifted, marking closer ties within the BRICS+ group.

Consider Russia's 2016 integration into the expanded OPEC+ alliance, which bolstered Russian–Saudi cooperation over global oil supplies. More recently, the pact between Saudi Arabia and its long-standing adversary Iran – brokered by China and signed in Beijing on 10 March 2023 – highlights this realignment. Simultaneously, Pakistan is drawing nearer to China, Russia is deepening its involvement in Syria and Libya, and making overtures towards Turkey, all of which indicates a strategic expansion of Sino-Russian influence in the region.

Moreover, nations such as Venezuela, Ecuador, Peru, Bolivia, Chile and Uruguay have all aligned themselves with China's BRI. This trend signifies a marked departure from the era of US dominance in the region, as we've seen historically enshrined in the Monroe Doctrine, which proclaimed Latin America as the US's sphere of influence ('America for the Americans'). The recent ascendance of left-wing populist leaders in Latin America appears to be catalysing this shift towards China, already the pre-eminent market for South American commodities.

China's influence in Africa is also expanding at an unprecedented pace. The lingering memories of European colonialism have made many African nations more receptive to Chinese investments, despite the neo-colonialist undertones of Beijing's approach. China's comprehensive proposals, including the development of digital payment infrastructures and strategic acquisitions, have solidified its position as a favoured partner. Numerous African countries have signed memorandums of understanding with China to join the BRI. The pressing challenge for Western nations now is to present more compelling alternatives.

INDIA'S SPECIAL POSITION

Against this complex backdrop, India emerges as a strategic fulcrum. With its burgeoning population – now surpassing that of China – rapidly expanding economy, democratic heritage, and English-speaking culture, India occupies a singular position between the superpowers of the West and East.

Currently, India's economy ranks as the fifth largest by nominal GDP and third largest by purchasing power parity, and is projected to maintain its vigorous growth trajectory.[14] This economic strength affords India a degree of strategic autonomy, enabling it to navigate the fraught relations between the US and China without committing fully to either side.

During the First Cold War, India stood as a foremost member of the Non-Aligned Movement, a coalition of states that refused to formally align with any major power bloc. Nevertheless, India arguably cultivated closer ties with the Soviet Union, particularly as the US became embroiled in conflicts in Korea and Vietnam.

India's contemporary strategy mirrors this historical approach. It maintains strong trade relations with both the US and China while carefully balancing its strategic interests. For example, India is a member of the Quadrilateral Security Dialogue (Quad), alongside the US, Japan and Australia, which serves as a counterbalance to China's growing influence in the Indo-Pacific region. Simultaneously, India engages with China through platforms such as the BRICS+ group and the Shanghai Cooperation Organisation, despite periodic clashes in the Himalayas over recent decades. In essence, India performs a delicate diplomatic balancing act, deftly manoeuvring between competing global powers.

On the one hand, critics argue, Prime Minister Narendra Modi's government has adopted a more assertive, nationalistic approach, reminiscent of the autocratic tendencies observed in Russia and China. This was starkly illustrated by India's decision to abstain from the UN resolution condemning Russia's invasion of Ukraine, aligning itself with China and against the majority of the international community – 141 countries voted in favour, while only thirty-two, including India and China, abstained.

Despite its nationalistic domestic policies, India has increasingly gravitated towards the United States and its allies in recent years. This shift can partly be attributed to President Biden's proactive efforts to strengthen ties with India.

In June 2023, Prime Minister Modi was invited for a state visit to Washington, D.C. During this visit, India and the United States forged a series of technological and strategic partnerships, particularly in the critical sectors of semiconductors and satellite industries. Furthermore, India agreed to purchase advanced military equipment from the US, signalling enhanced defence cooperation that could significantly alter the balance of power in the Indo-Pacific region and beyond.

India has also committed to joining the US-led Artemis programme, aimed at heralding a new era of space exploration. This collaboration is particularly noteworthy as it involves the exchange of critical information in both technology and defence – a privilege typically reserved for established allies – marking a significant milestone in US–India relations.

This burgeoning partnership was further solidified by a joint statement issued during the G20 meeting in New Delhi in September 2023, where Modi and Biden reaffirmed 'the close and enduring partnership between India and the United States'.[15] Perhaps more significantly, the conference announced the creation of the India–Middle East–Europe Economic Corridor (IMEC), an early milestone of President Biden's and the G7's Partnership for Global Infrastructure and Investment, designed to counter China's BRI.

The IMEC, a deal to build railways and ports, aims to establish a more integrated and efficient trade route connecting India, the Middle East and Europe. Key signatories to the memorandum of understanding include India, the United States, Saudi Arabia, the United Arab Emirates and European Union member states such as France, Germany and Italy.

The agreement envisions a trade corridor spanning approximately 4,800 kilometres, linking significant ports like Fujairah, Jebel Ali, Abu Dhabi, Haifa, Mundra, Kandla, Piraeus, Marseille and Messina. This network aims to enhance trade logistics, providing a reliable and cost-effective transit option that complements existing maritime and road transport routes.

The IMEC promises to significantly reduce transportation costs between Europe and its connected regions, with estimates suggesting reductions of 30–40 per cent. Ursula von der Leyen, President of the European Commission, also predicted that trade between India and Europe could be conducted approximately 40 per cent faster.[16] Additionally, the project includes plans for power and data cables, as well as a clean hydrogen pipeline, reflecting a commitment to sustainable and efficient trade practices. This initiative not only enhances economic ties but also underscores a strategic counterbalance to China's expanding influence.

However, the IMEC is not without its challenges, particularly the ongoing conflicts in the Middle East, which could impede progress. Concerns about financing also loom large, with estimates suggesting costs could soar up to $8 billion.[17] Nonetheless, the IMEC represents a strategic victory for the West in the tussle over supply chains and fortifies ties with India.

This initiative has already provoked counteractions. Excluded from the IMEC due to its affiliations with Russia and strategic alignment with China, Turkey has proposed the Iraq Development Road, aiming to involve countries such as Kuwait, Iraq, Qatar and the UAE. This corridor is intended to complement the North–South Transport Corridor connecting India, Iran, Azerbaijan and Russia.

In any case, these initiatives and their myriad acronyms – BRI, RCEP, PGII and IMEC – reveal a world sliding back into Cold War-era trading blocs. A 'war of corridors' has been ignited as the world's superpowers vie for control over critical supply chains. In the coming years, China and its allies intend to capture and secure these corridors – with the aid of smart money.

9

Digital De-dollarisation: The BRICS+ and the Rise of the Non-dollar World

'How did you go bankrupt?'
'Two ways. Gradually, then suddenly.'
ERNEST HEMINGWAY, *THE SUN ALSO RISES*[1]

In a bipolar monetary order, it is not merely the internationalisation of the yuan or its digital counterpart that imperils the dollar's dominance, but rather the potential shift of some of the world's largest economies – those within BRICS+ and BRI partner countries – to digital payment infrastructures constructed by China. This shift would enable China to control and regulate trade between these jurisdictions.

The question then arises: why have Western commentators persistently underestimated China and the BRICS+ alliance as a formidable challenge to the G7? As the BRICS+ group continues to expand, it demands greater scrutiny, especially given China's recent strides in digital currencies and multi-CBDC networks. The West, it seems, remains woefully unprepared to counter this threat, comforted by the sense that if de-dollarisation is happening at all, it is occurring at a slow pace. However, this gradual shift could soon become an abrupt upheaval.

THE BRICS+

The expansion of the BRICS group in January 2024 has ignited a vigorous public debate about its potential to coalesce into a homogeneous power bloc, capable of challenging the supremacy of the United States and the G7 nations. Admittedly, the group comprises a motley assortment of countries, and their past efforts to harmonise policies, particularly in the monetary and economic realms, have been routinely derided and dismissed by Western commentators. However, there is reason to believe that this time may indeed be different.

Central to this is the group's renewed focus on de-dollarisation. While this in itself is not new territory for the group, the current context – a world where new technologies have enabled the emergence of new forms of money – is unprecedented.

Although the BRICS+ members broadly concur on the desire to diminish the dollar's dominance in international trade, they diverge on the methods to achieve this. Some advocate for prioritising the Chinese yuan, others favour trading in local currencies, and yet another faction supports the idea of a common currency shared by the BRICS+ as a whole. In recent months, however, there appears to be a convergence towards the idea of moving trade onto multiple-CBDC bridges, indicating a potentially unified strategy in the making.

COMMON CURRENCY

On the eve of the BRICS summit that led to the group's expansion into the BRICS+, in Johannesburg in August 2023, Brazil's president Luiz Inácio Lula da Silva made a bold call for the group to establish a common currency for trade and investment, aiming to mitigate their exposure to the vicissitudes of dollar exchange rate fluctuations.[2] Although this proposal was not formally on the summit's agenda, it nonetheless sparked a range of responses from other BRICS+ leaders, spanning from interest to scepticism.

India's foreign minister dismissed the notion of a BRICS+ currency, preferring instead to focus on enhancing trade in national currencies. Russian president Vladimir Putin also pushed for the idea of conducting trade among member countries in their own currencies rather than the dollar. China's President Xi alluded to the broader ambition of reforming the international financial and monetary system, though he refrained from explicitly endorsing a common currency for the bloc.[3]

In theory, the potential benefits of a BRICS+ currency could be substantial for the group. It would mitigate the risks associated with fluctuations in US monetary policy, facilitate economic integration among member countries and, crucially, allow members to circumvent US trade sanctions.

However, the implementation of such a common currency is fraught with complexities and is unlikely to materialise in the near future. Establishing a common currency would run into significant challenges due to the economic, political, and geographic disparities among the member countries. South African central bank governor Lesetja Kganyago aptly described it as a 'political project' that would require macroeconomic convergence and the establishment of a common central bank.[4] Furthermore, trade imbalances, especially given China's predominant role as the main trading partner for most BRICS+ members, would add an additional layer of complexity to such an ambitious endeavour.

While the countries in the eurozone also have significant economic disparities – consider the chasm between Germany and Greece – the differences between the BRICS+ nations are even more pronounced. China's economy dwarfs those of its counterparts, while Brazil, Russia, India and South Africa contend with distinct economic structures and challenges. Inflation rates, for instance, vary wildly, with some BRICS+ nations regularly grappling with double-digit inflation while others maintain comparatively lower rates.

The establishment of the euro required member countries to cede considerable control over their monetary policy to a centralised institution, the European Central Bank. Achieving a similar level of political cohesion among the BRICS+ nations would be exponentially more challenging due to their disparate governance structures and divergent foreign policy agendas. The eurozone itself has struggled with maintaining cohesion, particularly during economic crises. A BRICS+ monetary union would face even greater risks, given the broader cultural and political divides.

Moreover, the expansion of the group has set a precedent, with an additional twenty to thirty countries expressing interest in joining. Most members appear enthusiastic about further enlarging the group.

At the 2023 conference, the anticipated announcement of a common digital currency gave way to discussions about trading in local currencies instead of the dollar. Consequently, the most plausible scenario at present is that the group will collaborate in launching their own interoperable digital currencies, which could be linked together to form a new international payment system.

MULTI-CBDC BRIDGES

In 2024, events began unfolding precisely along these lines. In January, the newly expanded group met for the first time, hosted by Russia, the group's chair for 2024. Iran – similarly hampered by US sanctions – called for prioritising the development of digital currency systems.

The notion of a unified payment system gained further momentum in February when Russia proposed the development and implementation of a BRICS-wide system utilising CBDCs. Russian finance minister Anton Siluanov introduced the concept of the 'BRICS Bridge', a system designed to address the fragmentation of the current payment system outside of the West's 'unfriendly infrastructure'. Siluanov asserted that the bloc was prepared to commence testing this system imminently.[5]

On 5 March 2024, additional details emerged, with the Russian news agency TASS announcing that the BRICS+ nations would collaborate to establish an independent payment system grounded in digital currencies and blockchain technology. Kremlin aide Yury Ushakov said in an interview with TASS:

> We believe that creating an independent BRICS payment system is an important goal for the future, which would be based on state-of-the-art tools such as digital technologies and blockchain. The main thing is to make sure it is convenient for governments, common people and businesses, as well as cost-effective and free of politics.[6]

Furthermore, the Kremlin asserted that the paramount objective for 2024 should be for the group to augment their influence within the international monetary and financial system. In line with this, Russia's statement also advocated for settling transactions in national currencies and fortifying correspondent banking networks to secure international transactions. An example of this is the development of the Contingent Reserve Arrangement, which aims to provide liquidity in response to balance of payments pressures.

The so-called BRICS Bridge could pose a formidable challenge to the dollar-dominated global order, but it is not the only contender on the horizon. Another sophisticated multi-CBDC initiative, mBridge, began gaining traction in 2023. This project, co-developed by China, Thailand, Hong Kong and the UAE, is explicitly designed to expand the reach of China's digital yuan and other CBDCs.

As Bastian Benrath, Alessandro Speciale and Christopher Condon argued in an extended feature in *Bloomberg* about mBridge in August 2023:

> The Beijing-backed digital prototype for sending money around the world without relying on US banks is advancing so quickly that some European and American observers now view it as an emerging challenger to dollar-denominated payments in global finance …

The stakes are enormous. The dollar features in an estimated $6.6 trillion of foreign exchange transactions every day, while half of the approximately $32 trillion in global trade each year is invoiced in dollars, according to BIS [Bank for International Settlements] and United Nations data. mBridge could eventually make it easier for China's yuan to be used as a dollar alternative by enabling its digital form to settle large corporate transactions.[7]

The platform has been in development since 2017, yet Western observers, in their customary myopia, largely dismissed this significant initiative until recently. However, with a proof of concept and a pilot programme involving a selection of commercial banks and payment service providers in the participating countries now completed, the project is poised to revolutionise cross-border wholesale payments.

Moreover, it is increasingly evident that Beijing is not merely participating but is likely leading – or even controlling – the initiative. In October 2023, Chinese media reported that mBridge was transitioning to the Dashing protocol, developed by the Digital Currency Research Institute of the People's Bank of China and Tsinghua University, an institution affiliated with and funded by China's Ministry of Education.[8] In an article titled 'A CBDC Alternative to SWIFT?' from November 2023, CoinDesk reporter Noelle Acheson emphasised:

> This is significant in that it highlights just how much mBridge is a Chinese project, with international add-ons. China is the main trading partner for all the other key participants, and the UAE has been making moves to also deepen its investment and military relationship with the region. The UAE central bank representative on the project, Shu-Pui Li, spent 17 years at the Hong Kong Monetary Authority (HKMA). And the CEO of the UAE's principal sovereign wealth fund is also the Presidential Special Envoy to China.[9]

Bloomberg corroborated this by reporting that 'according to two people with direct knowledge of the project, the technological backbone of mBridge is a Chinese-built blockchain'.[10]

China's Digital Currency Research Institute (DCRI) made clear mBridge doesn't support US dollar payments.[11] A critical factor in mBridge's success will therefore be its ability to provide competitive exchange rates and FX liquidity.

Activity on the platform is steadily escalating. On 29 January 2024, the Central Bank of the UAE executed its first cross-border digital dirham transfer using the mBridge CBDC platform, sending 50 million dirhams ($13.6 million) to China. Reportedly, Sheikh Mansour, the bank's chairman, personally conducted the CBDC transfer.[12]

The benefits for participants in the mBridge project are self-evident. Transactions conducted on these digital payment rails using blockchain technology can be completed almost instantaneously – mBridge payments take seven seconds, according to the DCRI, and it halves their cost. This is in stark contrast to traditional cross-border transfers, which can take up to five days.

Additionally, the platform simplifies currency conversion. For instance, a company in China could pay a vendor in the UAE by having its bank issue a digital e-yuan token on the mBridge blockchain, which would then credit the vendor's account with dirhams, the local currency.

mBridge also provides commercial lenders in one country with access to currency issued by another nation's central bank, without the need for intermediaries or correspondent banks, thereby making the process faster and more cost-effective.

Given these advantages, it is unsurprising that non-participating Western nations are increasingly anxious. If the BRICS+ group or a significant number of large BRI countries were to shift a meaningful proportion of their trade onto multi-CBDC platforms like the BRICS Bridge or mBridge, it would deal a substantial blow to the dollar.

In light of this, it is worth examining where the BRICS+ nations and key BRI countries stand regarding CBDC development.

BRICS+ CBDC DEVELOPMENT

The Russian government is currently putting the digital ruble through rigorous testing. This testing phase is projected to extend to the end of 2024. However, Anatoly Aksakov, the chief architect of Russia's crypto and CBDC legislation, expressed optimism in December 2023 that Moscow and Beijing might begin using their respective CBDCs for payments by 2025. Aksakov conveyed to TASS news agency that 'digital national currencies' would significantly facilitate the 'rapidly growing trade turnover of Russian and Chinese companies'.[13]

In March 2024, at a meeting of the Association of Banks of Russia, both the governor and deputy governor of the central bank provided an update on the digital ruble. They stated that testing was proceeding according to plan and announced that Russia's largest bank, Sber, had joined the nineteen other banks involved in the pilot programme. It was also confirmed that Russia would produce a comprehensive report on the BRICS Bridge project before the end of 2024.[14]

On 7 June 2024, Aksakov stated at the St Petersburg International Economic Forum that he expected international CBDC payments to be the norm within five years, and that Russia could start using the digital ruble for international transactions as soon as the second half of 2025.[15] In July 2024, Vladimir Putin urged his government to accelerate the rollout of the Russian CBDC. According to TASS, he stated that 'now we need to take the next step, namely to move to a broader, full-scale implementation of the digital ruble in the economy, in economic activity and in the field of finance.'[16]

The most significant new addition to the expanded BRICS+ group is, without question, the Kingdom of Saudi Arabia. The inclusion of Saudi Arabia, alongside the UAE, could mark a profound shift in these nations' international priorities.

Historically aligned with the United States, Saudi Arabia has seen these ties loosen in recent years. While Saudi Arabia's entry into BRICS+ represents another step away from Washington,

D.C., it does not necessarily equate to a complete severance of ties. Washington views this development with particular dread, given its potential impact on the global dollar-dominated oil market.

On 12 June 2024, a flurry of reports announced that the Kingdom had quietly let its fifty-year petrodollar agreement with the United States expire without renewal, causing a wildfire of rumours to spread on social media about the official end of US dollar hegemony.

The news quickly spread around the world, at least on the lower echelons of the media food chain. 'Saudi Arabia's petro-dollar exit: a global paradigm shift', read the headline in *The Business Standard*, a Bangladeshi local newspaper.[17] *FXStreet*, an American financial markets magazine, asserted that 'The petrodollar is dead and that's a big deal'.[18] In Australia, a blogger announced in the news section on the website of Ainslie Bullion, an obscure gold-dealer, that 'The petrodollar is history. CBDCs are here'.[19] Meanwhile, mainstream media seemed suspiciously quiet, with no major outlet reporting on the deal's expiry. It seemed the story had reached Brisbane without landing on the desk of the *Financial Times* or *Wall Street Journal*.

In reality reports of the petrodollar's demise had perhaps been somewhat exaggerated. While it is true that an agreement established on 8 June 1974 was allowed to expire, the petrodollar system is in reality based more on practical market realities than bilateral treaties. 'The United States–Saudi Arabian Joint Commission on Economic Cooperation' was a joint statement issued and signed on that date by Henry Kissinger, the US secretary of state at the time, and Prince Fahd, the second deputy prime minister (and later king and prime minister) of Saudi Arabia, which made mutual assurances about US–Saudi cooperation with regards to oil supplies. But it did not enshrine the Kingdom's obligation to sell oil only in dollars, the practice of which emerged organically over the years that followed the deal. We will remain in a *de facto* petrodollar system so long as the Saudis continue to hold the majority of their foreign reserves in US dollars and sell the majority of their oil in US dollars.

However, the timing of the reports was certainly ominous. Just a few days prior to the petrodollar's supposed 'expiry', on 6 June 2024, the Saudi Central Bank confirmed it was joining the mBridge multi-CBDC project as a full participant, as the initiative moved from the production phase to the 'minimum viable product' (MVP) phase.[20]

With the launch of the MVP stage, the project aims to integrate new technologies and use cases, including interoperability with other platforms. Saudi Arabia's participation could be a watershed moment for the US dollar's dominance over global oil transactions, signalling a strategic shift from West to East. This development suggests that the days of the dollar's unchallenged supremacy in global oil trade may be numbered. The potential for Saudi Arabia to embrace CBDCs, and, by extension, the financial architecture championed by BRICS+, poses an unprecedented challenge to the existing US-led global financial order.

Besides Saudi, the UAE's accession to the BRICS+ group is particularly noteworthy, as it stands as perhaps the most zealous advocate for advancing digital currencies and joining the multi-CBDC platforms that signify a move away from the dollar-dominated world. Its ambitious plans for developing a viable CBDC are well underway. In March 2023, the UAE announced its expectation to complete the first phase of its CBDC development strategy by mid-2024, which includes proof-of-concept work for both wholesale and retail CBDCs.[21] A significant component of this project is mBridge, along with a bilateral CBDC bridge with India.

As we've seen, the UAE marked a major milestone in this initiative on 29 January 2024, by conducting its first cross-border digital dirham transfer using the mBridge CBDC platform. Further developments are anticipated imminently, underscoring the UAE's commitment to leading the charge in the non-dollar digital currency arena.

The stance of India will be pivotal – if it were to join the non-dollar sphere, it would be another major blow for the West. For now, however, India's central bank, the Reserve Bank of India, appears to be adopting a measured approach to CBDCs. It is purportedly investigating technological solutions to address privacy concerns associated with the digital rupee. Indeed, the bank launched pilot programmes for both wholesale and retail CBDCs in late 2022 but has publicly declared that it is not in a rush to roll out a full-scale CBDC for general use.

This cautious approach underscores India's strategic deliberation in navigating its economic future. While the Reserve Bank of India's prudence may appear as hesitancy, it also reflects a deeper, more calculated engagement with the profound implications of a digital currency.

The Banco Central do Brasil (BCB) is ambitiously planning to launch a CBDC, the Drex, by the end of 2024. The Drex aims to complement traditional currency in circulation, with the potential to reduce operational costs, enhance financial inclusion and secure both wholesale and retail transactions.

Despite the Drex pilot programme being in its final stages, it is expected that the launch will be postponed until early 2025. This delay stems from the need for regulatory agencies to establish a new legal framework for the digital currency and its infrastructure.

Nevertheless, Brazil's leading position in various digital economy technologies indicates that the Drex will likely be widely adopted, improving the nation's business environment. Brazil's success in developing its digital economy supports this expectation. Pix, a digital payments system introduced in November 2020, quickly became popular, with nearly three-quarters of Brazilians (99 per cent of the adult population) now registered.[22] Its popularity has been attributed to increased financial inclusion and reduced transaction costs. The BCB anticipates that the Drex will advance the digital economy further, addressing gaps left by Pix and enhancing the country's digital financial infrastructure.[23]

Iran began its journey towards a CBDC in 2022, leveraging Hyperledger Fabric blockchain technology – a versatile distributed ledger known for its capacity to execute smart contracts. By March 2023, the Central Bank of Iran proudly announced the completion of the pre-pilot stage of its CBDC project.[24] This phase had thoroughly examined the legal, regulatory and technological implications of launching an Iranian CBDC, setting the stage for more advanced studies.

Iran is hellbent on developing the technology and building the networks necessary to sidestep US sanctions. The moment it joined the BRICS+, Iran wasted no time in pushing for cooperation around payment systems, digital currencies and common currencies. But the real kicker came in January 2023. Reports surfaced that Iran and Russia were toying with the idea of using a gold-backed currency for their bilateral trade.[25] At that moment, Russia's regulations on digital financial assets – tokenised real-world assets – prohibited such assets for payments. But by April 2023, Russia had published a draft law allowing digital financial assets to be used for cross-border payments.

In June 2024, Iran officially unveiled its CBDC during a ceremony attended by Central Bank of Iran (CBI) Governor Mohammad Reza Farzin and the chief executives of several major banks. A pilot project commenced in July on the island of Kish, involving two major Iranian banks, Mellat and Tejarat, and will focus on retail transactions.

Nigeria, which has announced its intention to join the BRICS+ within two years, has already taken a bold step by launching its CBDC, the eNaira. The goal was to enhance financial inclusion and reduce transaction costs. However, the rollout has been anything but smooth. Broader adoption of the eNaira has been sluggish, and the government's push towards a cashless economy has backfired in dramatic fashion. Restrictions on cash use have sparked public protests demanding the return of paper currency. Efforts to promote the CBDC, such as lifting access limits and offering payment discounts, have fallen flat. Meanwhile, the imposition of cash withdrawal limits has led to a cash shortage and increased public dissatisfaction. As it stands, CBDC usage in Nigeria remains abysmally low – under 0.5 per cent of the population have adopted the eNaira, compared to the 50 per cent using cryptocurrencies.[26]

Nigeria's experience highlights the complexities of adopting CBDCs, especially in developing countries. For CBDCs to succeed, they must be backed by public trust and acceptance. This necessitates educating the public about the benefits, risks and operations of CBDCs before they are introduced. Collaboration with banks, fintech firms and other stakeholders can bolster this effort. China's digital yuan, developed through a partnership between the government, major banks and tech giants like Alibaba and Tencent, exemplifies a successful domestic CBDC rollout.

The tale of the eNaira is a cautionary one. It underscores the critical importance of groundwork – laying a foundation of understanding and trust before expecting widespread adoption. Nigeria's struggles serve as a stark reminder that technological ambition must be matched with strategic, inclusive planning.

In June 2024, news emerged that Thailand – the country which initiated the mBridge project – had formally applied for BRICS+ membership.

Apart from Hong Kong, all other central bank mBridge members – China, the UAE and Saudi Arabia – are also part of BRICS+. Although Hong Kong remains a special administrative region with its own economic policies, one could argue it is technically part of the group due to its association with China.

'We hope to receive positive feedback and be accepted as a BRICS member at the next summit in Russia,' said Thai foreign ministry spokesperson Nikorndej Balankura – referring to the BRICS+ summit set to take place in Kazan between 22–24 October 2024. Malaysia also announced plans to apply for membership soon. Additionally, in February 2024, South Africa reported that thirty-four countries had expressed interest in joining the bloc. Momentum is significantly increasing, and the West underestimates this bloc and its eagerness to switch to digital currencies at its peril.

THE DIGITAL YUAN AND CBDC DEVELOPMENT IN THE BRI

While the BRICS+ nations are likely to use their own digital currencies, China is unmistakably positioning its digital yuan as a reserve digital currency for its BRI partner countries in the developing world. In his book *Cashless*, Richard Turrin explores various scenarios for the digital yuan's future role in global trade, focusing on its potential implementation with BRI countries and then with China's other major trading partners.[27] Turrin delves into the current use of the paper yuan in these markets and projects what could happen if the digital yuan captures a larger share of this trade over the next decade.

Writing in 2021, Turrin suggested that the proportion of BRI trade conducted in yuan could increase from 14 per cent to 60 per cent by 2031. Assuming the BRI market continues to grow at its historic rate of 6 per cent, resulting in a market size of $2.26 trillion by 2031, this would equate to a market value of $1.36 trillion for the yuan in BRI markets. If the *digital* yuan made up 60% of this total, that would represent a market value of $0.82 trillion, more than Japan's total global exports ($0.7 trillion).

Turrin then shifts his focus to Chinese trade outside of the BRI, predicting that China could increase the percentage of its trade settled in yuan from 20 per cent to 40 per cent by 2031. If 25 per cent of this trade were settled in *digital* yuan, it would result in a market value of $0.58 trillion. Combining these figures, we arrive at a total market value of $1.4 trillion for the digital yuan by 2031, or twice the total exports of Japan.[28]

However, this projection is likely conservative for several reasons. Firstly, since Turrin's predictions were made in 2021, several significant international alliances have emerged, such as the Sino-Russian pact of limitless cooperation. Both China and Russia have expressed their intention to increase the use of the yuan in their trade and to price key commodities in yuan. It is reasonable to assume that a portion of this trade will eventually shift to the digital yuan.

Secondly, global CBDC adoption has surged in the three years since Turrin's forecasts. Today, 134 countries are exploring CBDCs, compared to just thirty-five in May 2020. This includes key BRI partner countries like Indonesia, which is making rapid progress towards a CBDC. Having completed studies into a proposed CBDC – the digital rupiah – in January 2024, Bank Indonesia confirmed its plans to launch its CBDC, starting with full-scale trials in partnership with leading commercial banks.[29]

It's not far-fetched to suggest that digital payment rails could account for 30–40 per cent of global trade by 2040. This figure might seem unthinkable in the West, but we are not the ones driving this change. It's the growing populations of key BRI and BRICS+ countries who will make all the difference. These nations are likely to embrace digital finance and payment systems as their primary financial infrastructure, bypassing traditional Western financial institutions and mechanisms.

The West lags behind in innovation in this area partly because its legacy banking systems are still trusted and reliable. The urgency to find alternatives is lower, and the influence of established banks amplifies voices calling for the status quo. But the West is facing a new threat to which it must wake up. This is not just de-dollarisation – this is *digital* de-dollarisation.

THE NEW VARIANT: DIGITAL DE-DOLLARISATION

The push for de-dollarisation among America's rivals is not a novel phenomenon. China's petroyuan, for example, was an audacious attempt to challenge the US petrodollar as the principal currency in crude oil transactions. However, none of these efforts possessed the substantial clout required to genuinely threaten the dollar's supremacy – until now, with the impending rise of CBDCs. Digitally enabled de-dollarisation is an entirely new variant of this virus.

Digital money, moving faster and more cheaply than the US dollar, provides companies and governments with an effortless exit from the dollar's hegemony. As US treasuries begin to appear less attractive than other debt securities, or as the US government's reliability and impartiality is called into question due to geopolitical tensions, developing countries courted by China and Russia – or pressured to trade in the digital yuan or digital ruble – will find themselves able to make the switch instantaneously, facilitated by the digital infrastructure China has meticulously constructed for them, to which America offers no alternative.

We can think of digital de-dollarisation as a global bank run on the US dollar, occurring at the speed of light as funds transfer seamlessly across the internet. A microcosm of this played out in March 2023, when Silicon Valley Bank collapsed after facing withdrawal attempts totalling over $42 billion within a few days. This financial panic, ignited by rumours of insolvency that spread like wildfire on social media, starkly illustrated the potential speed and impact of digital bank runs.

The collapse of Silicon Valley Bank ranks among the most extraordinary bank failures in US history. The bank's downfall exposed a broader issue of undercapitalisation within the American banking sector, estimated to be in the vicinity of hundreds of billions of dollars.[30] The episode starkly illustrated the speed with which confidence in the US financial system could erode on a macro scale.

The SVB debacle serves as a harbinger of the vulnerabilities lurking beneath the facade of a robust US financial system. But what could trigger a global run on the US dollar? In chapter 1, we argued that the dollar's status as the global reserve currency relies on faith in the Federal Reserve's ability to manage and honour the nation's debt obligations, even to strategic competitors or adversaries. Yet, global confidence in the US government's willingness and ability to do so is eroding for two main reasons.

Firstly, there's the recent politicisation of the dollar by the US government, highlighted when it froze Russian foreign reserves. This move effectively constituted a default on its obligations to another sovereign nation, shaking trust in the dollar's reliability. Secondly, the United States holds the unenviable title of having the highest level of sovereign debt in global history. This has led some commentators, such as economic researcher and author Chris Martenson, to declare the United States functionally insolvent.

In an interview on 'The Bitcoin Standard Podcast' podcast, macro analyst Luke Gromen suggests that many countries, including China, are motivated to de-dollarise and re-price commodities away from the dollar not just to sidestep potential US sanctions, but to protect themselves from the inevitable bursting of the US debt bubble in the coming decades.[31] The US dollar's 'exorbitant privilege' seems more precarious than ever, burdened by the US government's exorbitant debt.

Add digital currencies to the mix – offering unprecedented levels of flexibility and efficiency – and we have the perfect recipe for digital de-dollarisation. Countries could soon switch their reserves from US dollars to digital yuan as swiftly and seamlessly as anxious depositors moved their funds from Silicon Valley Bank to J. P. Morgan. To date, de-dollarisation has been happening gradually. It could soon happen suddenly.

'BRETTON WOODS III'

Gromen explores another crucial, though often misunderstood, aspect of de-dollarisation, emphasising that the true measure of de-dollarisation lies not merely in the currency used for transactions but in how these transactions are ultimately settled.

While the US dollar remains a dominant player in global financial transactions, the settlements landscape has been quietly yet significantly shifting since 2014. Nations are increasingly opting for commodity-based settlements over traditional dollar settlements. This means that instead of settling trades with currency, transactions can be settled using tangible goods and resources like oil and gold. This shift marks a fundamental change in the mechanics of global trade.

This trend is underscored by the actions of central banks worldwide. In recent years, a growing number of major central banks have pivoted away from holding US Treasury bonds, opting instead to amass gold reserves, which are perceived as a more stable asset base. We are witnessing something of a gold boom.

The World Gold Council's April 2024 report noted that, in the first quarter of 2024, central bank demand for gold reached record highs, with China, India and Turkey leading the pack.[32] This surge in gold acquisition is not mere coincidence; it signals a strategic departure from the dollar-centric system that has dominated global finance since the mid-twentieth century.

As one might expect, China is at the forefront of this movement. It is pioneering a model where trade settlements can be made in a combination of Chinese yuan, goods and gold instead of dollars. This approach not only reduces China's dependence on the US dollar but also elevates the yuan's status as a global trading and reserve currency.

All of this is gradually realigning the world's financial architecture. The increasing acceptance of the yuan and commodity-based settlements speaks to a diversification of economic interactions, challenging previous systems and paradigms. As more countries engage in transactions using the yuan, the digital yuan, and other digital currencies, they will naturally be more inclined to bolster their foreign reserves with these currencies.

This pattern mirrors the historical trajectory of the US dollar, which became a cornerstone of global reserves due to its prevalence in international trade and commodities markets.

Zoltan Pozsar, a prominent financial analyst, distils these developments into what he terms 'Bretton Woods III'. As we've seen, the original Bretton Woods system was characterised by fixed exchange rates tethered to the US dollar, which in turn was convertible to gold.[33] This arrangement collapsed in the early 1970s, ushering in Bretton Woods II – a regime of floating exchange rates where the US dollar retained its supremacy as the world's primary reserve currency and the linchpin of global trade.

Pozsar's vision for Bretton Woods III foresees the global financial order fragmenting into currency blocs and nations increasingly relying on a diverse mix of currencies and commodities to settle international transactions.

But what would this mean for the West in practice? Should a substantial number of countries gradually pivot away from the US dollar for both their trade and reserves, the dollar will not only be dethroned from its lofty perch atop the global financial hierarchy, but its value will also depreciate significantly, wreaking havoc on exchange rates and Western imports.

The pound and the euro would likely suffer secondary depreciation effects if the dollar weakens appreciably. Global currencies are intricately interconnected, and fluctuations in the value of one major currency invariably impacts others. Investors, corporations and governments perpetually trade different currencies for myriad reasons – trade, investment and financial management. So any considerable depreciation in the dollar would inevitably trigger a ripple effect across other significant currencies, unsettling the delicate balance of global finance.

The United Kingdom and the eurozone are deeply entwined with global trade, exporting vast quantities of goods and services to markets where prices are often denominated in dollars. When the dollar weakens, goods and services produced in the United States become relatively cheaper and more competitive on the international stage. Conversely, goods priced in euros or pounds become more expensive. This shift in exchange rates can erode the competitiveness of UK and European exports, adversely affecting trade balances and potentially stifling economic growth.

Given that many commodities, particularly oil, are priced in dollars, a depreciation of the dollar would cause the prices of these commodities to rise in pound or euro terms. This would escalate the cost of energy and other essential commodities in Europe and the UK, triggering inflationary pressures. Thus, a weakened dollar could ripple through the global economy, creating a cascade of economic challenges for the West.

Moreover, the BRI and BRICS+ countries have historically been substantial holders of US government securities, drawn to the perceived safety and liquidity of these investments. However, as these nations increasingly diversify away from dollar-denominated assets, the United States would find itself contending with a diminished pool of international investors. This scenario would likely necessitate higher interest rates to attract alternative investors, thereby escalating the cost of borrowing. The repercussions could be profound, including soaring costs for servicing the national debt and potentially exacerbating the US fiscal deficit.

Furthermore, a significant shift away from the US dollar and an attendant reduction in investment in US assets could precipitate heightened volatility in Western financial markets. As investors navigate this evolving landscape, capital flows would become less predictable, impacting market liquidity and stability. The Federal Reserve could also encounter formidable challenges in managing monetary policy effectively should the US dollar's global role diminish, complicating efforts to influence global economic conditions through conventional mechanisms such as interest rates.

The broader strategic and geopolitical implications of de-dollarisation can't be underestimated. The potential depreciation of the dollar, increased borrowing costs and challenges to US fiscal and monetary policy will have serious and far-reaching consequences for economies worldwide. Mortgage and energy costs will rise, and higher government borrowing costs will necessitate spending cuts elsewhere. This isn't just about a few percentage points on exchange rates. It's about the redefinition of global financial power. It's about the mortgage on your house and the gas in your car. It's about governments around the world rethinking their budgets and policies. In short, it's about the world economy entering uncharted territory.

10

The Battle for Resources:
Energy, Food and Smart Money

Whoever controls oil controls much more than oil. And in
our time, much of the world's oil supply is controlled by
states, regimes, and a cartel for which America's wellbeing is
not exactly a priority.

JOHN MCCAIN[1]

In the twenty-first century, the indicators of geopolitical power have
changed profoundly. Unlike the twentieth century, during which
power was defined by economic output and military strength,
above all else, in the coming decades power will be defined by
natural resources – who controls them, and who has affordable
access to them.

In his seminal work *Resource Wars*, author and journalist Michael
T. Klare highlighted how technologically advanced countries, with
their insatiable energy demands, have become reliant on oil and
gas to fuel their economies and sustain their populations' lifestyles.[2]
But with the possibility of the period of cheap oil soon to be
over, we stand on the precipice of a crisis with the potential to
undermine living standards across the industrialised Western world.
Furthermore, as the economies and populations of the developing
world continue to grow and require more energy to sustain their
trajectories, we are fast approaching a crunch point.

As we saw in chapter 1, the dominance of the US dollar has historically been closely tied to its role in global oil trade. Yet we are now witnessing a realignment, with major oil-producing nations like Saudi Arabia and Venezuela gravitating towards China and Russia. This shift could significantly diminish the geopolitical influence of the G7's service-based economies, which will be overshadowed by the resource-rich autocracies in the Sino-Russian axis and the BRICS+ grouping.

To add to this, the world is becoming ever more dependent on China in the realm of rare metals, which are crucial for a range of technologies, from electric vehicles and fighter jets to renewable energy sources and everyday electronic devices. This dependence on China in an era of energy transition places the rising superpower in a formidable position.

In the emerging bipolar monetary order, where the majority of global trade in natural resources could be conducted on digital platforms dominated by China, currencies like the dollar, the euro and the pound risk seeing massive erosions in their value and relevance – which could, in turn, contribute to the breakdown of Western society as we know it.

ENERGY IS POWER: GROWTH AND DEPLETION

In the twenty-first century, to put it simply, access to affordable sources of energy, which is needed to sustain growth, is becoming increasingly restricted. This is not necessarily because sources of energy or even non-renewable energy are scarce – there is an active debate among geologists about the degree of scarcity or abundance of non-renewable energy sources such as oil and gas in the earth's crust – but because the process of extracting them is getting ever more expensive.

Against this backdrop, a nation's geopolitical power is defined by its access (or not) to affordable sources of energy, rather than economic output and military might – because the latter are dependent on the former. As Luke Gromen has succinctly stated, 'when push comes to shove, oil is the base layer of the global economy, not the dollar.'³ In recent decades, the West appears to have lost sight of this simple fact, lulled into complacency by abundant, affordable energy. There is a simple reason for this complacency. There has been little competition for resources, until now. As Klare stated in his other work *Rising Powers, Shrinking Planet*:

> Until recently, the global hunt for vital resources had been dominated almost entirely by the mature industrialised powers. Three centres of economic might – the United States, Japan and Europe – devoured the vast majority of the oil, natural gas, coal, uranium, and other primary sources of energy used worldwide … however, young competitors have been muscling their way onto the scene with roaring economies that devour mammoth quantities of raw materials just to sustain their explosive rates of growth.⁴

Among these new competitors, China is of course the biggest player. In 1980, China consumed 1.7 million barrels of oil per day. By 2024, this had skyrocketed to an astonishing 17.21 million barrels per day. The United States consumes roughly 19.1 million barrels per day.⁵

In the twentieth century, the United States was able to maintain its power and growth thanks in large part to its reliable access to cheap oil via the petrodollar system. Despite being a major producer of oil itself, the United States still relies on foreign oil due to several factors. Different oil fields produce different grades of crude oil. The US predominantly produces light, sweet crude oil, but many of its refineries are optimised for processing heavier, sour crude oil. These refineries were historically designed to handle imported oil from places like the Middle East and Venezuela. Therefore, the US imports heavier oil while exporting its surplus light oil. Since the oil market is global and prices are set internationally, the US exports oil and petroleum products to other countries where it can fetch higher prices and, at the same time, imports oil from countries where it can obtain it more cheaply.

Some foreign oil is processed into specific products that are more difficult or expensive to produce domestically. Refined products such as certain chemicals or fuel types may require unique crude oil properties, leading to the need for imports. Moreover, importing oil helps the US maintain strategic relationships with key allies and trading partners, such as Saudi Arabia. The US also maintains strategic petroleum reserves for emergencies. Domestic oil is sometimes conserved for national security reasons, while foreign oil imports help meet regular consumption needs.

The continued growth of the service- and manufacturing-based economies of the G7 has been predicated on continued access to cheap oil. These advanced economies are deeply integrated into global networks that rely heavily on stable energy supplies. But as the cost of traditional energy sources increases, these nations could face significant economic disruptions and crises.

What's worse, many of their geopolitical rivals, such as China and Russia, are endowed with vast – if different – natural resources of their own, which puts them in a position to leverage their energy supplies for strategic and economic advantage.

By investing in infrastructure projects across Asia, Africa and Latin America as well as Europe, both China and Russia are positioning themselves as key players in the global energy market, not only supplying traditional energy sources but also developing new supply chains for renewable energy.

Developing countries across these regions are also reliant on access to affordable and abundant energy to fuel their own economic development. By collaborating with the resource-rich China and Russia, they can manage their growing energy demands and even start transitioning to more sustainable energy sources. The digital payment rails that China is building will serve to pull these nations into the Sino–Russian orbit, creating the potential for cartel-like behaviours around resources.

PEAK CHEAP OIL: ASSUME A CAN-OPENER

So, we are witnessing a great bifurcation, with developing and commodity-rich nations increasingly coalescing around the autocratic Sino-Russian axis, while the manufacturing- and service-based economies of the West stick together, despite the perils of isolating themselves from the energy sources and emerging technologies on which their economies rely.

Luke Gromen points out the shaky foundations upon which many economic growth projections for the West are built by stating that they 'assume a can-opener'. He suggests that economists and financial models frequently make unjustified or oversimplified assumptions, particularly regarding the continued availability of cheap oil. This metaphorical 'can-opener' refers to the crucial yet assumed presence of a tool – in this case, affordable oil – without acknowledging the real challenges in securing it.

For over a century, cheap oil has been a bedrock of economic development and growth. However, Gromen argues that this reliance cannot be sustained indefinitely. While global oil reserves are not yet critically depleted, the cost of extracting and processing the remaining oil is climbing. Regulatory and environmental costs, combined with the increasing difficulty of accessing new reserves, mean we are nearing a point he terms 'peak cheap oil'.[6] This is the threshold beyond which oil production can no longer be economically viable at low cost.

Gromen contends that many economic forecasts fail to consider the ramifications of reaching this juncture. Ignoring the advent of peak cheap oil leaves economies exposed to a host of issues, from unexpectedly higher prices for goods and services to soaring transportation costs, which would inevitably drive inflation. This inflationary pressure could erode living standards, especially for lower- and middle-income groups. While wealthier individuals and businesses might adapt more readily to higher energy costs, poorer populations could suffer disproportionately, potentially igniting social and political tensions both domestically and internationally.

SMART MONEY: THE ACTUAL CAN-OPENER

Soon, the proverbial 'can-opener' that could actually ensure access to affordable energy sources – as well as key resources more broadly, such as rare metals, food and water – might just be smart money.

China is in the process of building a digital monetary order which operates independently of the US-controlled dollar-based monetary system – and it is China's order that will soon control a vast majority of these key resources. China has followed a meticulous plan to get to this point, not only developing the necessary digital infrastructure, but also building key alliances with commodity-rich nations across the globe. If, as predicted, these nations move more and more of their trade onto Chinese digital payment rails, this will have major implications across the Western world.

Take the Kingdom of Saudi Arabia, one of the most pivotal players in the global oil market. With Saudi Arabia now a part of BRICS+ and the Saudis denominating their oil trade away from dollars, it is potentially signalling the beginning of the end of the petrodollar system.

This would bring advantages for fellow CBDC-developing allies in the Organisation of Islamic Cooperation, OPEC+ and BRICS+, who would benefit from quicker and more streamlined transactions. But above all, this would benefit China: if global oil trade moved onto Chinese-led digital payment rails, China would gain access to huge amounts of data on the volume, timing and financial terms of oil purchases. This would in turn give Beijing unprecedented strategic insights into the energy dependencies, economic vulnerabilities and policy orientations of Western and developing countries alike. Such information could be leveraged to inform China's geopolitical strategy, negotiate trade terms or influence global oil prices to its advantage.

The shift is already being put into motion. In October 2023, Chinese oil and gas company PetroChina completed the first international crude oil trade using the country's digital yuan. The company – the listed arm of state-owned China National Petroleum Corporation – bought one million barrels of crude oil settled in digital yuan at the Shanghai Petroleum and Natural Gas Exchange.

In addition, it would be entirely possible for China to actively harness its control over the digital payment system to dictate terms for oil purchases, tying access to political compliance or concessions in other areas of international relations. Imagine a scenario where, amidst escalating tensions, China decides to delay or outright block payments made through the China-dominated CBDC system for oil shipments destined for Western countries, just as the US blocked Russian access to the dollar system.

This would generate a huge crisis, spiralling into broader economic turmoil and potentially triggering energy shortages, skyrocketing prices and social unrest. And beyond this, turmoil in the West could ultimately undermine confidence in traditional currencies and financial markets. So, the ripple effects of such manoeuvres extend beyond mere economic metrics, affecting geopolitical alliances and trade negotiations.

Finally, the digital currency system would also significantly undermine the efficacy of current sanctions, enabling sanctioned nations to engage in global trade independently of the US dollar or the traditional global financial system, which is dominated by the US and its allies.

This would have a major impact on nations like Venezuela, home to the world's largest known oil reserves, and Iran, another major oil producer, which have been seriously hampered by US-imposed economic sanctions in recent years. With sanctions severely limiting their access to global markets and financial services, Venezuela and Iran have not been able to monetise their vast natural resources. But the introduction of a CBDC system would allow these nations to bypass restrictions by facilitating direct trade with countries that are either sympathetic to their cause or else seeking to maintain a neutral stance in global geopolitical tensions.

Specifically, a CBDC system would allow Iran and Venezuela to set up direct transactions with countries within the BRICS+ coalition without needing to use the US dollar or process transactions through conventional financial institutions that comply with Western sanctions. So, a digital approach to international trade could considerably mitigate the impact of sanctions, allowing these countries to unlock new revenue streams and stabilise their economies despite ongoing geopolitical pressures.

In essence, smart money will enable the BRICS+ grouping to ring-fence their energy resources, leaving the West in search of alternative sources at much higher prices, leading to collapsing living standards.

RARE METALS

Guillaume Pitron's insightful book *The Rare Metals War* sheds light on another pressing global issue: China's monopoly over rare metals.[7] These rare metals, including elements like neodymium, dysprosium and praseodymium, are needed to power the energy transition, as they are crucial for the manufacturing of various high-tech products such as wind turbines and electric vehicles, as well as other electronic devices.

In 2024, China produces about 60 per cent of the world's rare metals and handles nearly 90 per cent of the global refining processes, giving it substantial control over the supply chain of these critical minerals.[8] This means China can control their availability and pricing.

As things stand, viable alternatives remain scarce, so Western nations don't really have anywhere else to turn to for these metals. This makes Western supply chains very vulnerable: any disruption in supply, whether due to political strife, economic fluctuations or natural disasters, could lead to critical shortages and inflated costs for key components in green technology. In light of this, China can leverage Western dependency as a tool in diplomacy.

Given that China supplied approximately 78 per cent of the rare earth metals imported by the United States in 2019,[9] the Asian giant has significant power over its rival, and could choose to dictate unfavourable trade terms that favour Chinese geopolitical objectives.

Western countries must devise strategies to address these risks. This could take a multifaceted approach, encompassing investment in alternative mining operations, development of technologies for recycling rare metals and diplomatic efforts to secure stable, ethical supply chains, thereby reducing reliance on a single dominant source and ensuring a sustainable and secure transition to green energy.

These efforts become ever more vital in light of rapid CBDC development. China could feasibly restrict Western access to both the materials and the CBDC system required for their purchase in future, thereby forcing Western nations into a corner where they must negotiate under pressurised conditions or face considerable disruptions to critical supply chains. What's more, by implementing a programmable CBDC, China could prioritise exports of rare earth metals to strategic allies or countries engaged in its BRI, squeezing other nations which depend on these materials.

Consider the implications for a nation heavily invested in the electric vehicle (EV) industry, which depends on rare metals for battery production and other components. Facing a scenario where China controls both the supply of these metals and the digital currency platform used for transactions, this nation could be pressured into accepting less favourable trade terms. Compounding this, China would be able to set higher prices or impose conditions that disadvantage Western competitors in these sectors, which would also hamper their progress. So, for example, Chinese BYD cars could undercut the price of Teslas, or the Chinese could choke supplies of materials needed to make Teslas so that BYD can have first use of them all.

Should the transactions for these critical resources in Western countries be mandated to occur through a Chinese-controlled CBDC system, the implications for privacy and national security would also be significant. China could monitor and analyse the financial activities of Western companies and even governments, gaining a strategic overview of their economic plans, supply chain vulnerabilities and investment priorities. This surveillance could potentially be used to manipulate market prices, restrict access to strategic materials or perform economic coercion.

FOOD SECURITY

No resources are more critical than food and water. Amidst the ongoing conflict between Russia and Ukraine, along with the broader geopolitical fractures reshaping the globe, the accessibility of agricultural exports is undergoing a dramatic shift, with profound implications.

Ukraine, often called the 'breadbasket of Europe', is central to global food supply chains, particularly for its grain exports. The war has significantly curtailed these exports, with dire consequences for numerous African nations that depend on Ukrainian grain. The global spike in food prices following the Russian invasion raised fears of impending famine in Africa, necessitating urgent and coordinated responses.

The United Nations, with Turkey acting as a crucial mediator, orchestrated the Black Sea Grain Initiative. Signed at Dolmabahçe Palace in Istanbul on 22 July 2022, this sought to mitigate the escalating global food crisis by ensuring the safe export of Ukrainian grain and other foodstuffs, despite the ongoing conflict.

Remarkably, the UN plan also encompassed efforts to boost exports of Russian food and fertilisers, which were similarly disrupted by the conflict and ensuing sanctions. Consequently, Russia initially agreed to the plan, permitting the export of commercial food and fertilisers, including ammonia, from three vital Ukrainian ports on the Black Sea: Odesa, Chornomorsk and Yuzhny/Pivdennyi. This was critical not only for the nations directly embroiled in the conflict but also for regions with precarious food security.

However, Russia later decided to withdraw from the Black Sea Grain Initiative, marking a significant shift in its international relations, particularly concerning Africa – albeit not in the expected manner. Rather than this withdrawal representing a blow to African countries, it precipitated a strategic pivot by Russia, which sought to fortify its ties with the African continent through a variety of alternative projects.

As we have observed, Putin's administration has undertaken the significant gesture of debt forgiveness, absolving a considerable portion of African nations' foreign debts to Russia. Moreover, Russia has independently secured a steady food supply for various African countries. In a noteworthy initiative, Russia also pledged to deliver substantial quantities of grain to several African nations, including Burkina Faso, Zimbabwe, Mali, Somalia, the Central African Republic and Eritrea. These countries are set to receive between 25,000 and 50,000 tonnes of grain each, with Moscow covering the delivery costs.

President Putin is clearly leveraging food (in)security to build trust and confidence between Moscow and African nations. He positions Russia as a reliable and economically supportive partner, in stark contrast to the United States and other Western allies, who are neither cancelling debts nor significantly investing in Africa.

Meanwhile, China and the BRICS+ members are positioning CBDCs and their prospective multi-CBDC platforms to significantly influence global food security dynamics. Given that BRICS+ nations include some of the world's largest producers of essential agricultural commodities such as soybeans, wheat and rice, the increasing use of CBDCs in agricultural trade could prioritise or restrict exports based on geopolitical considerations.

The same issues arise across various industries: by demanding payment for these exports in their CBDCs, major producers could effectively dictate which countries have access to their agricultural goods. This strategy would allow these nations to facilitate direct trade within their networks, bypassing traditional dollar-dominated markets and financial institutions. Such direct trade would be more efficient and less costly, promoting increased exchange of food commodities among BRI partners and BRICS+ countries, much to the detriment of Western nations.

With the advent of a multi-CBDC platform, BRICS+ countries could forge a more resilient and efficient food supply chain among themselves. This system would employ smart contracts for immediate payment upon delivery, reducing risk and uncertainty for exporters within the coalition. Enhanced supply chain resilience would directly bolster food security for BRICS+ nations and BRI partner countries, while Western nations, clinging to traditional payment methods, might face delays and increased costs.

Moreover, China's vast technological advancements and investments in agricultural technology could be leveraged through its
CBDC network, potentially encouraging other BRICS+ and BRI
partners to adopt these innovations. Such investments, conducted
in CBDCs, could be contingent on favourable trade terms, ensuring
a steady supply of food to China and its allies while marginalising
Western technologies and influence in the global agricultural sector.
Furthermore, China would be positioned to set standards and
regulations favouring their agricultural products, thereby exerting
greater control over the global food export market.

WATER SECURITY

Water security, already a global crisis, is exacerbated by pollution,
inefficient management and the unpredictable whims of climate
change. While the G7 nations, with their advanced technologies
and relatively stable political climates, generally possess the means
to invest in sustainable water management practices, innovative
purification technologies and climate resilience strategies, challenges
remain. Even these nations struggle with managing transboundary
water resources and adapting to the multifaceted impacts of climate
change.

Conversely, the BRICS+ countries, characterised by their
rapidly growing economies, diverse political systems, and varying
levels of environmental governance, confront a far more intricate
set of challenges. Water scarcity and pollution are acute issues in
many of these nations, including India, South Africa and Brazil.
Industrial growth, urbanisation and less stringent environmental
regulations exacerbate these problems. Furthermore, the effects
of climate change on water resources are more severe in several
BRICS+ countries, intensifying the challenge of ensuring water
security for their burgeoning populations.

Looking ahead to a future featuring multi-CBDCs, the scenario
becomes more complex. On one hand, such a system could furnish
BRICS+ nations with unprecedented mechanisms to finance large-
scale water infrastructure projects – dams, water treatment plants,

irrigation systems – without dependence on Western financial institutions. This newfound financial autonomy could accelerate investments in water security, allowing these nations to tailor solutions to their unique challenges.

However, as with many sectors, the use of programmable CBDCs may balkanise rather than unify the global economy. We are transitioning into an era of digital currency trading blocs, dominated by resource-rich autocracies, which may compel other nations to align with them based on geopolitical interests and access to critical resources.

While these new blocs present an alternative model, decentralising traditional Western dominance with some potentially positive outcomes, they also pose a significant threat to global economic stability and risk further fragmenting an already divided international community. The early repercussions are evident in the escalating conflicts of recent years – with numerous proxy wars being waged over these natural resources, and more likely to follow. These examples will be examined in greater detail in our next chapter.

11

Flashpoints and Proxy Wars: Ukraine, Taiwan and the Scramble for the 'Global South'

As the world's major powers grapple for control over supply chains, criticial resources and advanced technologies, a series of proxy wars and territorial disputes have erupted, with more likely to ignite soon. These conflicts challenge US hegemony and the supremacy of the dollar, shaping the emerging bipolar world order. Digital currencies will not only fuel these clashes but also play a decisive role in their outcomes.

The Ukraine conflict serves as a litmus test for the US dollar's ability to thwart the territorial ambitions of the West's adversaries. Despite Western sanctions, Russia's economy remains resilient, partly due to digital money and bolstered by increased trade with China, showing a 3.6 per cent growth in 2023.[1] This underscores the shift towards a bipolar monetary system.

Moreover, the Ukraine conflict offers a preview for China as it contemplates its move on Taiwan. A Russian triumph in Ukraine would embolden China.

Either way, with the invasion of Ukraine, Russia severed its ties with the West and aligned its fate with China, while Europe closed ranks and sought refuge under the US's protective wing. From this point onwards, the world was effectively split, with both China and the US presenting a stark ultimatum to other nations: 'You're either with me or against me.'

Against this backdrop, key regions are poised to become battle-grounds for intensified proxy wars between the US and China. For our purposes, the most important of these are Eastern Europe, Africa and Latin America, as well as exploration of newfound resources in the Arctic region.

UKRAINE

Russia's interest in Ukraine is deeply rooted in history. It's not a coincidence that Russia invaded the former USSR constituent just as Ukraine began to move closer to Western alliances like NATO and the EU. The invasion is part of a wider Russian aim to counter NATO's eastward expansion and to reassert Russian influence in the post-Soviet space.

However, Ukraine holds further attractions for Russia. To mention just a few of its valuable assets: Ukraine benefits from extensive fertile farmlands, as well as mineral resources, including coal, iron ore, manganese, titanium and uranium. Ukraine also has considerable industrial infrastructure, particularly in areas like aerospace, defence and shipbuilding. The country's coastline along the Black Sea is strategically significant, featuring ports that are vital for exporting food and key commodities. Finally, Ukraine is a key transit route for Russian natural gas exports to Europe. As such, controlling Ukraine would give Russia unprecedented influence over global food exports, infrastructure, shipping and energy supply chains, bringing the Kremlin sizeable economic and strategic advantages.

The conflict has served to unite Western Europe, rallying nations under the NATO banner in a show of solidarity with Ukraine and bringing about its expansion to include Sweden and Finland. Given Finland's extensive border with Russia, the NATO alliance is now right on Putin's doorstep.

Under the Biden administration, the US leapt into support for Ukraine and quickly became the country's chief financial supporter, providing $44.3 billion in military assistance by April 2024.

A significant portion of this aid materialised as military equipment and weaponry from American defence contractors, profoundly impacting the battlefield by enabling Ukrainian forces to reclaim occupied territories.

This arrangement is mutually beneficial: it enhances Ukraine's defensive capabilities while tangibly boosting the US defence industry, stimulating economic activity and supporting American jobs. The US has also leveraged its shale oil and gas boom to become a key energy supplier, replacing Russian resources in many markets, thereby shifting global energy supply chains and amplifying its strategic influence.

Consequently, the Ukraine situation has had positive domestic implications for the US and the Biden administration. Historically, wartime presidents often experience a surge in public support. Additionally, the conflict fosters cross-party cooperation, with the Democratic administration's military aid aligning with Republican interests in the military-industrial complex.

In April 2024, the US House of Representatives finally approved a delayed $61 billion aid package for Ukraine. This measure, fraught with opposition, required a fragile bipartisan deal and includes air defence systems, mid- to long-range missiles and artillery shells. While this aid is expected to support Ukraine into 2025, future assistance remains uncertain.

The war's outlook remains bleak, with potential escalation into unconventional warfare and concerns over Russia's possible use of tactical nuclear weapons. Regardless of the conflict's outcome, Russia is set to emerge as a highly militarised nation, possibly deploying its surplus military capacity to extend its influence in the region.

A Russian victory in Ukraine would not only signal the failure of Western sanctions but arguably mark an unambiguous shift to a bipolar monetary order, a world in which the Sino-Russian axis can pursue its territorial ambitions with impunity.

TAIWAN

Beijing is carefully observing events in Ukraine, calibrating its moves with respect to Taiwan, which China claims as its own. Should

China lay claim to Taiwan's strategic, economic, and technological treasures – a cache that can scarcely be overstated – we would be living in a new world.

Nestled in the Western Pacific, adjacent to the South China Sea, Taiwan straddles a pivotal maritime artery vital to international trade. A successful invasion would grant China dominion over one of the planet's busiest shipping lanes. This would severely impede the US Navy's operational freedom in the region and precipitate a profound shift in the military equilibrium of the Indo-Pacific.

The island is home to TSMC (Taiwan Semiconductor Manufacturing Company), responsible for most of world's semiconductor chips, essential for a vast array of high-tech products, from smartphones to military equipment. It remains unclear whether China would be able to control and use the TSMC factories if it gained control of Taiwan – it has been reported that the company has ways to disable their chipmaking machines in the event of an invasion[2] – but the disruption to supply chains would be momentous and potentially give China the ability to leverage its influence over these supply chains in geopolitical negotiations. When the Suez Canal was blocked for a few days, in 2021, it led to a delay in car supplies of weeks. But this would be far, far worse. There is little doubt that TSMC's recent decision to produce its most advanced chips in Arizona from 2028 was a direct response to this threat.

The US has long maintained a policy of 'strategic ambiguity' towards Taiwan, selling it arms to defend itself while not formally recognising it as a separate nation. President Biden has stated that the US military would defend Taiwan in the event of an invasion, but also said that the United States does not support the independence of Taiwan after Taiwanese voters spurned Beijing by giving the ruling (and pro-independence) Democratic Progressive Party a third presidential term in January 2024.[3] Republican nominee Donald Trump has suggested that Taiwan should pay the US for the defence it receives, while his running mate, J.D. Vance, has stated that: 'The thing that we need to prevent more than anything is a Chinese invasion ... It would be catastrophic for this country. It would decimate our entire economy. It would throw this country into a Great Depression.'[4]

A Chinese invasion would be seen as a direct challenge to US commitments and credibility in the region, precipitating a severe deterioration in US–China relations and even military confrontation.

Beyond this, a successful takeover of Taiwan by China would likely intimidate other nations in the region, potentially leading to a realignment of regional powers: countries like Japan, South Korea, the Philippines and Australia would need to reassess their security policies and alliances, possibly leading to an arms race or increased dependency on China. This could create a domino effect, encouraging other nations across Asia, Africa and Latin America to pivot towards China, in search of economic and political protection.

For China, Taiwan holds deep historical and symbolic importance. Taiwan has remained a democratic and self-governed entity since the end of the Chinese Civil War in 1949, which led to the establishment of the People's Republic of China under the CCP. For the CCP, reclaiming the island is seen as a correction, a reunification of the nation under one flag. The island's reintegration into the mainland would mark the completion of a journey that President Xi has prophesied for himself and his party, and solidify China's position as a pre-eminent world power.

China is taking a slower, more deliberate path towards Taiwan than its ally is in Ukraine. Beijing has already started trying to destabilise the Taiwanese administration with cyberattacks, among other tools in their arsenal. But, unlike Russia, it is biding its time, refraining from direct engagement until the right moment. Parallels can be drawn with its tactics in Hong Kong, which was transferred back to China by the UK in 1997, after two decades of measured CCP negotiations. In the case of Taiwan, President Xi is certainly aiming for reunification well before 2049, the centenary of the CCP's rise to power.[5] He is more likely to make a move before the end of the decade. But this broader timeline would afford China a quarter of a century to methodically work towards its goal, gradually increasing its pressure and influence over Taiwan via diplomatic isolation, economic leverage and military posturing – which will also allow Beijing to carefully calibrate international reactions.

From China's perspective, it does not necessarily want – or need – to hasten the process of taking control over Taiwan. For one thing, recent conflict simulations suggest that the US would emerge victorious in a hot conflict to defend the island's independence, albeit at a staggering cost, with serious losses in military equipment and personnel on both sides.

In a sense, China can also afford to be patient, and wait for Western democracies to elect appropriately weak leaders more likely to appease their ambitions. On the other hand, it has been argued that China's window of opportunity might not last long, as the country's slowing rates of growth and declining birth rate could mean that the US remains economically and militarily dominant for many decades to come. President Xi might well choose to strike while the iron is hot.

AFRICA

Both China and Russia are ardently courting emerging African markets, each with their own distinct strategies. China, through its BRI, has been pouring vast sums into infrastructure projects across the continent for years. Roads, railways, ports and telecommunications networks have all seen Chinese investment. Take the Mombasa–Nairobi Standard Gauge Railway in Kenya, for instance – a flagship BRI project that has markedly improved trade and travel within the region. Such investments have not only cemented China's economic foothold but have also bolstered its political clout.

Russia, albeit less economically entrenched than China, is deploying a different playbook, focusing on military and security arrangements. Russian private military contractors, such as the notorious Wagner Group, are active in nations like the Central African Republic and Libya, trading military assistance for political and economic sway.

Why this fervent interest in Africa? The continent harbours some of the world's most rapidly expanding economies and populations. Nations like Ethiopia, Rwanda and Ghana have seen GDP growth rates soaring above 6 per cent in recent years.[6] Moreover, according to the UN's World Population Prospects, Africa's population is expected to double by 2050, reaching an estimated 2.5 billion people.[7] This impending demographic explosion offers a vast future market and labour force, a particularly enticing prospect for China and Russia, both grappling with their own demographic declines.

China and Russia's interest in Africa is also driven by an unmistakable lust for the continent's bounteous natural resources. Africa is a veritable treasure trove, brimming with essential minerals like cobalt, copper, diamonds, gold and platinum. China has sunk vast investments into the mining sectors across the continent. Russia, not to be outdone, has ramped up its activities, with entities like Rosatom pursuing uranium mining and nuclear projects in nations such as Namibia and Tanzania.

Consider cobalt, for instance – vital for the production of batteries in electric vehicles (EVs), smartphones and other electronics. The Democratic Republic of Congo (DRC) boasts over 60 per cent of the world's cobalt supply.[8] China, with ambitions to dominate the EV sector, has significant stakes in major cobalt mines in the DRC, through companies like CMOC (previously known as China Molybdenum Company Limited).

American firms, including Tesla, also depend heavily on the DRC for their battery components. Yet, the contrast in approach is stark. While Western entities express concern over appalling working conditions, slave labour and environmental degradation, China exhibits a conspicuous nonchalance. The DRC, predictably, is more inclined to accept investment from Beijing, where such inconvenient questions are rarely posed.

In addition, the African continent has considerable oil and natural gas reserves in countries such as Angola, Nigeria and Algeria. China has invested heavily in the oil sector across Africa through state-owned enterprises like China National Offshore Oil Corporation and China National Petroleum Corporation.

Finally, with large tracts of arable land and significant freshwater resources, Africa also presents major opportunities for agricultural investments. Both China and Russia are interested in securing food resources for their populations. China, in particular, has been deeply involved in agricultural projects with this aim in mind, while also exporting agricultural technology and expertise to the region. For instance, China has invested in extensive rice farming projects in Mozambique, introducing advanced irrigation techniques and high-yield crop varieties. These initiatives not only aim to boost local food production but also ensure a steady supply of agricultural products for China's burgeoning population. Russia has increased its agricultural presence in Sudan, focusing on wheat production.

China has, of course, also focused on exporting its digital financial market infrastructure through which it will deploy its digital yuan and influence the CBDC development of African countries. These efforts are most visible through the widespread adoption of Chinese mobile payment systems like Alipay and WeChat Pay, which have been integrated into African markets via partnerships with local telecom operators and banks. Additionally, Chinese digital banking solutions have been deployed through collaborations with African financial institutions, facilitating the introduction of advanced technologies and services.

E-commerce platforms modelled after Alibaba have also found their way into Africa, fostering local e-commerce development and logistics. Support for African fintech start-ups has been substantial, with China investing in innovation hubs and accelerators across the continent. Blockchain technology and cryptocurrency exchanges, another area of Chinese expertise, have begun to influence African financial transactions and record-keeping systems.

China's microfinance and digital lending platforms, designed to offer credit and financial services to underserved populations, have seen significant implementation, particularly in countries like Nigeria, Kenya and South Africa. For instance, in Nigeria, Chinese mobile payment systems have been successfully integrated, and, in Kenya, partnerships with fintech companies have driven new financial services innovations. In South Africa, blockchain projects and microfinance initiatives have targeted both small businesses and individual consumers.

With great opportunities inevitably comes fierce competition. Africa, long a battleground for proxy conflicts, remains a stage where international actors vie for influence. This was glaringly evident during the Cold War, as the continent became a theatre for coups, often backed by the US and the Soviet Union. In the past seventy years, Africa has witnessed approximately one hundred coups.

This tug of war re-emerged in the Sahel and West Africa between 2020 and 2023, where a 'coup epidemic' swept across six former French colonies – Burkina Faso, Chad, Gabon, Guinea, Mali and Niger. These coups, driven by domestic challenges like underdevelopment, state fragility, corruption and economic mismanagement, were also influenced by renewed international competition, especially between the US and Russia, echoing Cold War patterns.

The governments in these regions, historically aligned with Paris, are now questioning Western democratic values and resenting perceived neocolonialism. As confidence in European influence wanes, countries like China, Russia, Turkey and members of the Gulf Cooperation Council are stepping in.

The unfolding saga of military coups in Africa provides fertile ground for Russia's expanding ambitions, offering Putin a chance to deepen his influence. The Kremlin has seized this opportunity by offering strategic and military support to various militia groups, resurrecting Cold War-era alliances. The Wagner Group, for instance, has bolstered the juntas in Mali and Niger following the ousting of Ibrahim Boubacar Keïta and Mohamed Bazoum, respectively. This has accelerated the collapse of French-influenced regimes and empowered new anti-Western military leaders, paralleling Iran's support for military-led regimes in Burkina Faso and Mali.

Russia's diplomatic manoeuvres in Africa are as audacious as they are calculated. At the second Russia–Africa Summit in St Petersburg on 27–28 July 2023, Putin announced the forgiveness of $23 billion in African debt.[9] This grand gesture, coinciding with Russia's exit from the Black Sea Grain Initiative, signals a deliberate strategy to strengthen economic ties and expand influence, effectively erasing 90 per cent of Africa's debts to Moscow.

Additionally, Putin pledged more funds for developmental projects and expressed strong interest in the African Continental Free Trade Area, which is poised to become a market exceeding $3 trillion in GDP.[10]

Observing from afar, the United States, long reliant on France's insights in the Sahel and West Africa due to historic colonial ties, is now re-evaluating its approach. Washington, once content to let Paris lead in addressing regional challenges, has been jolted by the recent spate of coups in former French colonies, exposing France's waning influence and necessitating a reassessment of US policies in this volatile region, home to numerous international terrorist organisations.

In response to the strategic advances of China and Russia, the US foresees a perilous drift towards autocratic regimes as Western influence wanes. Consequently, it is striving to bolster its presence and partnerships across Africa, aiming to sustain its geopolitical clout in a continent increasingly pivotal to global economic and political dynamics.

These efforts extend to economic engagement, marked by increased investment in critical sectors such as energy, technology and infrastructure through initiatives like Prosper Africa. Diplomatic manoeuvring accompanies this economic outreach, highlighted by a series of recent high-profile summits aimed at fortifying ties with African nations. For instance, the US–Africa Leaders Summit held in Washington, D.C. in December 2022 was a landmark event that convened leaders from across the continent to deliberate on trade, security, governance and shared interests, underscoring America's strategic intent to foster robust cooperation and partnerships in Africa.

Finally, the United States has also escalated its military presence in Africa, primarily through United States Africa Command, which collaborates with African nations on counterterrorism, security training and military assistance. Joint military exercises, such as the African Lion drills in Morocco, Tunisia and Senegal, are part of this effort.

However, with the US, China and Russia all ramping up their presence on the African continent, the stage is set for potentially explosive proxy conflicts. Economic competition for natural resources, influence over political processes and military posturing in politically unstable regions create a veritable tinderbox, primed to ignite at any moment.

LATIN AMERICA

In the twenty-first century, China has significantly bolstered its influence in Latin America through substantial investments in ports, roads and digital infrastructure under the BRI. Venezuela, Brazil, Argentina and Peru have eagerly signed up to big ventures. The $3.6 billion Port of Chancay in Peru, predominantly financed and constructed by China, is poised to become a pivotal maritime hub in the Pacific, offering China a strategic foothold in the region.

Latin America's abundance in vital commodities such as oil, lithium and copper aligns perfectly with China's voracious energy needs and its burgeoning technological and manufacturing sectors. Chile and Peru, as global leaders in copper production – a metal indispensable for electrical wiring, construction and renewable energy technologies – have attracted significant Chinese investments to secure its supply. Brazil, a major producer of iron ore, supplies another essential resource for China's vast steel-making industry.

Venezuela's colossal oil reserves, the largest proven reserves globally, estimated at over 300 billion barrels, are of profound strategic interest to China.[11] Chinese involvement in Venezuela's oil sector spans many years, with numerous Chinese firms forming joint ventures with Venezuela's state oil company, PDVSA. By the late 2010s, China had extended over $60 billion in loans to Venezuela, predominantly in exchange for oil.[12] These funds have been crucial in sustaining the Venezuelan economy amidst crippling US sanctions and severe economic instability.

Latin America is also a major source of agricultural commodities. Brazil and Argentina are among the world's largest producers of soybeans, a crucial import for China's livestock industry. South America also produces other important commodities like beef, poultry and grains, which China is focusing on in an effort to secure food resources and diversify its supply chains away from traditional suppliers like the United States.

Another locus of strategic interest for China is the so-called Lithium Triangle, spanning parts of Argentina, Bolivia and Chile. This region harbours a significant portion of the world's lithium reserves, a metal indispensable for batteries in EVs and energy storage systems.

China has emerged as the top trading partner for countries such as Brazil, Chile and Peru, and now stands as the second-largest trading partner for the region as a whole, doing its best to catch up with the United States. According to the World Economic Forum, trade between China and Latin America skyrocketed from $12 billion in 2000 to over $315 billion in 2020, reaching $489 billion by 2023. In the first two months of 2024, China's exports to Latin America rose by 20.6 per cent.[13]

China has been deeply embedded in the development of smart cities across Latin America, integrating a plethora of digital services such as surveillance, transportation systems and public utility management. Projects like the ECU-911 system in Ecuador and similar ventures in Bolivia are China's means of establishing its digital standards through urban management technology. Huawei has emerged as a dominant force in the Latin American telecommunications sector, particularly with the deployment of 5G networks, extending its technological tentacles deep into the continent.

Chinese firms like Alipay have also penetrated the Latin American market, establishing a notable presence in Mexico, helping transform financial transactions in regions with underdeveloped banking infrastructures, mirroring China's own digital financial ecosystem.

Unsurprisingly, the US has grown concerned over China's increased presence in what it considers its backyard, and has responded by revitalising its engagement with the region through initiatives like América Crece, aimed at promoting private sector investment in energy and infrastructure in Latin America.

The overlapping interests of the US and China in Latin America are likely to lead to increased tensions, manifesting in economic competition, diplomatic standoffs and support for rival political factions within Latin American countries.

The US has historically supported more conservative, market-friendly governments, while China finds alignment with governments favouring state-led economic models. But this 'support' could gradually slide into active engagement, with both sides using cyber- and information warfare to spread disinformation and even influence elections. This is a dangerous prospect, undermining the political autonomy of Latin American countries and reducing them to stages for renewed proxy wars.

THE ARCTIC

Even the uninhabited Arctic is emerging as a new potential flashpoint for international conflict, intensified by the disquieting effects of global warming. Research indicates that over the past three decades, Arctic sea ice has diminished at an alarming rate of 13 per cent per decade.[14] Yet, this environmental catastrophe also heralds new strategic and economic opportunities.

As the ice retreats, once impassable waterways are now becoming navigable, transforming the Arctic into a tantalising transit route for global shipping. Indeed, at least three new trade routes have recently become viable, with the Northwest Passage standing out. According to data from the World Economic Forum, this route could reduce transit times by up to four days.[15]

This development is a game-changer for many Asian companies trading with the east coast of North America. With cargo ship operating costs ranging from $9,259 to $24,140 per day, even a single day's reduction in travel can lead to substantial savings. When multiplied across the thousands of ships that traverse these routes, the cumulative cost savings are immense. Consequently, the Northwest Passage is set to experience a surge in maritime traffic, positioning itself as a preferred route for a significant volume of global trade.

Beyond its value as a shipping lane, the Arctic harbours untapped natural resources. The region is reputedly rich in oil, natural gas and a wealth of minerals, presenting an irresistible lure for countries aiming to enhance their energy security and resource reserves. Additionally, the opportunity to establish military and research bases on this frontier offers a strategic extension of national defence capabilities.

The geopolitical ramifications of these developments are profound. As nations jostle for influence in this once forbidding expanse, the Arctic is set to become a key theatre for global power dynamics. It has already captured the strategic imaginations of Russia, the United States, Canada and China, each crafting strategies to assert their presence and stake their claims.

China and Russia have recently asserted their dominion over the *Northeast* Passage, a previously impassable route along Russia's northern Arctic coastline that now provides a direct link to Shanghai. Rosatom, the Russian state nuclear corporation responsible for the passage and its fleet of nuclear-powered icebreakers, aims to increase trade along Russia's northern coast tenfold over the next decade. China sees this as part of a collaborative effort to create the 'Ice Silk Road', establishing a blue economic corridor that connects the major markets of China and Europe.

Canada occupies a unique position with regards to the Northwest Passage, possessing a substantial portion of the trade route along with several Arctic ports and mines. However, its infrastructure significantly lags behind that of other Arctic nations such as Norway, Sweden and Russia. Consequently, the Canadian government faces the formidable challenge of safeguarding its interests, maintaining control in this strategically crucial region and withstanding the overtures of eager foreign investors.

The relative underdevelopment of Canada's Arctic region makes it particularly vulnerable to external influences. The Canadian government must remain vigilant against aggressive manoeuvres, much as it did in December 2020 when it thwarted a Chinese investment firm's attempt to acquire a gold mine located in a critical area of the Arctic Northwest Passage.

Indeed, Canada might take inspiration from China's playbook in this regard, as China has implemented stringent regulations to prevent foreign investment in sectors deemed vital for national security. Adopting similar policies could fortify Canada's national interests and those of the West more broadly.

Ultimately, we should all be preparing for a world marked by conflict on multiple new fronts in the coming decades, as the New Cold War between the world's two power blocs compete over contested territories and resources that are diminishing in most spheres but continue to be uncovered amidst the receding ice caps.

The war in Ukraine represents the failure of 'dollar deterrence'. The prospective invasion of Taiwan would signal the tipping point towards a Chinese-led world order, which will run on smart money controlled – or largely influenced – by Beijing. The outcomes of the modern-day scrambles for influence in Africa and Latin America will dictate the cultural and geopolitical allegiances of the booming populations of the so-called Global South. The emergence of smart money-based alliances will go far in deciding the balance of power. In this world, nothing will be more important than the security of these new monetary paradigms.

12

Cyberspace:
The Fifth Dimension of Warfare

'The internet is about to start killing people, and the
government regulates things that kill people.'
BRUCE SCHNEIER[1]

Once upon a time – and for a substantial period thereafter – the
traditional operational domains of warfare were land, air and sea.
In the twentieth century, space was added as the fourth dimension.
By 2016, NATO acknowledged a fifth domain: cyberspace.[2]

Cyberwarfare has already become a central theatre in the New
Cold War. In March 2020, President Trump declared a national
emergency in cyberspace – the fourth such declaration by a US
president in five years.[3] In a retaliatory gesture, China, in April 2021,
called the US the biggest instigator of cyberattacks. The subsequent
month, G7 foreign ministers implored both Russia and China to
adhere to international norms in their cyber activities.[4]

With the advent of digital currency, this domain is set to become
the epicentre of twenty-first-century conflicts for two principal
reasons. Firstly, because digital money is likely to play a significant
role in cyberwarfare operations. Secondly, and more critically in
the context of an emerging bipolar monetary order, because data is
poised to become a new linchpin of geopolitical power, akin to oil
in its strategic significance.

China is cultivating remarkable capabilities to harvest, analyse and monetise data on an unprecedented scale. This isn't merely an economically advantageous tool; it is a formidable weapon in the realm of non-lethal geopolitical warfare. CBDCs hold the potential to disrupt foreign economies and reshape the global financial system, given the data they will collect – data that can be both monetised and weaponised by its recipients.

Needless to say, companies in both China and the West are already engaging in these practices. TikTok, with its affiliations with the Chinese Communist Party, is widely suspected of functioning as a spyware apparatus for Beijing. American tech behemoths like Meta, Google and X amass vast quantities of data but are not formally integrated into a system of sharing this data with their governments, although they comply when requested. As data becomes increasingly pivotal to governmental operations and capabilities in the West, maintaining this delicate balance will become ever more challenging. The tug of war over data sovereignty and control is set to intensify, with far-reaching implications for both privacy and power in the digital age.

Cyberspace unveils new battlegrounds unconfined by physical borders, which are defined instead by the expanse and intricacy of digital networks. The convergence of emerging technologies like AI with smart money introduces previously unimaginable dimensions to cyberwarfare. As these technologies entwine, they will redefine the very fabric of conflict, where the sophistication of code and algorithms supplants the brute force of traditional warfare.

The precise manner in which CBDCs will be employed in cyberwarfare remains to be seen, but we can certainly begin to make educated conjectures. What is indisputable is that state-issued digital currencies will become integral to state-sponsored cyberwarfare. Moreover, it is relatively clear that abstaining from developing a CBDC will not be the most secure path for the world's major powers, any more than abstaining from nuclear weapons or the AI race would shield a nation from the threats posed by these technologies in the hands of adversaries.

In essence, the race to develop CBDCs is not merely a concern for central banks; it is a significant issue for the US Department of

Defense, the UK Ministry of Defence and the defence departments of countries worldwide. This new frontier in the digital arms race demands attention at the highest levels of national security, as the implications of falling behind could be as dire as any in traditional military realms.

In his book *Softwar*, Jason Lowery, a US Space Force astronautical engineer and US National Defense Fellow at MIT, examines the geopolitical ramifications of Bitcoin.[5] He posits that this groundbreaking technology should be seen as a vector of digital warfare poised to revolutionise national security, cybersecurity and possibly even the foundational architecture of the internet.

Lowery contends that it would be folly for the United States to disregard this new technology, thereby allowing other nations to gain a strategic advantage in exploiting its capabilities. To illustrate the current governmental neglect of Bitcoin's potential applications for national defence and security, he references General Ferdinand Foch, the former Chief of Staff of the French Army, who in 1911 (in)famously remarked that 'airplanes are interesting toys, but of no military value'.

We are in danger of committing the same blunder regarding CBDCs – viewing them as curious technologies devoid of broader significance. In the midst of escalating cyberwars, the United States and other Western nations must utilise every available tool to counter global competition from the likes of China and Russia. CBDCs will swiftly evolve into instruments of cyberwarfare, and the West must, at the very least, understand how to defend itself against this emerging threat.

CYBERATTACK TARGETS

What, then, are the most glaring vulnerabilities or single points of failure when it comes to cyberattacks, and how might smart money be harnessed to exploit them? Hostile states could potentially leverage CBDCs to breach energy grids and other critical infrastructure, or to exert control over vital cyber infrastructure within their spheres of influence.

As we've observed, the deployment of CBDC technology allows nations to integrate their cybersecurity protocols into the digital infrastructure of countries to which they export such technology. This could create a scenario where essential cyber infrastructure, including energy grids, telecommunications and financial systems, become vulnerable to external manipulation.

Both China and Russia have a well-documented history of deploying advanced persistent threats to infiltrate and exploit critical infrastructure. CBDCs could introduce an additional avenue for these cyberattacks in multiple ways. By embedding malicious code or exploiting security loopholes within CBDC systems, these nations could extend their reach and impact, transforming digital currency into a formidable weapon in their cyberwarfare arsenals.

By obscuring the origins of funds, state-sponsored hackers could carry out intricate cyberattacks, such as phishing campaigns and malware deployment, without leaving a discernible trail.

With the advent of smart contracts, CBDCs could automate the execution of malicious activities once specific conditions are met. For instance, payments could activate malware embedded within energy grid management systems, resulting in significant disruptions.

Malware triggered by smart contracts could induce regional blackouts by shutting down power plants or substations. A striking example of such an impact was observed during the 2015 cyber-attack on Ukraine's power grid, where hackers remotely manipulated circuit breakers to cause widespread outages.

State actors could also destabilise financial operations within the supply chains of critical infrastructure companies, such as energy providers, precipitating systemic failures. A disruption in the energy sector can cause major economic losses. For instance, the 2003 blackout in the northeastern United States and Canada led to an estimated economic loss of $6 billion, stemming from halted industrial production, spoiled goods and lost wages.[6]

In 2021, a ransomware attack by the cybercriminal group DarkSide – believed to be based in Russia – compelled the Colonial Pipeline, a major fuel supplier for the US East Coast, to cease operations. The incident precipitated widespread shortages and panic buying.

Hospitals, water treatment plants and other critical services depend on a stable power supply. Disruptions could result in life-threatening situations, such as the inability to perform surgeries or maintain clean water supplies.

Also in 2021, a ransomware assault on Ireland's health service debilitated its systems, forcing the cancellation of medical appointments and surgeries. Patient data was compromised and the healthcare sector faced substantial disruptions.

In the financial sector, deploying malware to compromise banking infrastructure can paralyse financial transactions, while being left vulnerable to hacking incidents can erode trust in the entire system. The 2016 cyberheist on Bangladesh Bank illustrates the potential magnitude of such incidents. Hackers sent thirty-five orders from the SWIFT financial messaging system in an attempt to steal $951 million from the account of Bangladesh Bank at the New York Fed, though thankfully only five of the orders were executed, amounting to $101 million.[7]

Automated financial disruptions via CBDCs could also trigger market instability. A smart contract could be engineered to initiate large-scale sell-offs in stock markets, leading to crashes akin to the 2010 Flash Crash, where the Dow Jones Industrial Average plummeted about 1,000 points within minutes.

By embedding malware in CBDC transactions, state actors could also access sensitive data from critical national infrastructure, thereby facilitating espionage. This was starkly illustrated by the 2020 SolarWinds attack, wherein Russian hackers infiltrated several US federal agencies, gaining access to highly sensitive information.

Cyberattacks on military infrastructure have the potential to disable defence systems, as evidenced by the 2017 WannaCry ransomware attack, which disrupted the defence networks as well as healthcare systems of several countries, including the UK's National Health Service (NHS).

China, Russia and the BRICS+ coalition could also leverage cyber malware in CBDCs to exert economic pressure over developing nations, or even to blackmail them. By embedding malicious code in financial aid or investment transactions, they could encourage the victim nations to adopt their own cybersecurity technologies. The arsonist becomes the firefighter.

Election outcomes are also at stake. For instance, Russia frequently targets democratic processes with cyberattacks designed to sway political discourse and votes in the direction desired by the Kremlin, a practice that would likely be amplified through smart money channels.

So why not simply ban all interactions with CBDCs? If it's not too late for such measures? Sadly, the complexities and interdependencies of the modern digital economy may render such bans ineffective or even counterproductive.

DIGITAL DEPENDENCE

Today, most of our critical national and international infrastructure – and virtually all trade – depends on the internet. We cannot escape it, nor can we opt out of using it; our only recourse is to strive to protect it. This reality was starkly illustrated on 19 July 2024, when a global IT outage disrupted the operations of banks, airlines, TV and radio broadcasters and even supermarkets across the world, after US cybersecurity giant Crowdstrike suffered a technical glitch that debilitated Microsoft's Windows software – dubbed 'the largest IT outage in history'.[8]

The realm of cybersecurity gained heightened significance during the Covid-19 pandemic, as vast swathes of the population were compelled to rely heavily on technology for myriad activities. While the most conspicuous aspect was undoubtedly the consumer experience, the corporate world also found itself utterly dependent on digital platforms, cloud services (primarily furnished by behemoths like Google, Amazon, Microsoft and Alibaba) and enterprise resource planning systems. These systems, which aid businesses in automating and managing core processes such as finance, human resources, manufacturing, supply chains and data-related services, all rely on cyber infrastructure.

This cyber sphere enabled factories to continue operations, ensured the shipment of goods, maintained power supplies and kept the overall economy functional. Amazon, already a global juggernaut before the pandemic, became virtually indispensable across most advanced economies. On one hand, this underscores the increased resilience of a digitised world; even amidst major crises, digital technologies ensure that normal life continues.

On the other hand, the pandemic also laid bare the vulnerabilities within digital infrastructure, as cyberattacks surged. The stressful environment and inadequate security measures at both personal and corporate levels created a breeding ground for online scams and breaches. This highlighted the varying degrees of digital preparedness among smaller businesses and countries, exposing a digital divide both between and within societies. A country's digital resilience is profoundly influenced by its infrastructure, investment in technology and the digital literacy of its populace. This disparity creates chasms not only between those with access to advanced technologies like 5G and those without, but also between states that understand and harness critical cyber defence infrastructure and those that do not.

Cyberattacks using financial transactions can be perpetrated through various methods, such as phishing, malware, ransomware and distributed denial-of-service (DDoS) attacks. These techniques do not rely on the type of currency used but rather exploit vulnerabilities in software, networks and human behaviour. In essence, such cyberattacks mostly target weaknesses in digital infrastructure rather than the financial instruments themselves. For example, attackers might use CBDC networks to exploit software flaws and weak passwords, or use social-engineering tactics – like manipulating or deceiving a victim to gain control over a computer system – to infiltrate critical infrastructure, irrespective of whether the systems use CBDCs or traditional currencies.

International trade involves intricate networks of suppliers, manufacturers and distributors spanning multiple countries. Even if a nation bans CBDCs domestically, businesses engaged in international trade may still interact with foreign entities that use CBDCs, creating indirect exposure to potential cyber threats. Furthermore, businesses often depend on third-party services, such as cloud providers, logistics companies and financial intermediaries, which may operate in regions where CBDCs are used. The security practices of these third parties can affect the overall security posture of a business, rendering it vulnerable to attacks through interconnected systems.

Ultimately, determined attackers will always find ways to circumvent bans. They might use proxy servers, VPNs or other anonymising technologies to obscure their activities and launch attacks from seemingly unrelated sources. In our interconnected digital world, the challenge lies not in banning specific technologies but in fortifying our defences against the ever-evolving landscape of cyber threats.

CYBER DEFENCE

To counter these risks, nations must engage in international cooperation and implement robust cybersecurity measures, such as those introduced by blockchain technology, including multi-signature wallets and decentralised control, which can significantly enhance protection.

Initiatives like the Paris Call for Trust and Security in Cyberspace underscore the necessity of global cooperation to combat cyber threats. In the same vein, countries will have to collaborate to establish international cybersecurity standards for CBDCs. Engaging private companies in developing strong defences against potential CBDC-related cyber threats is also crucial.

But who is best prepared as things stand? In June 2021, the International Institute for Strategic Studies conducted a comprehensive assessment to evaluate and understand the cyber defence and cyberwarfare capabilities of fifteen countries, categorising them into three tiers.[9]

The United States stood alone in the first tier, excelling in all categories. Tier 2 included countries with world-leading strengths in several, but not all, categories, such as Australia, Canada,

China, France, Israel, Russia and the United Kingdom. The third tier comprised countries with some strengths but also notable weaknesses, including India, Indonesia, Iran, Japan, Malaysia, North Korea and Vietnam.

UNITED STATES

In the United States, the Cybersecurity and Infrastructure Security Agency (CISA) spearheads the nation's cybersecurity initiatives. Functioning under the Department of Homeland Security, CISA collaborates with governmental and industrial partners to fortify critical infrastructure against threats and vulnerabilities.

In 2019, the US launched the Cyberspace Solarium Commission, inspired by President Eisenhower's Project Solarium and established under the National Defense Authorization Act.[10] This bipartisan body was charged with evaluating cyberspace defence strategies and formulating a comprehensive approach. The commission examined two scenarios: the 'Slow Burn', involving a series of gradual cyberattacks eroding critical infrastructure, and the 'Break Glass', which looked at an abrupt, systemic failure. Dr Benjamin Jensen, Senior Research Director of the Solarium Commission, advocated for a national strategy that focuses not only on preventing attacks but also on absorbing and mitigating their impact, adhering to the principle of deterrence by denial. Public–private partnerships were identified as crucial for enhancing system resilience and diminishing the severity and frequency of cyberattacks.[11]

The commission proposed a layered strategy to stabilise the current system by coordinating activities across various levels, each aimed at mitigating the impact of cyberattacks. In alignment with this, the US Department of Defense developed a cyberwarfare strategy centred on five pillars: building and maintaining cyber capabilities, defending the Department of Defense information network, preparing to defend the US homeland from major cyberattacks, developing viable cyber options for conflict management and establishing international alliances to deter shared threats.

In 2011, the White House introduced an 'International Strategy for Cyberspace'.[12] Crucially, this asserted that nations have the right to use military force in response to a cyberattack.

CHINA

In China, the Cyberspace Administration of China (CAC) reigns supreme over the internet, embodying the state's vision of digital control. Established in 2011 as the State Internet Information Office and rebranded in 2014, the CAC now operates as an executive arm of the Chinese Communist Party (CCP). Its expansive mandate includes drafting regulations, issuing licences and enforcing disciplinary actions, managing usernames on online platforms, scrutinising online comments, regulating VPNs, and controlling internet content. The CAC's actions, closely aligned with CCP objectives, shape China's digital realm through rigorous censorship, surveillance, propaganda and stringent legal frameworks.

To further the CCP's authoritarian goals, the CAC wields several key instruments. The Great Firewall blocks access to numerous foreign websites and services, including Google, various Meta platforms including Facebook and Instagram, X, YouTube and Wikipedia, while targeting domestic sites critical of the government. The Golden Shield Project monitors the online activities and communications of Chinese internet users, collecting data from various sources to identify individuals engaged in activities deemed illegal or subversive. The 50 Cent Party, comprising paid online commentators, spreads pro-government narratives on social media and internet forums to sway public opinion and quell dissent. The Cybersecurity Law of 2017 establishes a legal framework for internet regulation, mandating user consent for data collection, data storage within China and cooperation with authorities. It imposes penalties for spreading 'misinformation' (or criticism of the CCP), disrupting network operations or threatening national security.[13]

China's aggressive cyberspace policies have inevitably attracted significant scrutiny. While the Chinese government justifies these measures as essential for maintaining sovereignty and stability, critics – ranging from human rights groups and foreign governments to internet users – condemn the CCP for violating freedom of expression, privacy and access to information.

The cybersecurity landscape is evolving rapidly across the EU and Europe, with individual nations establishing their own cybersecurity agencies, complemented by the overarching European Union Agency for Cybersecurity (ENISA).

In Germany, cybersecurity efforts are spearheaded by the Bundesamt für Sicherheit in der Informationstechnik (BSI); in France, by the Agence nationale de la sécurité des systèmes d'information (ANSSI); and in Italy, by the Agenzia per la Cybersicurezza Nazionale (ACN). These agencies manage computer and communication security, protect critical infrastructure, mitigate cyberattacks, oversee cryptography and certify security products within their respective countries. Their efforts are bolstered by ENISA, which aims to coordinate a robust, continent-wide approach to cybersecurity resilience.

The EU faces significant challenges in grappling with the need to harmonise and standardise legislative and regulatory frameworks across member states while developing central cyber-defence capabilities. Consequently, many EU member states advocate for 'cyber borders' extending beyond national boundaries to encompass the entire EU or potentially the European Free Trade Association (EFTA) countries, including Iceland, Switzerland and Norway. By pooling their skills and resources, the wider European community can position itself as a formidable global competitor alongside the US, China and Russia.

Some observers posit that Europe could establish its niche in the digital landscape through technological regulation, or regtech. While the United States dominates in data collection, China excels in data processing and Russia is notorious for its hacking capabilities, Europe's prowess in crafting meticulous regulations could crown it the global leader in data protection. Europe's pioneering efforts, such as the 'safe harbour' privacy principles of the late 1990s and the landmark General Data Protection Regulation (GDPR) introduced in 2016, ensure that data within the EU is stored in the world's safest environments, respecting the rights of its creators – EU citizens. With the GDPR and the seminal AI Act approved in March 2024, the EU has skilfully navigated its path between the technological superpowers of the USA and China.

The United Kingdom, in the post-Brexit era, faces a more complex predicament. It must decide whether to establish its own sovereign digital realm, integrate with the EU's digital space and cyber-defence efforts or align with an ally like the US, which could make sense given their mutual membership of the 'Five Eyes' intelligence alliance along with Australia, Canada and New Zealand.

DIGITAL SOVEREIGNTY: DATA LAWS OR DATA WARS

The problem is that cyberspace transcends national boundaries, and the domain of cybersecurity transcends traditional military domains, given that cyberattacks occupy ambiguous territory. These attacks can target a wide range of entities, from private-sector companies and governmental organisations to academic institutions. Such attacks often elude classification as acts of war, primarily due to the absence of an international consensus on what constitutes 'digital sovereignty'. Yet, this does not diminish their potential to be utterly crippling.

Indeed, the nebulous nature of cyberwarfare presents a unique challenge. While conventional warfare is bounded by clear rules and definitions, cyberattacks operate in a shadowy realm where the lines are blurred. The lack of a unified definition for digital sovereignty leaves a gaping void in international law, allowing perpetrators to exploit these grey areas with impunity. The consequences can be as devastating as any traditional military assault, undermining the stability and security of targeted nations in profoundly insidious ways.

The nascent realms of smart money and cyberwarfare represent entirely uncharted territory. Here, we confront a suite of unprecedented questions: what is the relationship between data and ownership? Does data belong to those it describes or to those who collect it? Should states possess data about their citizens? Should they possess data about foreign citizens? Does all this hinge on the data's physical location? Should states own data situated beyond their borders?

Digital sovereignty issues relate to everything from individual ownership of personal data to the digital dependencies that exist, for example, between the EU and the US. French president Emmanuel Macron and EU Commission president Ursula von der Leyen have both recently highlighted these issues, with von der Leyen discussing the importance of digital sovereignty in the context of her broader policy goals at the start of her tenure in 2019.[14]

To grasp the essence of digital sovereignty, we must revisit the traditional definition of sovereignty: 'supreme authority within a territory', historically maintained by military force. In the context of digital sovereignty, we need to recast the respective scopes of 'authority', 'territory' and 'army' across the realm of cyberspace. This involves redefining what it means to exercise control in an intangible, borderless digital domain and reconsidering what forms of power and protection are appropriate for upholding such sovereignty in a world increasingly shaped by technology.

It is evident that in the digital realm, borders become increasingly amorphous. One might imagine a boundary encapsulating the space where a nation's citizens' data resides. However, the advent of cloud technology renders this notion problematic. Although cloud-stored data is accessible globally, it physically resides on servers and within data centres situated within specific national borders, which may not coincide with the origin country of the data.

Consequently, the concept of data ownership has grown more convoluted. In this intricate system, to whom does the data belong?

Is it the citizens who generate it, the nation where it is physically stored or the country of the multinational company providing the storage service? Take, for instance, data from French citizens stored by Google, an American corporation, in Iceland – a nation that has positioned itself as a global data storage hub. How, then, does the French government access its citizens' data when it is stored abroad and ostensibly 'owned' by a foreign private entity?

In an era where data holds the same value as oil did in the twentieth century, these questions are laden with geopolitical implications and could potentially ignite conflicts. Many predict that nations will resort to applying pressure – or even deploying force – to safeguard their citizens' data.

DATA IS THE NEW OIL

The definition of digital sovereignty only becomes more urgent as the value of data increases. The analogy of data as the new oil is not only apt but also deeply revealing, highlighting the staggering value and profitability inherent in data management. Just as the extraction, refining and trading of oil have yielded immense profits for decades, so too is the process of collecting, storing, transmitting, analysing and selling data becoming a similarly lucrative enterprise. It is not far-fetched to imagine a future where nations might physically clash over data control, much as they have over oil resources in the past and present.

Countries will soon regard their data – the collective information of their citizens – as a national commodity, fiercely guarded and strategically leveraged. The rise of multi-CBDC platforms, championed by China and BRICS+ members, signals a monumental shift in the global data landscape. These platforms could become formidable instruments for amassing, scrutinising and weaponising vast quantities of data, granting participating nations enhanced control over BRI countries and posing a potential threat to Western interests.

Every transaction funnelled through these platforms can be meticulously tracked, monitored and analysed, yielding profound insights into the economic behaviours and trends of BRI nations. This trove of data might encompass details on trade volumes, financial flows, investment patterns and even the economic priorities of participating countries. For China and the BRICS+ coalition, such an extensive reservoir of information would be priceless, allowing them to fine-tune their economic strategies and policies to bolster their sway and dominance within the BRI network.

With access to granular economic data from BRI countries, China and its allies could secure a decisive edge in trade negotiations, investment decisions and strategic alliances. They could pinpoint economic vulnerabilities or dependencies within these nations and manipulate this intelligence to direct economic agreements or infrastructure projects to align with their geopolitical objectives.

For the West, the ramifications of this data-centric approach are profound. Its capacity to sway global economic and political dynamics could be significantly undermined as China and the BRICS+ consortium exploit their data-driven insights to consolidate power within the BRI network. Western nations might find themselves at a strategic disadvantage, bereft of the comprehensive economic intelligence that the multi-CBDC platform furnishes its operators. This could precipitate a realignment of global alliances, trade patterns and power structures, with China and BRICS+ nations increasingly setting the agenda in a world where data is the new currency of power.

In this context, the digital yuan has made a considerable impact in the corridors of the US Congress. Lawmakers have repeatedly attempted to counter its influence. The latest effort came on 8 November 2023, when Florida Republican Senator Rick Scott, alongside colleagues from both the House and Senate, reintroduced the 'Chinese CBDC Prohibition Act'.[15]

Scott's bill, initially presented in the previous Congress, aims to prohibit US financial services firms from engaging in transactions involving the digital yuan. Scott stated, 'Secretary Xi and his thugs have no business playing Big Brother to American citizens and how they spend their money. That is why I am fighting to prevent this problem from ever becoming someone's reality.'[16] But as we've seen, the horse has likely already bolted on this issue.

The military forces of the future will, in all likelihood, be spearheaded by cyber divisions – a reality already acknowledged by various governments as they develop such units. Advanced nations are fortifying their defences against these looming threats, bracing themselves for the oncoming storm. The private sector, too, is poised to play a crucial role, much like private contractors in conventional warfare. This heralds yet another paradigm shift – this time in the realm of modern warfare and national security, where digital acumen becomes as indispensable as traditional military might.

In this new epoch, cyber capabilities will be paramount, reshaping the very essence of how nations defend their interests and project power. The battlefield is no longer confined to physical terrains; it now encompasses the vast, intricate web of cyberspace. Here, the ability to protect and exploit information will define the victors and vanquished, making digital prowess the linchpin of twenty-first-century geopolitics. In this world, smart money could become the ultimate catalyst for success or failure.

13

The Wrong Conversation:
Culture Wars and the Future of Money

'The exploration of space will go ahead, whether we join in it
or not. And no nation which expects to be the leader of other
nations can expect to stay behind in this race for space.'
PRESIDENT JOHN F. KENNEDY[1]

President Kennedy's call to action for space exploration doesn't
seem entirely out of place in the realm of cyberspace and digital
money.

As we've seen, 134 countries and currency unions, which account
for 98 per cent of the world's GDP, are now navigating the waters
of CBDC exploration, according to the Atlantic Council. The G20
nations are at the forefront of this shift, with nineteen members
advancing towards the development of CBDCs.

The European Central Bank is gearing up for the digital euro pilot,
joining over twenty countries that ventured into CBDC trials in 2023.
Nations like Australia, Thailand and Russia are continuing their pilot
tests, while India and Brazil aim for launches in 2024 and 2025.

In the United States, the conversation has become highly
politicised and has been a sticking point for the 2024 presidential
election campaigns. Other G7 members like the United Kingdom
and Japan are advancing with their consultations and prototype
development.

In short, the race for the future of money is going ahead whether we like it or not. Blockchain technology is not going away. It is also a momentous technological innovation, which will be harnessed by the private sector to disrupt and upgrade a wide range of industries far beyond banking and finance, from healthcare and real estate to media, entertainment and education. It is akin to the invention of the internet in its range of applications and scope for impact on the economy and society.

Like the internet, blockchain is an innovation for all of humanity. In a sense, blockchain simply represents the next evolution of the internet, which is why blockchain technology is closely associated with the term 'Web3' in tech circles, representing a move away from centralised tech monopolies towards an era of a decentralised web that enables digital ownership rights for all participants.

There was never any doubt that the day would come when governments around the world would look into ways of availing themselves of this technology, for both good and ill. There is a natural and understandable aversion to this fact from many in the tech industry, which has spread across society more broadly.

Bitcoin and Web3 enthusiasts consider CBDCs to be the mortal enemy – an attempt by the state to co-opt the blockchain revolution and reverse its intended effects by centralising power and pushing back against the tide of decentralisation.

Granted, CBDCs must have a centralised ledger, because this is what central banks do. However, though we might be moving towards a world of increasingly decentralised finance, we will move along a spectrum, rather than play a zero-sum game. The world will still need governmental institutions, and these institutions cannot simply be left in the past. For all the inherent problems of central banking, and indeed of governments, the simple fact is that they are not going away anytime soon. Even the staunchest libertarian would be likely to admit this. The question is the extent to which these centralised ledgers can (or should) be designed to create 'liberal' – as opposed to authoritarian – forms of digital money.

As we've seen, the charge towards digital money is being led by China and Russia, and their autocratic allies are responding to their rallying call. If the West recuses itself from the race for the future of money, this territory will be ceded to them.

So Western leaders must ask their populations – is this a serious position to take? As the internet moves into its third act, and begins to cannibalise the global monetary order, is this the time to step away, and let the BRICS+ take it from here, while we continue to fiddle with our paper notes and punch credit card numbers into unfamiliar websites?

Or rather, is this the time to dive into the unknown, and seek to lead. When Tim Berners-Lee invented the World Wide Web in 1989 to meet the demand for automated information-sharing between scientists in universities and research institutes around the world, he did not anticipate that his creation would profoundly and permanently change the way we live and interact to this day.

The emergence of digital currencies represents the biggest technological revolution since then, the final step in the full digital transformation of the global financial system and the biggest transformation the industry has faced in more than 300 years. Today, the global race for the future of money is well underway, so what should the West do?

WHAT WE KNOW, AND WHAT WE DON'T...

'Reports that say that something hasn't happened are always interesting to me, because as we know, there are known knowns; there are things we know we know. We also know there are known unknowns; that is to say we know there are some things we do not know. But there are also unknown unknowns – the ones we don't know we don't know. And if one looks throughout the history of our country and other free countries, it is the latter category that tends to be the difficult ones.'

Donald Rumsfeld[2]

The cryptic phraseology that Donald Rumsfeld provided in response to a question at a US Department of Defense news briefing in the lead-up to the Iraq War is a fitting prism through which to consider how the West should approach CBDCs. There are things we already know about how they will affect our future, things we're aware we don't know and things we do not yet know that we don't know.

We know that a race for the future of money is underway and that China is leading this race. We also know that China intends to build a new system of digital payment rails along the fault lines of the BRI that will operate independently of the US dollar system. And we know that China's aspirations extend to a broader and more profound influence on the global financial architecture of the twenty-first century.

Additionally, we know of the dual-use nature of China's digital yuan, serving not only as a currency but also as an instrument of surveillance and control within its borders. Beijing is likely to roll out the same blueprint across the jurisdictions it is able to influence. The extension of this model on a global scale should be very worrying.

But what are our known unknowns? China's geopolitical strategy is clear, but its long-term impact and prospects for success remain to be seen. China's ability to persuade developing nations to pivot away from the US dollar and towards digital currencies for trade and reserves is still an open question.

The path that the BRICS+ nations will tread is shrouded in ambiguity. Will they prioritise the promotion of their local currencies in international trade and, by extension, their digital versions through multi-CBDC bridges, or will they gravitate towards the digital yuan to diminish the dollar's global dominance? And where will the allegiances of key states like India and Brazil fall?

While the trajectory seems to favour a blend of these strategies, their prospective success in undermining the influence of the dollar remains deeply uncertain. Equally nebulous is how China might leverage the digital yuan – and its influence over the digital payment rails it is constructing for its allies – as an instrument of non-lethal warfare. The potential for CBDCs to become tools in cyberwarfare is well-known, but the scope and nature of their deployment in that capacity remain speculative at best.

The full potential of programmability in digital money is also unknown. Its scope for impact ranges from the minutiae of daily transactions to the grand machinations of economic policy and governance. The extent to which it will become a part of civilian life, and a tool of statecraft, will depend on the decisions of authoritarian governments and the conversations of civil societies in democracies.

Moreover, the intersection of CBDCs with artificial intelligence introduces a fascinating yet daunting frontier. AI is poised to augment CBDCs, potentially enabling micropayments and offering novel approaches to monetary policy and labour market controls. However, the specifics of this fusion – the manner in which it will materialise, its benefits and its challenges – remain largely speculative.

By definition, we cannot know what Rumsfeld called the unknown unknowns – those outcomes that cannot be expected because there has been no prior experience or theoretical basis for expecting them. But we can speculate as to which category of threat or opportunity they might belong to, namely their application to national security, access to energy and control over global supply chains.

In many ways, what we might call the 'knowledge landscape' of digital currencies is strikingly similar to that of artificial intelligence. Both are alien life forms whose risks and opportunities remain largely unbeknownst to us, requiring exploration, regulation and international collaboration. Both are the subject of a geopolitical arms race with uncertain outcomes. Both are likely to bring about technological and economic paradigm shifts on a global and long-lasting scale. We just don't know exactly how yet.

Western countries should seek to lead the race for the future of money in much the same way that they are seeking to lead in the conversation regarding the appropriate design, effective deployment and safe regulation of AI. We require an attitude of leadership and open enquiry.

However, for a variety of cultural reasons, Western societies are presently on course to have the *wrong conversation* about CBDCs, and are in danger of missing the forest for the trees, causing them to retreat from the race for the future of money entirely.

THE WRONG CONVERSATION – AND THE CULTURE WARS TO COME

In the West, CBDCs have become the latest battleground in the domestic culture wars. We need a conversation about the future of money, and the future of the global monetary order. Instead, there is a strong sense in which the conversation has become hopelessly myopic and effectively hijacked, focused on a narrow set of issues surrounding privacy and the potential for government overreach. These issues should of course be discussed and addressed, but our society's prevailing mindset – perhaps unsurprisingly, in the wake of the pandemic – is presently overly paranoid and conspiratorial.

We know that our emails could be hacked by malicious actors, or even spied on by the government, but we still send and receive emails every day. We also know that companies like Google and Meta possess more private information about us than we can possibly imagine, and we know that they actively monetise this data, and yet we continue to voluntarily provide them with our information almost every hour of the day. We also know that these companies have far greater resources than our governments do, and that their business is specifically designed to harness personal data and use it for their commercial benefit. None of us have a say in these companies' policies, and we are not admitted to take the minutes of their board meetings.

However, when it comes to our elected governments, despite their best efforts to convince us otherwise, many of us seem determined to believe that the only possible incentive for bringing money into the digital age is an overwhelming desire to spy on us and to control what we spend our money on. We are certain that our governments not only have the resources to do this but will also have the technological know-how and the unrelenting energy to do so.

There is no question that this is an incentive in China, and will be in many other countries. If the race for the future of money is left to China, much of the developing world could succumb to digital money that is surveillance based, and fundamentally serves as a tool for centralised state-power, rather than an instrument for free trade, as the US dollar has served for decades.

This begs a simple but important question: does the West – and the United States specifically – have a *responsibility* to engage in a global discussion about the future of money? Does it have a responsibility to ensure – or at least attempt to ensure – that the properties of money in the digital age remain fundamentally liberal and democratic?

If so, this starts with the conversation we have as a society. Unlike the citizens of China, we in the West have the opportunity to influence our governments' direction of travel when it comes to the future of money.

In the coming years, likely between 2025 and 2026, governments in the West will ask their populations and parliaments for their opinions about digital money. There is much at stake, so we need to understand what we are being asked.

Public sentiment in the United States, the United Kingdom and the EU is presently a mixture of scepticism, overt opposition and lack of interest. A survey by the Cato Institute revealed that only 16 per cent of Americans support the adoption of a CBDC, with twice as many Americans opposing it. Almost half (49 per cent) have not formed an opinion, likely due to 72 per cent of Americans not being familiar with CBDCs.[3]

The two issues that have most animated Western populations are overwhelmingly those of privacy and programmability. Though the issues are separable, they are also two sides of the same coin. What we might term 'the privacy concern' is the fear of being surveilled, while 'the programmability concern' is the fear of being controlled.

The same CATO survey highlighted these major concerns, with 68 per cent of Americans opposing a CBDC if it meant the government could monitor their spending. This opposition rises to 74 per cent if the government could control what they spend their money on. Republicans are more likely to oppose a CBDC than Democrats, but both groups show notable wariness once benefits and risks are considered.[4] Interestingly, some potential advantages like reducing financial crime did garner support.

When the Bank of England received over 50,000 responses to its consultation on a digital pound, the majority of concerns expressed were over privacy.[5] A public petition in the UK also expressed concerns that programmability would erode freedom by granting the issuer control over how individuals use the currency.

In Europe, the European Central Bank (ECB) conducted a public consultation that included 8,221 respondents, revealing that privacy was the most important cited concern.[6]

PRIVACY AND PROGRAMMABILITY

So, what exactly is the privacy risk? The best way to understand this is to look at how the most draconian version of this fear is currently being played out in China. It is no secret that the CCP utilises its CBDC as a powerful instrument for extensive state monitoring and control over economic activities. This surveillance is conducted in a number of ways.

The digital yuan allows the Chinese government to track all transactions in real time. Every purchase, transfer and monetary interaction can be monitored, logged and analysed by government authorities.

The addition of the digital yuan to China's existing surveillance infrastructure, which includes its vast network of CCTV cameras and social credit system, provides a holistic view of an individual's behaviour and economic activities.

The social credit system in China is an extensive framework designed to monitor and assess the creditworthiness, trustworthiness and loyalty of businesses, individuals and government entities. In its earliest iteration, it primarily targeted rural individuals and small businesses that lacked formal documentation and financial histories. After initial regional trials in 2009, the programme then expanded to a national level in 2014. The system plays a pivotal role in China's state surveillance apparatus, assessing financial behaviour alongside broader social conduct to score its citizens.

All of this is buttressed by increasingly sophisticated mobile phone tracking functionalities, thanks in part to the Covid-19 pandemic. The Chinese government enforced strict lockdowns as part of its zero-Covid policy, which lasted much longer than in most other nations. This extended period of confinement allowed for an unprecedented expansion of social control mechanisms, with the government deploying advanced facial recognition technology, as well as 'Skynet', an elaborate network of surveillance cameras.

In their recent book *Surveillance State*, Josh Chin and Liza Lin outline how China is transforming into an Orwellian police state, marked by AI-enhanced security forces that maintain an omnipresent watch over millions of citizens.[7] The digital yuan is likely to become the apotheosis of this spyware strategy.

It is therefore no surprise that citizens of the West associate CBDCs with dystopian visions of state surveillance. However, the 'programmability concern' seems to be the greater of the two fears about state-issued digital currencies, and that which has garnered the most media attention to date in the West. It is likely to remain a focal point of enormous contention and controversy in the years to come.

It is important to clarify some misconceptions about programmability. Programmability in money is not novel, unique to digital currencies or inherent to digital currencies. In other words, it has long been possible to programme *payments* in various ways, although this is different from programming *digital currencies*, and digital currencies are not *necessarily* programmable.

However, programmability has become a dirty word for two reasons. Firstly, because of observation of how China is seeking to intertwine its digital currency with its social credit score system, and fears that programmable money represents the means through which governments will exercise the kind of overreach many thought they demonstrated during the pandemic, leading to similar social credit score systems being stealthily implemented in Western countries.

Many fear that our governments will *programme* our money in such a manner as to control or manipulate our spending, whether by designating which goods and services we can buy, like limiting the amount of alcohol or cigarettes we might purchase, or by aligning our spending with carbon reduction goals, or even worse by freezing our accounts when we fall out of line with prevailing political orthodoxies.

While some of these fears might be dismissed as paranoid hangovers from the pandemic, they are not without foundation. The Canadian trucker protest is rightly one of the most frequently cited examples in this regard.

In early 2022, a series of protests and blockades began in Canada against Covid-19 vaccine mandates and restrictions, called the Freedom Convoy by organisers. The initial convoy movement was created to protest about vaccine certificates being required for crossing the United States border, but later evolved into a protest about Covid-19 mandates in general. Beginning on 22 January, hundreds of vehicles formed convoys from several points and traversed Canadian provinces, before congregating in Ottawa on 29 January 2022 for a rally at Parliament, at which pedestrians joined. Other related protests blockaded provincial capitals and border points with the United States.

Outrageously, funds being sent to the protesters from sympathetic organisations were legally frozen through government orders. The attorney general of Ontario was granted an Ontario Superior Court of Justice court order under Section 490.8 of the Criminal Code of Canada against 'GiveSendGo' to freeze the funds collected from two campaigns, 'Freedom Convoy 2022' (for US$8.4 million) and 'Adopt-a-Trucker' (for over $686,000), and prohibit their distribution. By 19 February 2022, at least seventy-six bank accounts directly related to the protests, totalling $3.2 million CAD, had been frozen under the Emergencies Act.[8]

In the eyes of many in the West, this episode crystallised the dangers of endowing governments with further power to control or programme the money of its citizens.

However, the clear overreach of the Canadian government during the trucker protest should also remind us of a simple but important fact – that governments already have the ability, or propensity, to exercise such overreach, they don't need CBDCs in order to do so.

As the disclosures of Edward Snowden demonstrated, in times of heightened panic and national security fears – such as during the aftermath of the 9/11 attacks and the war on terror that followed – governments have often overreached and infringed on civil liberties. During this period, Snowden disclosed how the US intelligence services were spying on millions of people's emails. However, nobody has ever suggested abolishing emails or raised the possibility that, while email might be an appropriate tool of communication for the Chinese, it is not suitable for Western countries.

To make digital currencies synonymous with government control is to conflate a political issue with a technological issue. As we will discuss, the introduction of CBDCs – if they are to be introduced – should be preceded by laws which set parameters over their use.

Nevertheless, before CBDCs have even been piloted in the West, let alone implemented, they have already become tools of surveillance and systems of control in the popular imagination of millions in Western countries. In August 2023, the world's biggest podcaster Joe Rogan hosted a discussion with the singer Post Malone, during which Malone asks Rogan, 'So how do you feel about the government's digital currency that they're working on?':

> ROGAN: 'No fucking way. No way, that's what I think. I think that's checkmate. That's game over.'
> MALONE: 'That is fucking checkmate.'
> ROGAN: 'Because if they apply that to a social credit score, they decide somehow or another that you need some social credit score system, it's for the benefit of society, and they outline that they can track your behaviour and your Tweets and you get a score …'

MALONE: 'They're already doing that, they just haven't released
  the fucking report cards.'

ROGAN: 'They just control you to the extent that they would
  like. What they would like to do is to be able to strip you
  of your money, and to be able to lock you down, and to
  make sure that you comply, so that all of the other people
  also comply, because they don't want to be stripped of their
  money.'[9]

In an episode of the dystopian Netflix drama *Black Mirror*, a
young woman on her way to a high-profile wedding goes through
a series of misfortunes that adversely impact a form of social credit
score, which is made publicly visible on a popular social networking
application. By the time she gets to the wedding, nobody wants to
talk to her anymore.[10]

There is certainly truth to the idea that programmable money
can be used for nightmarish means, and there is ample evidence
that this is happening in China.

But is there any realistic reason to fear that Western governments
are hellbent on designing CBDCs in such a manner that would
enable state surveillance and implement the kind of programmability
that will lead us down the inevitable slippery slope of Orwellian
credit scores? A good place to begin will be to look at what Western
governments have so far said about these issues.

FEDERAL RESERVE

In the United States, the privacy issue has taken centre stage. The
debate has become starkly partisan, with Republicans leading calls
for CBDCs to be outlawed before the research phase has even
finished.

As we've seen, Donald Trump plans to ban the creation of a
digital dollar on the premise that it is a road to government tyranny.[11]
Some might point out that this is somewhat ironic coming from
the man who encouraged his supporters to storm the US Capitol
building on 6 January 2021.

On 26 February 2024, Republican senator for Texas, Ted Cruz – joined by fellow Republican senators Bill Hagerty, Rick Scott, Ted Budd and Mike Braun – introduced legislation to ban CBDCs, titled 'the CBDC Anti-Surveillance State Act'.[12]

Commenting on the bill, Senator Cruz stated: 'The Biden administration salivates at the thought of infringing on our freedom and intruding on the privacy of citizens to surveil their personal spending habits.'[13]

The bill was entirely focused on privacy and programmability. Senator Rick Scott added, 'Big government has no business spying on Americans to control their personal finances and track their transactions.'[14]

This was despite the bill going on to acknowledge that – much like email – surveillance capabilities were a contingency, not an inherent feature of CBDCs, stating 'a CBDC is government-controlled programmable money that, *if not designed to emulate cash*, could give the federal government not only significant transaction-level data down to the individual user, but also the ability to programme the CBDC to choke out politically unpopular activity'.[15] Nevertheless, the bill showed no interest in exploring the design of a digital dollar that emulates cash; it encouraged a ban before finding out how this might be done.

The bill made no mention of the role the dollar has played in maintaining free trade across the globe since the end of the Second World War, or in projecting American values and interests. It did not ask whether bringing the world's global reserve currency into the digital age might be worth a more nuanced discussion. 'A CBDC would open the door for the federal government to surveil and control the spending habits of all Americans,' said Senator Budd.[16]

In the face of this chorus, US officials have made repeated attempts to make clear that financial surveillance would never happen. On 7 March 2024, Federal Reserve Chairman Jerome Powell appeared before the US Senate Banking Committee to try to offer assurances that a digital dollar wouldn't be built in a way that gave the government an ability to spy on people. 'We're nowhere near recommending – or let alone adopting – a central bank digital currency in any form,' Powell told the hearing, adding 'people don't need to worry about it.'[17]

Powell also made clear a two-tier model would be adopted, even if they did go ahead, meaning that banks, rather than the government, would manage people's accounts. 'If that were a government account, that the government would see all your transactions, that's just something we would not stand for or do or propose here in the United States,' Powell said, before going on to contrast the US thinking with China's approach.[18]

By reflecting the relationship citizens presently bear to paper money, such a two-tier model would effectively solve many of the issues with which the public are concerned. Certainly, the central bank's ledger would be automatically updated with every transaction, but any personal or identifying information about the transactions would be the sole preserve of the retail bank, as it is today.

This approach was underscored in the Federal Reserve's report titled 'Money and Payments: The U.S. Dollar in the Age of Digital Transformation', which suggests that a potential CBDC should use an intermediated model in which the private sector would offer accounts or digital wallets to facilitate the management of CBDC holdings and payments, drawing on the private sector's existing privacy and identity-management frameworks.[19]

On 23 May 2024, a similar bill also titled 'The CBDC Anti-Surveillance State Act' – first introduced into the House of Representatives by Republican representative Tom Emmer in February 2023 – was passed by the House.[20] The bill 'requires authorizing legislation from Congress for the issuance of any CBDC — ensuring that it must reflect American values'; it went on to state that 'if not open, permissionless, and private, a CBDC is no more than a CCP-style surveillance tool waiting to be weaponized'.[21] During the debate, frequent references were made to the digital yuan and the blockage of bank accounts in Canada during the truck drivers' protest.[22]

EUROPEAN CENTRAL BANK

On 24 June 2024, the ECB released its first progress report on developing a digital euro. Privacy was front and centre of the update, with promises made about pseudonymous transactions and encryption features designed to act as bulwarks against tracking and identifying individuals by transaction. Furthermore, within the ECB's proposed framework, payment service providers will have to obtain explicit consent from individuals before using their financial data for commercial services.

The update also outlined methods for conducting offline transactions between parties without requiring a third-party intermediary. These payments would be settled directly on the users' payment devices, such as smartphones and future 'smart cards', which may be battery-powered or use bridging relays to synchronise transactions with the CBDC blockchain.

The report concluded by providing a timeline for a newly established 'Rulebook Development Group' to complete the first draft of its technical and regulatory CBDC framework. According to the ECB, the group will deliver its initial draft by the end of 2024, following consultations with service providers, infrastructure builders, and the general public.

The ECB has also expressed openness to programmable payments but has firmly opposed the idea of programmable money. Fabio Panetta, the governor of the Bank of Italy and former member of the executive board of the ECB between 2020–23, emphasised during his time in office that while the digital euro could enable users to set conditions for payments in advance (akin to direct debits or standing orders), it would not carry conditions as part of the currency itself. Panetta stated, 'the digital euro would never be programmable money. The ECB would not set any limitations on where, when, or to whom people can pay with a digital euro.'[23] In other words, for consumers, the digital euro would behave in the same way that euros held on banking apps already do, in the sense that programmability decisions would be made by the currency's users, not the central bank.

EU public discourse appears more open to the benefits of a retail CBDC. A June 2024 survey conducted by the Bundesbank showed that half of Germans are open to the idea of using a digital euro.[24] The EU's approach seems to be focused on creating a new payment rail that benefits the public sector and European financial institutions. The aim is to reduce reliance on non-European card networks and mitigate the risks posed by big-tech firms in the payment sector, such as the development of monopolies and single points of failure.

BANK OF ENGLAND

In the UK, the former Deputy Governor for Financial Stability of the Bank of England, Sir Jon Cunliffe, has stated that users of the digital pound would have the same level of privacy as they currently enjoy with electronic payments and that the central bank would not have access to individual data. He also said that the digital pound would not be programmable by the central bank.[25]

Responding to a public petition on this issue, the Bank of England sought to reassure the public that it has no intentions to programme a CBDC or to impose spending restrictions. It clarified that any programmability features would only be developed at the private-sector level, not by the government, and that users would always retain the option to utilise them or not.[26]

This position reflects a conscious effort to preserve public trust by eschewing programmability that could be seen as restrictive or controlling. Nevertheless, the private sector would have room to innovate with programmability, suggesting a two-tier model where the central bank fosters innovation while maintaining its distance from public money, so to speak. This would enable both traditional high street banks and neobanks to offer customers the option to engage with programmable features, should they choose to do so.

In January 2024, the Bank of England and HM Treasury announced that they were progressing to the design phase of a digital pound, following a joint consultation they conducted which received over 50,000 responses from members of the public, businesses, civil society and academia. In their response to the consulation, the Bank of England and the Treasury made a series of clear commitments with regards to both privacy and programmability, and the place of anonymous cash in society.[27]

Far from signalling the end of physical cash, this response explained that the digital pound would complement existing forms of money, providing individuals with greater flexibility and choice in how they conduct transactions. Indeed, no Western government has ever suggested that a CBDC would replace cash.

In a move underscoring its commitment to democratic oversight and the protection of individual freedoms, the then-Conservative UK government also pledged to navigate the introduction of a digital pound through the rigorous process of primary legislation.[28] This step promises an unprecedented level of parliamentary scrutiny, ensuring that any launch is predicated on safeguarding users' privacy and maintaining a clear separation between personal spending decisions and state or central bank interference. In essence, legislation will first be introduced to determine how the digital pound would be designed, before any greenlight is given for its development. Though the UK's new Labour government has said little about CBDCs since its landslide victory in July 2024, a plan for financial services it published in January showed 'more of a commitment than any other political party' to developing a digital pound, according Jannah Patchay, executive board director at the Digital Pound Foundation.

In his speech titled 'New Prospects for Money' delivered on 10 July 2023, Bank of England governor Andrew Bailey stated that 'there should be a public debate about the future of money in the UK'.[29] He is right, as there should be such a debate in the United States, and across Europe and the world, in the coming years.

So, what should these national conversations look like?

14

What Should the West Do?
Trade-offs and Opportunity Costs

'In any moment of decision, the best thing you can do is the right thing, the next best thing is the wrong thing, and the worst thing you can do is nothing.'

THEODORE ROOSEVELT[1]

In essence, governments in the West have three options: develop fully fledged retail CBDCs – digital dollars, digital pounds and digital euros for consumers; find a middle way, by either developing only wholesale CBDCs or otherwise regulating stablecoins; or abstain from CBDC exploration entirely and recuse themselves from the race for the future of money. In the words of Thomas Sowell, 'there are no solutions, there are only trade-offs'.[2] So, which option holds the best set of compromises?

OPTION I: RETAIL CBDC

When we talk about a digital dollar or digital euro or digital pound, what we are really talking about is a retail CBDC – a state-issued digital currency that is used by the public. What purpose would it serve for the US, UK and EU to introduce a retail CBDC?

If there are good reasons to develop retail CBDCs, they will not be the reasons which Western officials have so far alluded to, such as providing central banks with a safeguard against the decline of cash. These are reasons, but they are not good enough reasons. Indeed, if these were the only reasons to pursue retail CBDCs, we might be inclined to agree with the conclusions of the House of Lords report from January 2022 that characterised CBDCs as a 'solution in search of a problem',[3] and with *The Economist*'s conclusion from its 2024 forecasts that CBDCs appear to solve few problems while creating new ones.[4]

The only good reasons for introducing retail CBDCs would be geopolitical. We have argued that the past ten years have slowly given rise to real problems for the West, problems which should have been detected and planned for sooner but seem only to have crystallised in the last two years – namely the rise of China, the blueprint for the internationalisation of the digital yuan and, more importantly, the prospect of China's monopoly over the digital financial market infrastructure of the twenty-first century, granting it significant control over the global CBDC ecosystem and especially that utilised by BRI partner countries and the BRICS+ grouping.

The key question we should seek to ask is the following: what are the benefits for the West of entering an expensive arms race for the future of money?

To be sure, a decision to issue a digital dollar (or pound or euro), is not just a yes or no question. It is a decision to begin a decades-long odyssey, to enter a discussion, debate and competition regarding alternative visions for what money should look like, who should control it, what properties it should have, what threats or dangers need to be mitigated against, and who should build and control the payment rails on which it runs.

The main purpose of embarking on this journey would be to provide an alternative future for state-issued digital money to the one being developed by China and its allies. In a world in which 134 countries and currency unions are looking into digital money, most countries will eventually issue digital money options for the public. The question for the US, UK and EU is whether they want to take part in the discussion about the future of money by offering a 'liberal' vision of digital money that aligns with their historic political and cultural values, and in turn encourages other countries to develop and implement similar models. The point would not necessarily be to distribute a digital dollar around the world, but to set standards and precedents for liberal digital money, and have a stake in its global governance.

In the US, this discussion has started in policy circles. J. Christopher Giancarlo, chairman of the Commodity Futures Trading Commission and the founder of the Digital Dollar Project, has argued that the United States needs to launch a 'freedom coin' to counter China's 'surveillance coin'.[5]

A digital freedom coin might sound good on paper, but is it even possible to design one, let alone project its blueprint around the world?

WHAT WOULD A 'LIBERAL' RETAIL CBDC LOOK LIKE?

In liberal democracies, the design and functionality of a CBDC should be informed by values, and values should be encoded in law. The best way to distinguish a Western 'liberal' CBDC from an autocratic CBDC would be to set rigid legal parameters within which it can operate.

This is what the UK consultation has stipulated in its reference to 'primary legislation'. However, besides introducing new legislation, it might also be necessary to revisit existing legal frameworks. For example, in the United States, current legislation could make it almost impossible to guarantee user privacy in the case of a retail CBDC.

Norbert Michel, the vice president and director of the Cato Institute's Centre for Monetary and Financial Alternatives, has argued that Giancarlo's conception of a 'freedom coin' would not be possible without first revisiting the Bank Secrecy Act.[6] This act enshrines the legal requirements for financial institutions to share customer information with law enforcement without a valid search warrant. While this remains in place, Michel argues it would be 'absurd to talk about a CBDC that respects Americans' constitutional rights'.

Setting up laws informed by public consultations before digital currencies enter pilot phases would be smart. These discussions will give different groups – such as regular citizens, money experts and privacy supporters – a chance to share their worries and ideas. This feedback will be crucial for creating laws that work well and that people actually support.

The technical design of a 'liberal' CBDC would be informed by these laws and likely centre around four key issues: maintaining privacy and anonymity in transactions to the greatest degree possible; limiting programmability to 'layer 2', meaning that programmable functions would only be afforded to the private sector and not the state; prioritising a design that is interoperable, so that it is compatible with other digital currency ecosystems; and the need to adopt a multi-stakeholder governance model.

These principles would all be facilitated by cooperation with the private sector. By working with retail banks and fintechs, central banks would not only have access to the best and most appropriate technology, but would also be able to stay at arm's length from citizens, assuaging concerns surrounding government oversight and overreach.

PRIVACY AND ANONYMITY

In addition to revisiting existing legislation, any new privacy laws relating to the introduction of CBDCs would need to be comprehensive and robust. They must explicitly prohibit the unauthorised collection and sharing of personal financial data. These laws can draw inspiration from existing privacy regulations like the EU's General Data Protection Regulation (GDPR), ensuring that citizens' financial transactions remain confidential and protected against surveillance, unless mandated by law (e.g. for anti-money laundering purposes).

In the US, Project Hamilton has looked into the issue of privacy in depth.[7] The multiyear research project of the Federal Reserve Bank of Boston and the MIT Digital Currency Initiative has outlined design principles through which transactions are recorded as having happened, but information about the transactions themselves is not recorded. In this sense, a CBDC would more closely resemble a bearer asset, like cash.

This could be done by using pseudonyms or anonymous transactions to keep users' identities hidden. For instance, zero-knowledge proofs could confirm transactions without showing who is involved or how much is being sent to the government or central bank. In the same way, techniques like homomorphic encryption let data be processed without decoding it first, which keeps users' information private.

Identity verification would be a critical initial step, ensuring that all participants, whether individuals or institutions, undergo a rigorous Know Your Customer process, which would likely be facilitated by commercial and retail banks in a two-tier model. Upon successful verification, participants would receive unique identifiers or pseudonyms, allowing them to conduct transactions with a high degree of anonymity. This design would ensure privacy in everyday transactions, while still providing a mechanism for authorised entities to 'unmask' participants when legally required, such as in cases of suspected financial crimes.

To ensure that transaction data cannot be weaponised against citizens, the CBDC system would need to be designed without logs that could be used to track and profile users' financial behaviour. Data minimisation principles would be paramount, collecting only the data absolutely necessary for the operation of the CBDC.

To date, most if not all attempts to describe or suggest ways to design state-issued digital money that retains the key properties of cash have been routinely dismissed as impossible, pointless or even sinister ('a wolf in sheep's clothing', as Cato Institute analyst Nicholas Anthony described privacy-minded CBDC proposals in Cointelegraph in June 2024). It is also difficult to ensure that emails cannot be hacked, but we do not give up on email. So the question is, if digital money is coming anyway, shouldn't we at least try to make it private?

PROGRAMMABILITY

Regarding programmability, laws should clearly outline what is permissible. Clear boundaries should be delineated to prevent misuse, ensuring that programmable features are used solely for public welfare and not for intrusive control over spending.

The two-tier approach would be critical to maintaining this boundary when it comes to a retail CBDC for public use. The system's architecture would explicitly separate the base layer (Layer 1), responsible for the CBDC's issuance and primary ledger functions, from the programmability features, which would reside at Layer 2. Layer 1 would be under the purview of the central bank, ensuring the stability and integrity of the currency itself, but would deliberately lack programmability to prevent government overreach.

Programmability, including smart contracts and other automated financial instruments, would be exclusively developed and managed at the Layer 2 level by the private sector. This separation ensures that innovative use cases are driven by private enterprises to which citizens can voluntarily opt in or opt out.

For instance, banks, fintech companies and other financial institutions could develop smart contract-based applications for loans, savings products or automatic tax payments, without direct government control over the functionality of these applications.

This two-tiered approach not only decentralises the development and management of financial services but also encourages innovation in the private sector.

INTEROPERABILITY

The concept of interoperability stands as a cornerstone in the architecture of a liberal state-issued digital currency, ensuring it can freely flow across various financial ecosystems without barriers. This principle is paramount not only for fostering innovation and competition but also for preventing the entrenchment of new digital monopolies that could arise if certain platforms or services become gatekeepers of the CBDC world.

The EU's digital market strategy emphasises the importance of interoperability, aiming to ensure that new technologies can integrate with existing financial infrastructures and services. This approach encourages a competitive market where innovation can thrive, exemplified by the EU's Payment Services Directive, which mandates banks to open their payment services to third-party providers. By adhering to similar principles of interoperability, a liberal CBDC would enable consumers to transact across different platforms without being locked into a single provider, thereby enhancing consumer choice and fostering a vibrant, competitive ecosystem.

A user-friendly CBDC should be designed to be accessible to everyone, especially those who typically don't have access to banks. Creative solutions could bridge this gap, so no one misses out on the digital economy. For instance, by using simple mobile phones (feature phones) that are common in many developing countries, people could make transactions via USSD (Unstructured Supplementary Service Data) technology, which sends messages over the phone network.

This approach has been successfully implemented in mobile money services across Africa, where platforms like M-Pesa have revolutionised financial inclusion by allowing users to send and receive money, pay bills and access loans and savings products directly from their feature phones.

Additionally, the use of physical cards equipped with secure elements presents another avenue for inclusivity. Similar to how contactless debit cards work, these CBDC cards could facilitate offline transactions, making digital currency accessible to those without mobile phones or internet access. Such cards could be used to make purchases, transfer funds or withdraw cash from ATMs and participating retailers, ensuring that the benefits of a CBDC extend to the entire population.

GOVERNANCE

A liberal CBDC should not only represent a leap forward in financial technology but also a reimagining of monetary governance itself, embracing a multi-stakeholder model.

Central banks and financial institutions would provide the backbone. Their role will be pivotal in ensuring that the CBDC integrates seamlessly with existing financial infrastructures, maintaining the integrity and efficiency of national and international economic systems.

However, in a liberal CBDC model, governance should extend far beyond these traditional pillars of financial authority. Privacy advocates and consumer protection groups should be accorded a central role, championing the rights and interests of individual users. Their involvement would ensure that privacy is not an afterthought but a foundational principle of the CBDC, with mechanisms built in from the outset to safeguard personal data and ensure user autonomy in the digital age.

Experts and innovators would add another layer of governance to consult on the blockchain, cybersecurity and digital payments technologies involved, ensuring that the CBDC is not only secure but capable of evolving with future advancements.

Perhaps most crucially, the general public and representatives of civil society would also be integral to the governance model of a liberal CBDC. By involving end-users in the decision-making process, the system becomes truly democratic, reflecting the needs, concerns and aspirations of wider society.

The model would involve a variety of mechanisms designed to facilitate collaboration and consensus building. Advisory councils could offer a forum for representatives from each stakeholder group to discuss strategies, policies and technical updates. Public consultations would open the floor to broader input, ensuring transparency and allowing for the CBDC to be continually refined in response to feedback from the community it serves.

A multi-stakeholder model should aspire to the promise of a CBDC that is built not just *for* citizens, but *with* them, embedding democratic principles into the very fabric of our future monetary systems.

This all sounds very idealistic, but clearly the successful development and maintenance of a 'liberal CBDC' is an enormous undertaking. So, let's return to what the main purpose would be of Western governments going down this path. In other words, why bother?

PROJECTING VALUES

Developing digital money that reflects the values of liberal democracies – like privacy, free speech, the rule of law and the protection of individual rights – could be a powerful tool through which the West can project and uphold these values abroad. This soft-power approach isn't about forcing change or using money to influence people. Instead, it's about attracting others through shared values. How a country innovates and shares new tech says a lot about its moral standards and government.

Liberal democracies could set an example by showing that a financial system rooted in these values can work well and offer real benefits. This is all the more important since most of the world's liberal democracies have, for various reasons, seemed uninterested in leading these efforts to date, while China has made significant strides in binding countries in financial relationships that are tough to escape.

As we have seen in Sri Lanka, for example, China has heavily invested in ports and infrastructure, leading to large debts that the country struggled to pay off. Despite Sri Lanka being part of the British Commonwealth, the UK's interest has dwindled, leaving China as a dominant influence in the region.

Making government (but not consumer) CBDC transactions transparent would mean that government investments would be traceable, thereby reducing corruption and increasing public trust. When people know how government money is spent, they are more likely to believe that their taxes fund projects fairly and honestly. Estonia is a case in point, where transparent digital financial infrastructure has made it one of the least corrupt countries in the world, setting a standard for others.

Adhering to the rule of law means that financial regulations apply to everyone equally, without favouritism. A liberal CBDC system could ensure that all users follow the same rules when sending or receiving money, reducing risks of fraud or money laundering.

Protecting individual rights ensures that people control their money and privacy. With a liberal CBDC, people could have safer and easier ways to make digital payments without fear of their information being misused or weaponised.

Liberal democracies can inspire other nations by setting high ethical standards for CBDCs, creating a more open and fair global financial system that reflects the values of democratic governance. Taking these steps will be critical to winning influence in the New Cold War.

FINANCIAL INCLUSION AND ECONOMIC DEVELOPMENT

We know that autocratic digital money is coming. So, while a 'liberal CBDC' might sound fanciful, we have to consider seriously the idea that it might be worth fighting for, and investing in, as much as we have to consider the trade-offs involved in giving up on the idea of a liberal CBDC before we have started.

Simply put, the development of a CBDC by leading liberal economies such as the United States, United Kingdom or European Union presents an opportunity to wield soft power across the developing world and exercise a voice in the future of money, which is only going to become 'more digital' as time goes on.

The potential of a liberal CBDC to promote financial inclusion in a positive manner cannot be overstated. According to the latest World Bank's Global Findex Database, approximately 1.4 billion adults worldwide remain unbanked as of 2021, with a significant proportion residing in developing countries.[8] This gap in financial inclusion not only limits individual economic opportunities but also hampers broader economic development.

A liberal CBDC, by design, could address several barriers to financial inclusion. Firstly, it could greatly reduce transaction costs, which are often prohibitively high for traditional banking services in many parts of the developing world. As we've seen, the World

Bank reports that the global average cost of sending $200 remains at about 6.20 per cent in 2023, a figure that could be drastically reduced with the adoption of a CBDC.[9] By leveraging blockchain or similar technologies, a CBDC could streamline transactions, cutting down the intermediaries and the associated fees, thereby making it cheaper for people to send and receive money.

Remittances, or money sent home by people working abroad, are also crucial for many developing economies. In 2020, the World Bank estimated that these remittances to low- and middle-income countries totalled $540 billion.[10]

However, sending this money is often slow and expensive. A CBDC could radically change this process. For instance, by using a CBDC, a foreign worker in the United States would be able to send money to their family in just a few minutes without losing as much to fees.

Digital wallets, which securely hold and manage money, would also make CBDCs more convenient for people who don't have bank accounts. This is especially helpful in areas where many people distrust banks or don't have the documents needed to open an account. With a CBDC, they can store their money safely and access it whenever they need it.

These wallets could also facilitate a range of financial services, from savings and loans to insurance, directly from a mobile device, thereby integrating millions into the formal financial system.

The democratisation of financial services through a liberal CBDC could have profound implications for economic development and poverty reduction. Access to affordable financial services can empower individuals to start businesses, invest in education or healthcare and improve their overall quality of life. Furthermore, by bringing more people into the formal economy, a CBDC could improve tax collection and increase the effectiveness of social welfare programmes. The simple reality is that China is pushing its technological standards across the developing world, and will soon be ready to offer its digital payment rails to boot. If the West does not offer an alternative vision for the future of money, these unbanked populations will fall under the influence of Beijing.

TRADE AND INVESTMENT

There is no question that CBDCs can make cross-border payments radically more effficient and that they could represent a huge boon for international trade.[11]

For developing countries, the ramifications are profound. By slashing the costs and complexities of international transactions, a liberal CBDC could drastically lower the barriers to global trade for businesses. This improved access could ignite a surge of economic activity, empowering small and medium-sized enterprises to transcend domestic confines and seize new market opportunities.

Simplifying cross-border payments could also stimulate foreign investment. Currently, high fees and erratic processes deter investors, making international ventures appear daunting and costly. A CBDC could decisively address this issue, smoothing the path for capital flows and reducing investment risks.

The United Nations Conference on Trade and Development underscores that foreign direct investment is indispensable for emerging economies, to create jobs, improve infrastructure and fortify industries.

With a CBDC, an investor in Germany could transfer funds to a company in Nigeria with negligible fees and no delays. This secure, efficient system would incentivise investments in the Global South, fostering economic growth and development. The smoother the transactions, the more confident investors will be in allocating their capital to these regions.

A liberal CBDC that strengthens trade and investment connections would also improve diplomatic relationships. Economic interdependence often promotes peaceful international relations, reducing the likelihood of conflict. For instance, if the US and India used a CBDC for trading, they could easily exchange funds at low cost, simplifying transactions and fostering mutual trust. This partnership would not only enhance business ties but also encourage cooperation on global issues like climate change and security.

STABILITY AND SECURITY

A stable and secure digital currency, underpinned by robust economies and advanced technology, could shield less developed nations from economic uncertainties and cyber vulnerabilities.

Developing countries often grapple with economic instability due to fluctuating commodity prices, unpredictable politics and global economic upheavals. When oil prices plummet, oil-dependent nations like Nigeria and Venezuela suffer severely. Similarly, political instability deters foreign investment, complicating long-term planning. Financial instability can trigger higher inflation, discourage investment and stifle economic growth, exacerbating the challenges faced by these nations.

Governments holding some reserves, and individuals and businesses holding some savings in a CBDC from a more stable economy, could offer a solution. With a reliable digital currency, people and businesses in these less developed countries would have a secure way to save, invest and transact. This could reduce their exposure to economic shocks, allowing them to focus more on growth and long-term planning. Governments could build infrastructure, improve education or invest in healthcare without worrying so much about sudden currency volatility. For instance, during Argentina's recent financial turmoil, citizens sought refuge in more stable foreign currencies.

Unlike traditional currencies, a CBDC would benefit from the efficiency of instant settlement, reducing costs and enhancing security. The owner of a small shop, for example, could seamlessly receive payments digitally, with minimal fees and reduced risks of fraud or theft. This stability would safeguard savings and foster economic resilience.

Moreover, a well-designed CBDC with robust protections against hacking and fraud could help developing nations fight financial crime. Weak regulations and corruption exacerbate these issues, with the United Nations Office on Drugs and Crime estimating that 2–5 per cent of the global economy is tied up in money laundering annually.[12] Advanced security features and traceability inherent in blockchain-based CBDCs would allow better monitoring of financial systems, preventing illicit activities and promoting economic stability.

As cyber attacks become increasingly common and sophisticated, the security of financial systems is more important than ever. The FBI's Internet Crime Complaint Center has reported a surge in cybercrimes costing billions across the globe annually.[13] Liberal CBDCs, engineered with state-of-the-art security measures – such as advanced encryption, secure ledger technologies and robust authentication mechanisms – could set new global standards, ensuring digital currencies offer both convenience and stringent security. The question is: will the financial cybersecurity systems of the twenty-first century be built and controlled by China, or will there be alternatives?

TRADE-OFFS

Creating a retail CBDC would bring about pros and cons for Western governments and their citizens, though the challenges would be more significant for governments. The trade-offs can be grouped into three main areas: financial costs, political costs and the risk of failure.

Developing and implementing a retail CBDC will require a lot of money. Building a new digital financial system from scratch needs advanced technology, cybersecurity measures and infrastructure upgrades. The Bank of England has estimated that a CBDC could cost hundreds of millions to develop. Governments will need to justify using taxpayers' money for these expensive projects, especially when there are other priorities like healthcare and education.

CBDCs require state-of-the-art systems that can securely and efficiently handle large numbers of transactions. For instance,

China's e-CNY has been designed to handle millions of payments per second.

Digital currencies need strong protection to prevent hacking and fraud. In 2022, cyberattacks led to more than $3 billion in cryptocurrency losses,[14] making it essential for CBDCs to have advanced security.

CBDCs will need stable networks to ensure that even people in remote areas have access. For example, Nigeria's eNaira had to ensure that mobile banking worked well in rural regions.

Governments will also have to work hard to convince voters that CBDCs are necessary. They will have to articulate how digital currencies will help people and businesses, and they must outline how they are rapidly developing a geopolitical significance, all while handling the polarised political debates that surround CBDCs. Many fear government overreach and surveillance, while others are concerned about technological disruptions to traditional banking.

Governments will need to spend significant time and effort explaining the pros and cons of various CBDC strategies. This includes discussing the risks and opportunity costs involved in not developing one at all, which we'll shortly explore further.

The challenge is made harder because today's political environment is so divided that misinformation can spread easily. To tackle this, governments will not only need to present a convincing argument for CBDCs but will also need to engage with sceptics and address concerns about privacy, personal freedom and the government's role in finances.

Beyond the privacy and programmability concerns we have looked at, some worry that CBDCs could exclude people who don't have access to digital technology. For instance, in Kenya, nearly 60 per cent of the population didn't use the internet in 2022.[15] Governments need to reassure the public that digital currencies will not leave anyone out.

Governments will need to open channels for public dialogue, including debates, online forums and collaboration with tech experts to explain how CBDCs can provide faster, safer and cheaper transactions.

And, most importantly, as we have argued throughout this book, governments will need to make the global case for developing liberal CBDC infrastructure, and explain why it is necessary to compete with strategic adversaries like China and Russia in this space.

There's also the risk that the CBDC project might not work out as planned, whether due to technical glitches, unexpected economic outcomes or changing political winds. Technology could struggle to scale up, leading to outages or data breaches. Economically, a CBDC might disrupt the banking system, causing financial instability. Politically, if the public loses faith in the new system or a government changes, the project could be abandoned altogether.

It is not difficult to imagine the sight of some future president or prime minister being flown out of his or her capital city in a helicopter – Nixon-like – after being ousted from office for having invested hundreds of billions of dollars into a freedom coin vanity project that imploded on take-off.

The decision to implement a retail CBDC is not one to be taken lightly by Western governments. It requires a careful calculation of the economic investment against the potential costs and benefits, a nuanced understanding of the political landscape to effectively communicate and advocate for the initiative, and a robust strategy to mitigate the risks of technological, economic and political failures.

In light of this, most governments will be thinking – or hoping – that there is an easy way out. Perhaps an alternative route would be to adopt a halfway house and either simply regulate stablecoins or develop a wholesale CBDC? Here, too, of course, we encounter trade-offs.

OPTION 2: WHOLESALE CBDC OR STABLECOIN REGULATION

In the United States, support for a fully fledged digital dollar or 'freedom coin' along the lines articulated by J. Christopher Giancarlo and the Digital Dollar Project is relatively weak. However, the political sphere has been more receptive to the concept of a wholesale CBDC.

In November 2022 – as we've seen, the year when everything changed – Kevin Warsh, the former Republican appointee to the Federal Reserve Board of Governors, argued for the need to develop an 'American-style' CBDC in order to counter Chinese influence.[16] Writing for the American Enterprise Institute, he stated that Beijing's clear head start in the CBDC race 'represents a consequential threat to the extant American-led financial architecture'.

Warsh suggested that a wholesale digital dollar, which was not extended to consumers but only used by the Federal Reserve and the banking system, could challenge the Chinese model on the international stage without igniting concerns about government overreach.

A wholesale CBDC is designed for large-value financial transactions, typically between financial institutions rather than individual consumers. Its development by the United States could enhance the efficiency and security of cross-border transactions involving the dollar. This improvement stems from the inherent advantages of digital currencies, such as improved transaction speeds, reduced operational risks and potentially lower costs, compared to traditional banking systems.

A US wholesale CBDC could, in one aspect, reinforce the global dominance of the dollar by making large-scale settlement of transactions in USD more efficient and appealing. This efficiency gain could incentivise international banks and financial institutions to maintain or even increase their use of the dollar for international settlements and reserves. For the reasons outlined in chapters 3 and 4, it would make sense for the central bank to take advantage of programmable capabilities when it comes to a wholesale CBDC (unlike with a retail CBDC).

The effectiveness of a wholesale CBDC in countering de-dollarisation would depend on its design and governance, particularly in terms of interoperability with other digital currencies and financial systems. If the digital dollar is perceived as a tool for extending US financial oversight and control, it could exacerbate concerns that fuel de-dollarisation. Conversely, a CBDC that emphasises collaboration, respects privacy, and adheres to international norms could bolster the dollar's position in the global financial system.

However, consensus in the US has begun to pivot away from the issuance of a full-blown digital dollar – whether retail or wholesale – and towards the regulation of stablecoins. The Atlantic Council, which has been tracking CBDC development across the world closely, reported in November 2023 that the United States has become far more cautious than the UK and Europe when it comes to prospects of CBDC issuance.[17]

Though the Fed had been taking firm steps towards the creation of a digital dollar throughout 2022, including its 'Project Cedar' wholesale experiment, according to the Atlantic Council direction of travel was entirely derailed by events in the private sector, namely the 'FTX implosion in late 2022, followed quickly by the "speed-of-light" bank run at Silicon Valley Bank in March 2023'. This meant that 'by the time the final report regarding the Project Cedar experiment had been published in May 2023, the policy landscape in the United States regarding digital currencies had shifted significantly'.[18]

In other words, the conversation was derailed and the bigger picture obscured. The collapse of a fraudulent private cryptocurrency exchange and the downfall of a depository institution favoured by the technological elite of America's West Coast should have had little relevance to the future of the US dollar on the global stage, against the backdrop of Beijing's rising assertiveness.

If anything, the events might have been used to the Fed's advantage in its development of a digital dollar. With regards to FTX, the Fed could have argued that the private sector's digital currency landscape was too volatile and required an anchor – a digital, interoperable flight to safety with state backing. And, as we've seen, the digital domino effect which caused Silicon Valley Bank to collapse, following $42 billion of withdrawal requests almost overnight, might have served to illustrate the future fate of the US dollar if China's allies and dependants suddenly decided that it was more beneficial to transact with the digital currency system built by the BRICS+. Instead, unsound cryptocurrencies were conflated with the broader future of digital assets, and the digital dollar lost momentum.

The conversation has since shifted to the need for – and the benefits of – bringing dollar-denominated stablecoins under regulation. A bill that has passed the House Financial Services Committee seeks to foster private stablecoin issuance, effectively creating an alternative to a digital dollar because the vast majority of stablecoins (98.9 per cent) are backed by the US dollar. If passed into law and implemented, the bill would place the Federal Reserve at the core of oversight regarding privately issued digital dollars, in addition to delivering regulatory clarity regarding cryptocurrencies.

On 8 August 2023, the Federal Reserve formally promoted stablecoin issuance by banks. In a closed-door meeting with Democrats from the House Financial Services Committee in February 2024, Federal chairman Jerome Powell further emphasised the need for a legislative framework for stablecoins.[19]

Proponents of a stablecoin alternative to a CBDC effectively argue that stablecoins retain all of the purported advantages of a CBDC with none of the drawbacks or complications. In April 2023, *Forbes* policy editor Avik Roy stated in his magazine's pages that, 'there's no such thing as an "American-style" CBDC'.[20] His piece was a direct attack on the policy proposals of Giancarlo and Warsh – for a retail digital dollar and wholesale digital dollar respectively – and an argument for the idea that 'stablecoins are superior to CBDCs'.

However, Roy's viewpoint deals squarely with implications for US consumers. Writing that 'what's particularly strange about the Warsh-Giancarlo position on CBDCs is that we already have blockchain-based versions of the US dollar that do all the things Warsh and Giancarlo want a CBDC to do, but with much stronger privacy protections'. Roy goes on to say: 'it is inconceivable that, all else being equal, global markets will prefer an e-CNY based on surveillance and censorship to a constellation of dollar-backed stablecoins with built-in privacy protections'.[21]

Roy's claims fit into a broader narrative that has emerged in US tech circles that stablecoins might be sufficient to contribute to 're-dollarisation'.

Granted, stablecoins combine the intrinsic stability of the US dollar with the efficiency of blockchain technology, enabling instant transactions, minimal fees and 24/7 operability. By bridging the gap between traditional finance and the burgeoning digital economy, stablecoins could ensure the continued preference for the dollar for international trade, remittances and as a reliable store of value, particularly in regions with less stable currencies.

What's 'particularly strange' about Roy's position, however, is that it is quite evident that 'all else being equal' does not apply here. As we have seen, China has spent ten years not only developing its digital currency, but rerouting and reprogramming the developing world's supply chains and laying out the digital payment rails for its BRI partners. Beijing is also building a coalition of oil-rich allies with whom it will conduct trade through the mBridge and BRICS Bridge platforms. Meanwhile, the United States has merely slapped some tariffs on half-a-dozen Chinese tech firms and toyed with the idea of banning TikTok.

An enormous act of faith would be required to leave the global fate of the US dollar entirely in the hands of the private sector. There is the potential for misalignment with national monetary policies, systemic risks posed by the failure of private entities and the fragmentation of the digital dollar ecosystem. The ideal approach might lie in a hybrid model, where regulated private stablecoins coexist with a retail or wholesale CBDC, combining the innovation of the private sector with the authority and stability of the federal government.

There is simply no universe in which the United States government would – or should – leave it to the private sector alone. Or rather, there is perhaps one universe, the one inhabited by Donald Trump.

OPTION 3: NO CBDC – WHO NEEDS A DIGITAL
DOLLAR ANYWAY?

Much of this book has been dedicated to suggesting that CBDC networks being developed by China and its allies could pose a grave danger to the West. But it is equally important to test the strongest arguments from the other side.

Let us consider that sceptics are correct in their suspicion that CBDCs are really a solution in search of a problem, and that our existing payments infrastructure – our brick-and-mortar banks, mobile banking systems and fintechs – together with our traditional reliance on paper money and the benefits it confers in terms of being a bearer instrument with a greater sense of anonymity, are perfectly sufficient. What would happen if the US, UK and EU all decided, or were persuaded by their intractable populations, to abandon CBDC development entirely, both wholesale and retail. What would be the consequences? And what trade-offs might be faced?

Even if our contention that de-dollarisation would be vastly accelerated were true, is this necessarily a bad thing?

Left to its own devices, for the reasons we have discussed, we contend that it is reasonably conservative to assume that the proportion of global trade denominated in yuan or digital yuan could increase from 2.3 per cent to 10–15 per cent – potentially on a par with China's contribution to global GDP. To reflect this, the Chinese yuan and digital yuan's proportion of global foreign currency reserves would be likely to augment from its current 2.79 per cent to 10 per cent in the next ten years.

We suggest that we can safely add another 20 per cent to both metrics in terms of the increase in the combination of all other non-dollar currencies and digital currencies, such that between 30–35 per cent of global trade will be conducted in non-dollar digital currencies under the BRICS+ sphere of influence, who are currently pressing ahead for multi-CBDC development. Combined, this would roughly diminish the global trade conducted in dollars to around 50 per cent of global trade, down from around 88 per cent presently.

This will represent a momentous shift in the global monetary order. Nevertheless, some have argued that de-dollarisation on this scale could still be a desirable outcome both for the United States and the world as a whole.

Lyn Alden has argued that the United States has suffered considerably by virtue of maintaining the world's global reserve currency. In *Broken Money*, Alden describes – in the chapter titled 'Heavy is the Head That Wears the Crown' – how the dollar's global reserve status has for decades enabled the United States to maintain a current account deficit to the detriment of its industrial base:

> It becomes expensive to pay American workers compared to
> workers in other countries, including both developed and
> developing countries.... Over time, more manufacturing
> facilities leave the United States and head to places like
> Germany, Japan, Taiwan, China, and Mexico.[22]

This is true, and it means that, over time, the United States' consistent current account deficits have caused it to enter a deeply negative net international investment position, a measure of a country's financial position relative to the world. If the value of this measure is positive, it indicates that the domestic economy is a net creditor, and if the value is negative, the domestic economy is indicated to be a net debtor. For this reason, Alden goes on to argue that 'Losing dollar hegemony at this point would ... lead toward a more neutral and balanced global economy and provide the opportunity for US revitalisation'.[23]

There is certainly truth to the claims that the dollar's dominance in global trade has enabled the US to run persistent current account deficits to the detriment of its manufacturing base, that the spiralling sovereign debt levels of the United States do not appear to be under control, and that an international trading system whose range of currencies used for trade more closely correlated with each country's respective contribution to global GDP might represent 'a more neutral and balanced global economy'.

But the question is: more balanced in whose favour? China's digital currency vision effectively enables it to have the best of both worlds – to have its cake and eat it. China – still being the world's factory – does not want to run vast current account deficits or hollow out its manufacturing base, but it does still want to internationalise its currency, as well as to have influence over the governance of the international financial system. As we've seen, a digital currency ecosystem enables them to do this. They can still keep their capital controls on the paper yuan, while dictating the terms of trade across the international digital payment rails it has built.

TRADE-OFFS

We have explored at length where this leads with regards to the battle for resources. In an era marked by escalating resource scarcity and rising oil prices, the ability to dictate terms in the global market for these resources could grant the BRICS+ group unparalleled leverage. This shift could realign traditional power structures and influence global economic policies in favour of the preferences and priorities of the BRICS+ nations.

If China and its allies are able to ring-fence the internet for money, dire consequences could ensue, but there are further trade-offs that would arise in the absence of a Western alternative to the future of digital money.

These are twofold: the West's diminished influence on the global conduct of trade, supply chains and the rule-making protocols that govern them; and the likelihood that the fate of the hundreds of millions of unbanked individuals will fall under the control of the CCP and its allies.

The dollar's role as the primary medium for international trade and finance has long afforded the US and its allies considerable power over the global economic architecture – from setting trade standards and lending terms to influencing policies on human rights and environmental, social and governance (ESG) practices within global supply chains.

Should China's digital yuan, or a collective digital currency system spearheaded by the BRICS+ nations, gain widespread acceptance, the consequences could be profound.

Critical aspects of international trade, such as debt mechanisms, interest rates and regulations pertaining to human rights and ESG concerns in supply chains, would increasingly reflect the preferences and standards of the BRICS+ bloc rather than those of the US and its allies.

If the West were to drop out of the race for the future of money, another crucial trade-off which both Western governments and Western citizens must consider is the virtual monopoly that China and its allies will be able to exercise over the roughly 1.4 billion people in the world who remain 'unbanked', representing 18 per cent of the world's population. This trade-off is arguably much closer to being a 'known known' than a 'known unknown'. It is almost certain to happen, for it is happening already.

The rise of CBDCs is of course crucial in the context of a rapidly digitising global economy. But the stakes of the technological advancement that CBDCs represent are not just economic but are also tied to principles of global freedom, global governance and global influence.

Two-thirds of the world's unbanked nevertheless own a mobile phone, which could help them access financial services. Digital currencies, by their nature, can be designed to be accessible to anyone with a mobile device, thereby potentially integrating hundreds of millions into the formal financial system. This can spur economic growth and development where traditional banking infrastructure is lacking.

However, CBDCs deployed by authoritarian countries will come with strings attached, such as surveillance capabilities that will be used to monitor and control the economic behaviour of citizens, or even international users, in line with the political objectives of the issuing government.

Simply put, allowing China and its allies to dominate the global digital currency landscape could leave billions at the mercy of the CCP.

In a world where the digital yuan and digital currencies modelled on its technology and system of incentives become dominant, freedoms and privacy will be affected worldwide. If authoritarian states can dictate who has access to their digital currencies, they could exclude entire populations or countries from the financial system for political reasons.

Take the military government in Myanmar, which has persecuted the Rohingya Muslim minority with violence and mass displacement. If Myanmar had a state-controlled digital currency, the government could easily freeze out these people financially.

China's government has taken similarly harsh measures against the Muslim Uyghur minority, including forced labour and internment camps. The digital yuan is not likely to be used in their favour.

There is therefore a moral argument to be made that it is imperative for Western countries to develop their own 'liberal' CBDCs, not just as a matter of national interest, but as a bulwark for a liberal, rules-based international order. By doing so, they can leave open the possibility that the financial systems of the future are built on the principles of democracy and freedom, rather than on authoritarianism and control.

This brings us on to a related point. The failure to develop a liberal CBDC will not just bring about trade-offs for citizens in developing countries, or among citizens of China's BRI partners. Now that we have entered the race for the future of money, citizens of a globalised world must expect to encounter them, and even be forced to use them, wherever they go.

So, while citizens of developed Western countries might think that the price of implementing a CBDC at home is too high, this does not mean they won't incur costs to their civil liberties when they are abroad, where their paper money will be refused, and they will be forced to transact in an authoritarian CBDC that harvests their data and spies on their behaviour. There are always trade-offs.

Those who object to CBDCs will say that this implies a sense of inevitability about their development and roll-out, when their existence should be a matter of democratic consent. This is true. But since it is inevitable that other countries will develop CBDCs, the more important question is whether citizens would be more comfortable using a digital currency designed by their own government, or that of another.

There is no turning back from the race for the future of money, just as there was no turning back from the space race in the 1960s. The country you live in will trade with the CBDCs of other countries. Your national currency will be exchangeable and interoperable with a host of foreign CBDCs. The only question is, how should they be designed and what properties should they have? Do you want to have control over the money you use, or do you want the money you use to be in control of you? At the end of the day, who should control the ledger?

Conclusion

For the United States and its allies, the choice is clear. Take part in the race for the future of money with the same spirit of leadership, innovation and international engagement that helped secure and maintain the dollar's status as the global reserve currency, or risk being left behind, and allow some of the most groundbreaking technologies to have been invented since the internet be harnessed by China, Russia and their allies.

The swift rise of digital money marks a tectonic shift in the world's financial architecture. This metamorphosis, destined to extend its reach through China's Belt and Road Initiative (BRI) partners and the recently bolstered BRICS+ coalition, presents a stark challenge to the strongholds of liberal democracy in the West. The fault lines of the New Cold War have been drawn, and the shape and magnitude of the rifts will to a large extent be determined by the fast-growing kudzu vines of smart money.

China's vigorous push into the realm of CBDCs is a deliberate strategy to shift the global balance of power from West to East. For the United States, the European Union and the United Kingdom, the consequences are monumental. To date, the supremacy of the dollar, euro and pound in global commerce and reserves has served as a bedrock of geopolitical power and influence. The spread of CBDCs threatens to erode this supremacy, offering alternative digital payment systems designed to bypass traditional Western financial institutions and diminish Western influence and soft power across the developing world.

For the fast-growing economies and populations of the so-called Global South, multi-CBDC platforms offer attractive alternatives to the dollar-dominated world built and controlled by the West. By facilitating instant settlement in international trade, these platforms will not only make trade faster and cheaper, but allow countries to circumvent Western financial regulations or sanctions where inconvenient. This shift will significantly diminish – if not entirely eliminate – the power of the US dollar as a mechanism for promoting and projecting the West's economic priorities and values globally, as it was used to do over the course of the twentieth century.

These changes will have tangible impacts on the lives of many millions – if not billions – of people, both in the West and across the Global South. The strategic composition of the BRICS+ nations, rich in natural and energy resources, stands in contrast to the resource constraints of the US, UK and Europe. While the US has somewhat mitigated its dependency through the shale revolution, the UK and Europe remain heavily reliant on external energy sources to fuel their service-oriented economies. The BRICS+ countries, many of which are net energy exporters, are positioned to gain substantial geopolitical leverage as global energy demands continue to grow, giving these nations an upper hand in dictating terms and potentially coercing other states into adopting their digital currency systems.

The global race to develop CBDCs is also a battle for influence over the world's unbanked population – hundreds of millions of individuals in developing countries without access to traditional banking services. The architecture of these digital currencies could lead to financial inclusion or exclusion, substantially impacting the economic and political destinies of these populations. The contrast between engaging in a world economy dominated by 'liberal' digital dollars and pounds, or the digital yuan or ruble, will be a stark one.

The West is presently behind in this race, and faces an uphill battle to catch up with China's decade-long head start. There are many different conversations to be had about CBDCs, but there is no question that they will soon be used by millions of people, and then billions. The West must decide whether it wants to lead the conversation about the future of money, or let others lead it. Where do we see state-backed money one hundred years from now? Still existing purely in paper form, or also existing digitally? And if the future of money is to be digital, who should govern its design, build its infrastructure and control its operations?

When we speak of 'the West' in the context of money and markets, we are also talking about the triumph of political and economic freedom. For decades, global dominance of the US dollar has reflected Western values of free trade and free markets around the world. This has led to the free exchange of ideas, the promotion and protection of free speech, and the flourishing of artistic, cultural and technological innovation across the world. If the prevailing money of the twenty-first century does not reflect these values, we will cultivate very different societies.

By the middle of this decade, the US, UK and EU are likely to make definitive decisions about whether or not to develop state-issued digital currencies. In the US, Donald Trump has committed to banning a CBDC if he is elected in 2024. The Democrats seem more inclined to pursue CBDC development, and would be likely to explore avenues through which it could reflect American values. In January 2024, the UK confirmed it was moving towards the design phase of the digital pound, and stated that it would make a decision about its roll out by 2026 at the latest, and that a parliamentary vote would be required to greenlight this. The ECB started the digital euro preparation phase in October 2023.

Clearly, a conversation about CBDCs will be necessary in every country, but these conversations will be especially important in the US, the UK and EU. The problems posed by CBDCs to the West are clear. But the key question remains: would the introduction of a digital dollar, a digital pound or a digital euro really represent a solution to these problems? In a sense, there is probably only one way to find out. Perhaps Western leaders will concoct ingenious plans to counter China's influence in this sphere without resorting to the development of digital money – but we are yet to hear of them.

No matter which way the decisions go, there will be momentous consequences for the global monetary – and therefore geopolitical – order. In the words of Thomas Sowell, there are no solutions, only trade-offs. The right conversation needs to take a realistic view of these trade-offs, on the understanding that there are no perfect solutions. Abstaining from the race for the future of money would also bring about irreversible consequences.

However, for a variety of cultural and political reasons, we seem to be on course to have exactly the wrong kind of conversation about CBDCs. It's time to have a smarter conversation about smart money, before it's too late.

Notes

INTRODUCTION

1   Pok, Caden. 'Donald Trump Promises To "Never Allow" CBDCs During New Hampshire Speech'. *Benzinga*, 30 January 2024. Available at: https://www.benzinga.com/markets/cryptocurrency/24/01/36852864/donald-trump-promises-to-never-allow-cbdcs-during-new-hampshire-speech.

2   Council on Foreign Relations. 'The Dollar: The World's Reserve Currency'. CFR, July 2023. Available at: https://www.cfr.org/backgrounder/dollar-worlds-reserve-currency.

3   McCauley, Robert N. 'Does the US dollar confer an exorbitant privilege?'. *Journal of International Money and Finance*, 57 (2015), pp. 1–14.

4   Munroe, Tony, Osborn, Andrew and Pamuk, Humeyra. 'China, Russia partner up against West at Olympics summit'. *Reuters* (4 February 2022).

5   White House. 'Executive Order on Ensuring Responsible Development of Digital Assets' (9 March 2022).

6   UK Government. 'Government Sets Out Plan to Make UK a Global Cryptoasset Technology Hub' (4 April 2022).

7   Ministry of Foreign Affairs of the People's Republic of China. 'A Journey of Friendship, Cooperation and Peace That Attracts Worldwide Attention' (22 March 2023).

8   Pozsar, Zoltan. 'Great power conflict puts the dollar's exorbitant privilege under threat'. *Financial Times* (20 January 2023).

9 Barrett, Jonathan. 'Silicon Valley Bank: Why did it collapse and is this the start of a banking crisis?'. *Guardian* (13 March 2023).

10 BBC News. 'Bowie talks to Paxman about music, drugs and the internet'. *Newsnight* (1999).

I. THE WASHINGTON CONSENSUS

1 Fox News. 'Biden scoffs at concerns supporting two international wars: We're the US "for God's sake!"' Fox News, 8 October 2023. Available at: https://www.foxnews.com/media/biden-scoffs-concerns-supporting-two-international-wars-us-gods-sake.

2 Zeng, Wendy, Johnson, William and Davis, James C. 'United States and Global Macroeconomic Projections to 2033' (US Department of Agriculture, Washington, D.C., 2024).

3 Brown, Sheldon. 'Patent statistics'. *Patent Experts* (22 March 2023).

4 Hegel, Georg Wilhelm Friedrich. *The Phenomenology of Spirit* (Cambridge Hegel Translations) (Cambridge University Press, Cambridge: 2019).

5 United States Census Office. 'Twelfth Census of the United States Taken in the Year 1900, Population, Part 1' (Washington: 1901).

6 Galati, Gabriele and Wooldridge, Philip. 'The euro as a reserve currency: A challenge to the pre-eminence of the us dollar?'. *International Journal of Finance & Economics*, 14/1 (2009), pp. 1–23.

7 Ibid.

8 Eichengreen, Barry. 'Bretton Woods after 50'. *Review of Political Economy*, 33/4 (2021), pp. 552–69.

9 Newton, Scott. 'Sterling, Bretton Woods, and Social Democracy, 1968–1970'. *Diplomacy & Statecraft*, 24/3 (2013), pp. 427–455.

10 Brook, Anne-Marie, Sédillot, Franck and Ollivaud, Patrice. *Channels for Narrowing the US Current Account Deficit and Implications for Other Economies*. OECD Economics Department Working Papers, 390 (OECD Publishing, Paris: 2004).

11 Frankel, Jeffrey. *The Plaza Accord, 30 Years Later.* NBER Working Paper Series, 21813 (National Bureau of Economic Research, Cambridge, Massachusetts: 2015).

12 Hobsbawm, Eric. *The Age of Extremes: The Short Twentieth Century, 1914–1991* (Abacus, London: 1995).

13 Fukuyama, Francis. 'The end of history?'. *The National Interest*, 16 (1989), pp. 3–18.

14 Williamson, John. 'A short history of the Washington Consensus'. In: *The Washington Consensus Reconsidered: Towards a New Global Governance*, Narcís Serra and Joseph E. Stiglitz (eds.) (Oxford University Press, Oxford: 2008), pp. 14–30.

15 Park, Zachary, Chon, Jake, Jiang, Eddy and Suzuki, Ryosuke. 'The effects of foreign direct investments on major economic metrics: A case study of post-colonialism Republic of Korea'. *Journal of Student Research*, 11/4 (2022).

16 Pemmaraju, Satya Prem. 'Marine trading sector in Singapore'. *International Journal of Science and Research Archive*, 11/1 (2024), pp. 1562–72.

17 Mann, Yossi. 'The global oil market and the status of the Suez Canal'. In: *The Suez Canal: Past Lessons and Future Challenges*, Carmela Lutmar and Ziv Rubinovitz (eds.) (Palgrave Macmillan, Cham: 2023), pp. 95–114.

18 Asif, Muhammad and Khan, Muhammad. 'Possible US-Iran military conflict and its implications upon global sustainable development'. *Journal of Sustainable Development*, 2/1 (2009).

19 Xiao, Yijia, Chen, Yanming, Liu, Xiaoqiang, Yan, Zhaojin, Cheng, Liang and Li, Manchun. 'Oil flow analysis in the Maritime Silk Road region using AIS data'. *International Journal of Geo-Information*, 9/4 (2020), 265.

20 World Bank. 'GDP (Current US$) – United States'. World Bank national accounts data, and OECD National Accounts data files (n.d.).

21 World Bank. 'Patent Applications, Residents – United States'. World Intellectual Property Organization (WIPO) Patent Report: Statistics on Worldwide Patent Activity (n.d.).

22 Roten, Ivan C. and Mullineaux, Donald J. 'Equity underwriting spreads at commercial bank holding companies and investment banks'. *SSRN* (December 2020).

23 Chang, Shun-Chiao and Tsai, Pei-Hsuan. 'A hybrid financial performance evaluation model for wealth management banks following the global financial crisis'. *Technological and Economic Development of Economy*, 22/1 (2016), pp. 21–46.

2. THE DRAGON AWAKENS — THE RISE OF CHINA

1   This statement is often attributed to Napoleon, but no known source can be found to verify the attribution. Gartner, S., Huang, C.-H., Li, Y., & James, P. (2023). *Identity in the Shadow of a Giant: How the Rise of China is Changing Taiwan*, Bristol: Bristol University Press, 2021., p. 6.

2   Wang, Yan and Yao, Yudong. 'Sources of China's economic growth 1952–1999: Incorporating human capital accumulation'. *China Economic Review*, 14/1 (2003), pp. 32–52; Hc, Qiang, Bertness, Mark D., Bruno, John F., Li, Bo, Chen, Guoqian, Coverdale, Tyler C., Altieri, Andrew H., Bai, Junhong, Sun, Tao, Pennings, Steven C., Liu, Jianguo, Ehrlich, Paul R. and Cui, Baoshan. 'Economic development and coastal ecosystem change in China'. *Scientific Reports*, 4 (2014), 5995.

3   Siddiqui, Kalim. 'The political economy of growth in China and India'. *Journal of Asian Public Policy*, 2/1 (2009), pp. 17–35.

4   Ibid.

5   Bassino, Jean-Pascal, Broadberry, Stephen, Fukao, Kyoji, Gupta, Bishnupriya and Takashima, Masanori. 'Japan and the great divergence, 730–1874'. *Explorations of Economic History*, 72 (2019), pp. 1–22.

6   Broadberry, Stephen, Guan, Hanhui and Li, David Daokui. 'China, Europe, and the great divergence: A study in historical national accounting, 980–1850'. *The Journal of Economic History*, 78/4 (2018), pp. 955–1000; He, Bertness, Bruno., Li, Chen, Coverdale., Altieri, Bai, Sun, Pennings, Liu, Ehrlich and Cui. 'Economic development and coastal ecosystem change in China', https://www.nature.com/articles/srep05995

7   World Bank. 'GDP Growth (Annual %) – India'. Available at: https://data.worldbank.org/indicator/NY.GDP.MKTP.KD.ZG?locations=IN; Worldometer. 'GDP by Country'. Available at: https://www.worldometers.info/gdp/gdp-by-country/

8   Vogel, Ezra F. *Deng Xiaoping and the Transformation of China* (Harvard University Press, Cambridge, Massachusetts: 2011).

9   Genov, Nikolai. 'Strong individualization in managing Asian societal transformations'. *Journal of Social Sciences Transformations & Transitions*, 2/5 (2022).

10 World Bank. 'Trade (% of GDP)'. World Bank national accounts data, and OECD National Accounts data files (n.d.).

11 Weinland, Don. 'China is rapidly rolling out its new digital currency'. *The Economist* (18 November 2022).

12 Stringer, Thomas and Ramírez-Melgarejo, Monserrat. 'Nearshoring to Mexico and US supply chain resilience as a response to the COVID-19 pandemic'. *Findings Press* (22 December 2023).

3. THE NEW ERA OF MONEY

1 ElBahrawy, Abeer, Alessandretti, Laura, Kandler, Anne, Pastor-Satorras, Romualdo and Baronchelli, Andrea. 'Evolutionary dynamics of the cryptocurrency market'. *Royal Society of Open Science*, 4/11 (2017); Fabus, Jurai, Kremenova, Iveta, Stalmasekova, Natalia and Kvasnicova-Galovicova, Terezia. 'An empirical examination of bitcoin's halving effects: Assessing cryptocurrency sustainability within the landscape of financial technologies'. *Journal of Risk and Financial Management*, 17/6 (2024), 229.

2 World Bank. 'Remittance Prices Worldwide Quarterly: An Analysis of Trends in Cost of Remittance Services', 48 (World Bank Group, Washington, D.C.: 2023).

3 Demirgüç-Kunt, Asli, Klapper, Leora, Singer, Dorothe and Ansar Saniya. *The Global Findex Database 2021: Financial Inclusion, Digital Payments, and Resilience in the Age of COVID-19* (World Bank Group, Washington, D.C.: 2021).

4 Alden, Lyn. *Broken Money: Why Our Financial System is Failing Us and How Can We Make it Better* (Timestamp Press: 2023).

5 United Nations Office on Drugs and Crime. 'Money Laundering' (n.d.).

6 The Global Economy. *Venezuela: Inflation Forecast* (n.d.); Hotez, Peter J., Basáñez, María-Gloria, Acosta-Serrano, Alvaro and Grillet, Maria Eugenia. 'Venezuela and its rising vector-borne neglected diseases'. *PLOS Neglected Tropical Diseases*, 11/6 (2017), e0005423.

7 Taylor, Mark P. 'Long-run purchasing power parity and the dollar-sterling exchange rate in the 1920s'. *IMF Working Papers*, 118 (1990); Kirch, Wilhelm (ed.). *Encyclopaedia of Public Health: Purchasing Power Parity* (Springer, Dordrecht, Germany: 2008), p. 1220; Park, Hail and Son, Jong Chil. 'Dollarization, inflation and foreign

exchange markets: A cross-country analysis'. *International Journal of Finance & Economics*, 27/3 (2022), pp. 2724–36.

8   Alpher, Stephen. 'Javier Milei wins Argentine presidency: Bitcoin gains nearly 3%'. *CoinDesk* (20 November 2023).

9   Ledesma, Lyllah. 'BlackRock CEO Larry Fink seeing client demand for crypto "around the world"'. *CoinDesk* (17 October 2024).

10 Khanna, Parag and Srinivasan, Balaji S. 'Great protocol politics', *Foreign Policy* (11 December 2021).

11 Ibid.

12 Kumari, Ishika. 'Elon Musk slams US dollar again, compares it to a "scam coin"'. *AMB* Crypto (14 March 2024).

13 Roubini, Nouriel. ' "Flatcoins" are the way forward'. *Financial Times* (14 December 2024).

4. SMART MONEY

1   Wolf, Martin. 'The time to embrace central bank digital currencies is now'. *Financial Times* (20 July 2021).

2   Federal Reserve. 'The Federal Reserve Payments Study 2022: Triennial Initial Data Release' (2023).

3   Finextra. 'Capgemini World Payments Report: Non-cash transactions to reach 1.3 trillion' (14 September 2023).

4   PwC India. 'Trends in the APAC Payments Landscape' (n.d.).

5   Ibid.

6   Adams, Michael. 'Top 10 cryptocurrencies of July 16, 2024'. *Forbes Advisor* (16 July 2024).

7   'Digital Tenge Rail Project in Kazakhstan to Pilot in China'. *Cointelegraph*, accessed 18 July 2024. Available at: https://cointelegraph.com/news/kazakhstan-digital-tenge-rail-project-china-pilot

8   Audu, Victoria. 'The back end of genocide: How the rush for Congo's cobalt is killing thousands'. *The Republic* (19 November 2023).

9   Benchmark Mineral Intelligence. 'Analysis: Lithium industry needs $42 billion to meet 2030 demand'. *Benchmark Source* (13 May 2022).

10 IMF. 'GDP Based on PPP, Share of World' (n.d.).

11 Shen, Samuel and Wee, Rae. 'Cheap yuan catapults China to second-biggest trade funding currency'. *Reuters* (17 November 2023).

12 Bertaut, Carol, von Beschwitz, Bastian and Curcuru, Stephanie. ' "The International Role of the US Dollar" Post-COVID Edition'.

FEDS Notes (Board of Governors of the Federal Reserve System, Washington D.C: 2023).

13 Atlantic Council. 'Dollar Dominance Monitor' (2024).

14 Gould, Stephen Jay. 'Nonoverlapping Magisteria'. *Filozoficzne Aspekty Genezy*, 11 (2021), pp. 7–21.

15 'Yuan' and 'renminbi' are both used to refer to China's currency, but they describe different aspects of the currency system. Renminbi is the official name of the currency of China, which translates to 'people's currency' in Mandarin. 'Renminbi' is analogous to 'sterling' in the UK, describing the currency in a broad, official sense. The yuan is the unit of account of the currency. Yuan is to renminbi what the pound is to sterling or what the dollar is to USD. In practical everyday use, when people discuss prices or costs in China, they typically refer to the amount in yuan. It is the term more commonly used in financial transactions.

16 Kumar, Ananya. 'A report card on China's Central Bank Digital Currency: The e-CNY'. *Atlantic Council* (1 March 2022).

17 Kumar, Ananya. 'Practice makes perfect: What China wants from its digital currency in 2023'. *Atlantic Council* (24 April 2024).

18 Finextra. 'China's digital yuan hits $250 billion milestone' (21 July 2023).

19 Statista. 'Number of Mobile Payment Transactions in China Between 2009 and 2023' (2024).

5. THE FAULT-LINES OF DE-DOLLARISATION

1 Reuters. 'China ramps up yuan internationalisation under Belt and Road Initiative' (19 October 2023).

2 Turrin, Richard. *Cashless: China's Digital Currency Revolution* (Authority Publishing, Gold River, CA: 2021).

3 Pardee School of Global Studies. 'Assessing China's Belt & Road Initiative (BRI)'. Center for the Study of Asia, Boston University (n.d.).

4 Witte, Michelle. 'Xi Jinping calls for regional cooperation via new Silk Road'. *Astana Times* (11 September 2013).

5 Jiao, Wu. 'Xi in call for building of new "Maritime Silk Road"'. *China Daily* (4 November 2013).

6 Areddy, James T. 'How China became the world's top development financier'. *Wall Street Journal* (6 November 2023).

7 Parks, Bradley C., Malik, Ammar A., Escobar, Brooke, Zhang, Sheng, Fedorochko, Rory, Solomon, Kyra, Wang, Fei, Vlasto, Lydia, Walsh, Katherine and Goodman, Seth. *Belt and Road Reboot: Beijing's Bid to De-Risk its Global Infrastructure Initiative* (AIDDATA at William & Mary, Williamsburg, Virginia: 2023).

8 Carney, Richard. *China's Chance to Lead: Acquiring Global Influence via Infrastructure Development and Digitalization* (Cambridge University Press, Cambridge: 2023).

9 Austin, Greg. 'Can there be any winners in the US–China "tech war"?'. *International Institute for Strategic Studies* (20 January 2020).

10 Kennedy, Scott. 'Made in China 2025'. *Center for Strategic & International Studies* (1 June 2015).

11 Lin, Chengyi. '3 drivers of China's booming electric vehicle market'. *Harvard Business Review* (3 January 2024).

12 Duesterberg, Thomas. 'US efforts to counter Huawei 5G dominance making progress: Open RAN playing growing role'. *Forbes* (22 March 2021).

13 People's Bank of China. 'Payment System Report' (2023) (*People's Bank of China*, Beijing: 2023); CIPS (Cross-Border Interbank Payment System). 'CIPS Participants Announcement No. 95' (n.d.).

14 Swift. 'Swift reports strong annual growth' (3 February 2022).

15 Alden, Lyn. *Broken Money: Why Our Financial System is Failing Us and How Can We Make it Better* (Timestamp Press: 2023).

16 Carney. *China's Chance to Lead.*

17 McCarthy, Niall. 'China now boasts more than 800 million internet users and 98% of them are mobile [infographic]'. *Forbes* (23 August 2018)

18 China Daily. 'China's 5G subscribers exceed 850m in February' (31 March 2024).

19 Sandle, Paul. 'BT warns of 500 million pounds hit from British limits on Huawei'. *Reuters* (30 January 2020).

20 Miller, Chris. *Chip War: The Fight for the World's Most Critical Technology* (Scribner, New York: 2022).

21 Reuters. 'China sets up third fund with $47.5 bln to boost semiconductor sector' (27 May 2024).

22 McKinsey & Company. 'Quantum Technology Monitor: April 2023' (McKinsey & Company, New York City: 2023).

23 Tett, Gillian. 'Quantum computing: Investment surges as talent gap persists'. *Financial Times* (12 June 2023).

6. THE LOST DECADE

1 Sanoski, Steve. 'Trans-Pacific Partnership would benefit La. ports and economy, US ag secretary says'. *Business Report* (26 January 2015).
2 US Government. 'Economic and Trade Agreement Between the Government of the United States of America and the Government of the People's Republic of China'. Office of the United States Trade Representative, Executive Office of the President of the United States (2022).
3 New Zealand Ministry of Foreign Affairs and Trade. 'Regional Comprehensive Economic Partnership' (n.d.).
4 Bown, Chad P. 'China bought none of the extra $200 billion of US exports in Trump's trade deal'. *PIIE* (Peterson Institute for International Economics) (19 July 2022).

7. WEEKS WHEN DECADES HAPPEN

1 Vladimir Ilyich Lenin, 'The Chief Task of Our Day', Moscow, 1918. *Lenin's Collected Works*, Fourth English Edition, Progress Publishers, Moscow, 1972. Volume 27, pages 159-63. Available at: marxists.org/archive/lenin/works/1918/mar/11.htm
2 Munroe, Tony, Osborn, Andrew and Pamuk Humeyra. 'China, Russia partner up against West at Olympics summit'. *Reuters* (4 February 2022).
3 Wright, Robin. 'Russia and China unveil a pact against America and the West'. *New Yorker* (7 February 2022).
4 President of Russia. 'Joint Statement of the Russian Federation and the People's Republic of China on the International Relations Entering a New Era and the Global Sustainable Development' (4 February 2022).
5 Wright. 'Russia and China pact'.
6 Moritsugu, Ken. 'Russia, China push back against US in pre-Olympics summit' (4 February 2022), https://apnews.com/article/winter-olympics-putin-xi-meet-0e9127176250c0cab19b36e758 00052e
7 Rao, Sujata and Jones, Marc. 'Russia's economic defences likely to crumble over time under sanctions onslaught'. *Reuters* (25 February 2022).

8 Prasad, Eswar S. *The Dollar Trap: How the US Dollar Tightened its Grip on Global Finance* (Princeton University Press, NJ: 2015).

9 White House. 'Executive Order on Ensuring Responsible Development of Digital Assets' (9 March 2022).

10 Ibid.

11 Ibid.

12 Ibid.

13 US Department of the Treasury. 'The Future of Money and Payments: Report Pursuant to Section 4(b) of Executive order 14067' (US Department of the Treasury, Washington, D.C.: 2022).

14 Ibid.

15 *Bill Cassidy, M.D.* 'Cassidy, Blackburn Introduce Bill to Crack Down on China's Digital Currency'. US Senator for Louisiana (9 March 2022).

16 Economic Affairs Committee. 'Central Bank Digital Currencies: A Solution in Search of a Problem?' (House of Lords, London: 2022).

17 UK Government. 'Government Sets Out Plan to Make UK a Global Cryptoasset Technology Hub' (4 April 2022).

18 UK Government. 'Mansion House Speech 2021'. Speech by Rishi Sunak, UK Chancellor, Mansion House, London (1 July 2021).

19 UK Government. 'Global Cryptoasset Technology Hub'.

20 Ibid.

21 European Central Bank. 'Eurosystem Launches Digital Euro Project' (14 July 2021).

22 European Central Bank. 'For a Few Cryptos More: The Wild West of Crypto Finance'. Speech by Fabio Panetta, Member of the Executive Board of the ECB, Columbia University (25 April 2022).

23 Kroeber, Arthur. 'Digital renminbi will not help Russia evade sanctions'. *Financial Times* (16 March 2022).

24 Ministry of Foreign Affairs of the People's Republic of China. 'A Journey of Friendship, Cooperation and Peace That Attracts Worldwide Attention' (22 March 2023).

25 Allison, Graham. 'Xi and Putin have the most consequential undeclared alliance in the world'. *Foreign Policy* (23 March 2023).

26 Ibid.

27 Davidson, Helen and Hawkins, Amy. 'Western leaders give cool response to China's plan for Ukraine peace talks'. *Guardian* (24 February 2023).

28 Stognei, Anastasia. 'Russia embraces China's renminbi in face of western sanctions'. *Financial Times* (26 March 2023).

29 Prokopenko, Alexandra. 'What are the limits to Russia's "Yuanization"?' *Carnegie Politika* (27 May 2024).

30 Aizhu, Chen. 'Vast China-Russia resources trade shifts to yuan from dollars in Ukraine fallout'. *Reuters* (11 May 2023).

31 Johnson, Carter and Tanzi, Alexandre. 'Yuan Usage Extends Global Climb as Euro Share Slips, Swift Says.' *Bloomberg* (18 April 2024) https://www.bloomberg.com/news/articles/2024-04-18/yuan-usage-extends-global-climb-as-euro-share-slips-swift-says

32 Aizhu, Chen. 'Vast China-Russia resources trade shifts to yuan from dollars in Ukraine fallout'. *Reuters* (11 May 2023).

33 Kroeber. 'Digital renminbi'.

34 McElwee, Lily, Snegovaya, Maria, Chopenko, Alexandra and Dolbaia, Tina. 'Xi goes to Moscow: A marriage of inconvenience?'. *Center for Strategic & International Studies* (28 March 2023).

35 Leonard, Mark. 'China is ready for a world of disorder: America is not'. *Foreign Affairs* (20 June 2023).

8. WHAT'S AT STAKE?

1 Pound, Richard W. Quotations for the Fast Lane (Montreal: McGill - Queens University Press, 2013).

2 Kihara, Leika. 'G7 to discuss digital currency standards, crypto regulation'. *Reuters* (11 April 2023).

3 President of Russia. 'Joint Statement of the Russian Federation and the People's Republic of China on the International Relations Entering a New Era and the Global Sustainable Development' (4 February 2022).

4 Economist Intelligence. 'Democracy Index 2023' (2024).

5 Roubini, Nouriel. 'A bipolar currency regime will replace the dollar's exorbitant privilege'. *Financial Times* (5 February 2023).

6 Tang, Hsin-Wei and Feng, Yuan. 'International anarchy in perpetuity? A re-examination based on the perspectives of classical political thinkers and ancient historical experience'. *Issues & Studies*, 52/3 (2016), 1650012.

7 Press Trust of India. 'States must uphold territorial integrity, says Delhi G20 declaration'. NDTV World (9 September 2023).

8 Rasheed, Moshin. 'Renewable energy adoption and CO_2 emissions in G7 economies: In-depth analysis of economic prosperity and trade relations'. *Journal of Environmental Science and Economics*, 3/2 (2024), pp. 41–66; Tuo, Siele Jean, Li, Chang, Brou, Ettien Fulgence, Kassi, Diby Francois and Gnangoin, Yobouet Thierry. 'Estimating carbon dioxide emission levels of G7 countries: A count data approach'. *Energy & Environment*, 35/4 (2022).

9 Rasheed. 'Renewable energy and CO_2 emissions in G7 economies'.

10 Statista. 'Share of Global GDP (PPP) Held by G7 and BRICS Countries from 2000 to 2024.' Statista (2024). https://www.statista.com/statistics/1412425/gdp-ppp-share-worldgdp-g7-brics/

11 de Castro Camioto, Flávia and Pulita, Alícia Cristina. 'Efficiency evaluation of sustainable development in BRICS and G7 countries: A data envelopment analysis approach'. *Gestão & Produção*, 29 (2022), e022; Ponomarev, S. V., Bukhonova, N. M., Saifutdinova, L. R. and Garayeva, C. R. 'Comparative analysis of the scientific, educational and digital potential of the BRICS and G7 countries: Conclusions for public administration systems'. *Proceedings of the Southwest State University. Series: Economics. Sociology. Management*, 13/2 (2023), pp. 39–52.

12 Ruzima, Martin and Boachie, Micheal Kofi. 'Exchange rate uncertainty and private investments in BRICS economies'. *Asia–Pacific Journal of Regional Science*, 2 (2018), pp. 65–77; Glauben, Thomas and Duric, Ivan. 'BRICS: World heavyweight in agricultural trade'. *Intereconomics*, 59/3 (2024), pp. 160–6.

13 Ibrahim, Ridwan Lanre, Al-mulali, Usama, Solarin, Sakiru Adebola, Ajide, Kazeem Bello, Al-Faryan, Mamdouh Abdulaziz Saleh, Mohammed, Abubakar. 'Probing energy transition-environmental sustainability hypothesis in post COP26 era: Do technological advancement, structural change, and demographic mobility matter for G7?' (4 November 2022), https://link.springer.com/article/10.1007/s11356-023-27472-6

14 Gajapathy, Manickam and Vasagan, V. T. 'Retrospect of gross domestic product of India and China: A comparative analysis'.

   Asia–Pacific Journal of Management and Technology, 4/3 (2024), pp. 31–44.

15 White House. 'Joint Statement from India and the United States' (8 September 2023).

16 Gauba, Sucheta and Singh, Juhi. 'From geo-political to geo-economics: The significance of IMEC for India'. *VEETHIKA: An International Interdisciplinary Research Journal*, 10/1 (2024), pp. 42–9.

17 Dawson, Ian G. J. and Zhang, Danni. 'The 8 billion milestone: Risk perceptions of global population growth among UK and US residents'. *Risk Analysis* (2024).

9. DIGITAL DE-DOLLARISATION

 1 Hemingway, Ernest. *The Sun Also Rises* (Scribner, New York: 1926).

 2 Savage, Rachel. 'What is a BRICS currency and is the US dollar in trouble?'. *Reuters* (24 August 2023).

 3 Ibid.

 4 Bull, Alister. 'South Africa's Kganyago plays down common African currency'. *Bloomberg UK* (4 July 2023).

 5 BRICS Russia 2024. 'First BRICS meeting of finance ministers and central bank governors under Russia's chairship held in Brazil' (28 February 2024).

 6 TASS. 'Kremlin announces creation of blockchain-based payments system in BRICS' (5 March 2024).

 7 Benrath, Bastian, Speciale, Alessandro and Condon, Christopher. 'China sprints ahead in race to modernize global money flows'. *Bloomberg UK* (9 August 2023).

 8 Kaaru, Steve. 'China integrates new blockchain consensus protocol into mBridge cross-border CBDC project'. *CoinGeek* (21 October 2023).

 9 Acheson, Noelle. 'A CBDC alternative to SWIFT?'. *CoinGeek* (7 November 2023).

10 Benrath, Speciale and Condon. 'China sprints ahead'.

11 Kapron, Zennon. 'Cross-border CBDC focused project mBridge moves forward'. *Forbes* (23 June 2024).

12 CBUAE. 'The CBUAE Successfully Launches Project mBridge Minimum Viable Product Platform for Early Adopters' (5 June 2024).

13 Crypto News. 'Russia-China CBDC payments may debut in 2024 – Moscow' (15 December 2023).

14 Ledger Insights. 'Russia to start using CBDC for cross border payments in 2025' (11 June 2024); *BRICS Russia 2024*. 'Meeting of finance ministers held in Brazil'.

15 'Putin wants to speed up deployment of Russia's CBDC'. *Ledger Insights*, 19 July 2024. Available at: https://www.ledgerinsights.com/ putin-wants-to-speed-up-deployment-of-russias-cbdc/

16 Crypto News. 'Russia-China CBDC payments may debut in 2024 – Moscow' (15 December 2023).

17 The Business Standard. 'Saudi Arabia's petro-dollar exit: A global finance paradigm shift' (12 June 2024).

18 Maharrey, Mike. 'The petrodollar is dead and that's a big deal'. *FXStreet* (14 June 2024).

19 Ainslie Bullion. 'The petrodollar is history. CBDCs are here' (14 June 2024).

20 Jones, Marc. 'Saudi Arabia joins BIS- and China-led central bank digital currency project'. *Reuters* (5 June 2024).

21 Singh, Amitoj. 'UAE unveils CBDC strategy: First phase to be completed by mid-2024'. *CoinDesk* (24 March 2023).

22 Economist Intelligence. 'Brazil Prepares to Launch Digital Currency by Early 2025' (7 March 2024).

23 Ibid.

24 Binance. 'Iran completes pre-pilot phase of central bank digital currency' (6 March 2023).

25 Dudley, Dominic. 'Russia and Iran eye up trade using cryptocurrencies to avoid dollars and sanctions'. *Forbes* (18 January 2023).

26 Anthony, Nicholas. 'Nigeria restricts cash to push central bank digital currency'. *Cato Institute* (19 December 2022).

27 Turrin, Richard. *Cashless: China's Digital Currency Revolution* (Authority Publishing, Gold River, CA: 2021).

28 Turrin, Richard. *Cashless: China's Digital Currency Revolution*. (Gold River, CA: Authority Publishing, 2021), pp. 202-204; 206-208

29 Pessarlay, Wahid. 'Indonesia's central bank eye CBDC trial for 2024'. *CoinGeek* (5 January 2024).

30 Money and Banking. 'The extraordinary failures exposed by Silicon Valley Bank's collapse' (20 March 2023).

31 The Bitcoin Standard Podcast. '194. The Debt Bubble with Luke Gromen'. *YouTube* (7 November 2023).

32 World Gold Council. 'Gold Demand Trends Q1 2024: Central Banks' (2024).

33 Pozsar, Zoltan. 'Bretton Woods III', *Credit Suisse* (Zürich: 2022).

10. THE BATTLE FOR RESOURCES

1 https://www.nytimes.com/2008/06/17/us/politics/17text-mccain.html

2 Klare, Michael T. *Resource Wars: The New Landscape of Global Conflict* (Henry Holt & Company, New York: 2002).

3 Gromen, Luke. 'Energy is the Base Layer of Money'. 13 June 2024. https://www.youtube.com/watch?v=xpRUEjuY_Qs

4 Klare, Michael T. *Rising Powers, Shrinking Planet: The New Geopolitics of Energy* (Henry Holt & Company, New York: 2008).

5 Kwok, Yun-Kwong and Zhang, Yanchun. 'Impacts of external oil supply shocks on the Chinese economy'. Refereed paper presented at the ACESA 2006 Conference – Emerging China: Internal Challenges and Global Implications, Victoria University, Melbourne, 13–14 July (2006); *Bloomberg UK*. 'China's oil demand outlook darkens as OPEC+ prepares to meet' (29 May 2024); *Statista*. 'Oil Consumption in the United States From 1998 to 2023' (2024).

6 Nate Hagens. Luke Gromen: 'Peak Cheap Oil and the Global Reserve Currency'. 'The Great Simplification #91'. YouTube (4 October 2023).

7 Pitron, Guillaume. *The Rare Metals War: The Dark Side of Clean Energy and Digital Technologies* (Scribe UK, London: 2021).

8 Baskaran, Gracelin. 'What China's ban on rare earths processing technology exports means'. *Center for Strategic & International Studies* (8 January 2024).

9 Van Veen, Kelsi and Melton, Alex. 'Rare Earth Elements Supply Chains, Part 1: An Update on Global Production and Trade'. *Executive Briefing on Trade* (United States International Trade Commission, Washington D.C.: 2020).

11. FLASHPOINTS AND PROXY WARS

1 Reuters. 'Russian 2024 GDP growth seen matching 2023 at 3.6%, finance minister says' (19 April 2024).

2 Baazil, Diederik, Koc, Cagan and Robertson, Jordan. 'ASML and TSMC can disable chip machines if China invades Taiwan'. *Bloomberg UK* (21 May 2024).

3 Holland, Steve, Bose, Nandita and Hunnicutt, Trevor. 'US does not support Taiwan independence, Biden says'. *Reuters* (14 January 2024).

4 Vance, J. D. 'Pick as Trump VP signals support for Taiwan over Ukraine'. *Nikkei Asia*. Available at: https://asia.nikkei.com/Opinion/J.D.-Vance-pick-as-Trump-VP-signals-support-for-Taiwan-over-Ukraine. Accessed 18 July 2024.

5 Haime, Jordyn. 'China's Xi Jinping makes televised pledge to absorb Taiwan'. *Telegraph* (1 January 2024).

6 World Bank. 'Africa's Pulse: An Analysis of Issues Shaping Africa's Economic Future', volume 8 (World Bank, Washington D.C.: 2013).

7 Sinha, Saurabh and Getachew, Melat. 'As Africa's population crosses 1.5 billion, the demographic window is opening; getting the dividend requires more time and stronger effort'. *United Nations Economic Committee for Africa* (12 July 2024).

8 Honorato, Felipe Antonio and de Freitas, Guilherme Silva Pires. 'Cobalt exploration is vital for the Democratic Republic of Congo and the world'. *London School of Economics* (4 April 2024), https://blogs.lse.ac.uk/africaatlse/2024/04/04/cobalt-exploration-is-vital-for-the-democratic-republic-of-congo-and-the-world/

9 Madden, Payce. 'Africa in the news: Russia-Africa summit, Botswana's election, and Africa's new growth projections'. *Brookings* (26 October 2019).

10 President of Russia. 'Article by Vladimir Putin "Russia and Africa: Joining Efforts for Peace, Progress and a Successful Future"' (24 July 2023).

11 Hayley, Andrew. 'China's oil trade and investment in Venezuela' (12 September 2023), https://www.reuters.com/business/energy/chinas-oil-trade-investment-venezuela-2023-09-12/.

12 The Dialogue. 'China-Latin America Finance Databases' (n.d.).

13 Zhang, Pepe and Prazeres, Tatiana Lacerda. 'China's trade with Latin America is bound to keep growing. Here's why that matters'. *World Economic Forum* (17 June 2021); He, Laura. 'China's exports jump thanks to demand from India, Russia and other emerging markets'. *CNN* (7 March 2024).

14 Carrington, Damian. 'Too late now to save Arctic summer ice, climate scientists find'. *Guardian* (6 June 2023).

15 LePan, Nicolas. 'The final frontier: How Arctic ice melting is opening up trade opportunities'. *World Economic Forum* (13 February 2020).

12. CYBERSPACE

1 SecureWorld. 'How Bruce Schneier sees security in 2019'. *SecureWorld News Team* (16 May 2019).

2 NATO. 'Cyber Defence' (n.d.).

3 Winder, Davey. 'Trump declares national emergency as foreign hackers threaten US power grid'. *Forbes* (2 May 2020).

4 UK Government. 'G7 Foreign and Development Ministers' Meeting: Communique, London, 5 May 2021', policy paper (UK Foreign, Commonwealth & Development Office, London: 2021).

5 Lowery, Jason P. *Software: A Novel Theory on Power Projection and the National Strategic Significance of Bitcoin* (Independently published: 2023).

6 ELCON. 'The Economic Impacts of the August 2003 Blackout' (ELCON, Washington, D.C.: 2004). pp. 1–2.

7 Lieberman, David. 'Congresswoman Wants Probe of Brazen $81M Theft from New York Fed.' New York Post, March 22, 2016. Available at: https://nypost.com/2016/03/22/congresswoman-wants-probe-of-brazen-81m-theft-from-new-york-fed/

8 'Companies around the world hit by IT outage.' Financial Times, July 17, 2024. https://www.ft.com/content/fba9b61d-efcf-4348-b640-ccb1f9d18ced.

9 IISS. 'Cyber Capabilities and National Power: A Net Assessment' (IISS, London: 2021).

10 Cyberspace Solarium Commission. 'Introduction' (n.d.).

11 Jensen, Benjamin. 'When systems fail: What pandemics and cyberspace tell us about the future of national security'. *War on the Rocks* (9 April 2020).

12 White House. 'International Strategy for Cyberspace: Prosperity, Security and Openness in a Networked World' (White House, Washington, D.C.: 2011).

13 LawInfoChina. 'Cybersecurity Law of the People's Republic of China', Order No. 53 of the President, as adopted at the 24th Session of the

Standing Committee of the Twelfth National People's Congress of the People's Republic of China (7 November 2016).

14 Pannier, Alice. 'Digital Sovereignty: Review of Macron's Term and Debates in the 2022 Presidential Campaign'. (French Institute of International Relations, Paris: 2022); Burwell, Frances and Propp, Kenneth. 'Digital sovereignty in practice: The EU's push to shape the new global economy'. *Atlantic Council* (2 November 2022).

15 Rick Scott. 'Sen. Rick Scott Introduces Bill to Combat CCP Influence in Digital Banking'. *US Senator for Florida* (8 November 2023).

16 Ibid.

13. THE WRONG CONVERSATION

1 John F. Kennedy Presidential Library and Museum. 'Address at Rice University on the Nation's Space Effort'. Speech by John F. Kennedy, President of the United States of America, Rice University, Houston, Texas (12 September 1962).

2 US Department of Defense. 'DoD News Briefing – Secretary Rumsfeld and Gen. Myers'. Speech by Donald Rumsfeld, US Secretary of Defense (12 February 2002).

3 Ekins, Emily and Gygi, Jordan. 'Poll: Only 16% of Americans support the government issuing a central bank digital currency'. *Cato Institute* (31 May 2023).

4 Ibid.

5 Shumba, Camomile. 'Digital pound consultation received over 50,000 responses, with privacy a major concern'. *CoinDesk* (27 October 2023).

6 European Central Bank. 'Eurosystem Report on the Public Consultation on the Digital Euro' (European Central Bank, Frankfurt, Germany: 2021).

7 Chin, Josh and Lin, Liza. *Surveillance State: Inside China's Quest to Launch a New Era of Social Control* (St. Martin's Press, New York: 2022).

8 BBC News. 'Canada protests: Police push back demonstrators in Ottawa'. BBC News (19 February 2022).

9 CoinDesk. 'Post Malone, Podcaster Joe Rogan Slam Prospects of a US Digital Dollar: That's "Game Over".' 'The Hash' team's reflection on comments from The Joe Rogan Experience podcast, episode #2018 – Post Malone, *Spotify* (August 2023).

10 Brooker, Charlie, Schur, Michael and Jones, Rashida. 'Nosedive'. *Black Mirror*, series 4, episode 1, Netflix (2016).

11 Guida, Victoria. '"Tyranny": Trump vows to block any Fed effort to launch digital currency'. *Politico* (18 January 2024).

12 Ted Cruz. 'Sen. Cruz Introduces Legislation to Ban Central Bank Digital Currencies'. *US Senator for Texas* (26 February 2024).

13 Ibid.

14 Ibid.

15 Ibid.

16 Ibid.

17 Hamilton, Jesse. 'US Fed Chair Powell says "Nowhere near" pursuing CBDC, won't spy on Americans'. *CoinDesk* (7 March 2024).

18 Ibid.

19 Board of Governors of the Federal Reserve System. 'Money and Payments: The US Dollar in the Age of Digital Transformation' (Federal Reserve System, Washington, D.C.: 2022).

20 Emmer, Tom. 'Emmer's Flagship CBDC Anti-Surveillance State Act Passes House of Representatives'. Congressman and Majority Whip (23 May 2024), https://emmer.house.gov/2024/5/emmer-s-flagship-cbdc-anti-surveillance-state-act-passes-house-of-representatives.

21 US Government. 'H.R.5403 (CBCD Anti-Surveillance State Act)'. Union Calendar No. 409, 118th Congress, 2D Session (US Government Publishing Office, Washington, D.C.: 2024).

22 Emmer, Tom. 'CBDC Anti-Surveillance State Act Passes'.

23 European Central Bank. 'The Digital Euro: Our Money Wherever, Whenever We Need It'. Speech by Fabio Panetta, Member of the Executive Board of the ECB, Committee of Economic and Monetary Affairs of the European Parliament, Brussels (23 January 2023).

24 Deutsche Bundesbank. 'Bundesbank Survey: Widespread Acceptance of Digital Euro Among General Public' (4 June 2024).

25 Bank of England. 'The Digital Pound'. Speech by Jon Cunliffe, Deputy Governor of Financial Stability at the Bank of England, UK Finance (7 February 2023).

26 UK Government. 'Response to Petition: "Prevent the Introduction of Any 'Programmable' CBDC in the UK"' (21 December 2022).

27 Bank of England. 'Bank of England and HM Treasury Respond to Digital Pound Consultation' (25 January 2024).

28 Ibid.

29 Bank of England. 'New Prospects for Money'. Speech by Andrew
   Bailey, Governor of the Bank of England, London (10 July 2023).

14. WHAT SHOULD THE WEST DO?

1 This statement is often attributed to Theodore Roosevelt, but no
   known primary source can be found to verify the attribution. Available
   at: https://www.theodorerooseveltcenter.org/Learn-About-TR/TR-
   Quotes/In%20any%20moment%20of%20decision%20%20the%20
   best%20thing%20you%20can%20do%20is%20the%20right%20
   thing%20%20the%20nex
2 Sowell, Thomas. *A Conflict of Visions*. William Morrow & Co, 1987.
3 Economic Affairs Committee. 'Central Bank Digital Currencies: A
   Solution in Search of a Problem?' (House of Lords, London: 2022).
4 Ramani, Arjun. 'The roll-out of central-bank digital currencies will
   slow in 2024'. *The Economist* (13 November 2023).
5 Giancarlo, J. Christopher and Harper, Jim. 'Fight China's
   "surveillance coin" with a US "freedom coin"'. *The Hill* (13 March
   2023).
6 Michel, Norbert. 'Central bank digital currencies, under any name,
   threaten privacy and freedom'. *Cato Institute* (2 May 2023).
7 Digital Currency Initiative. 'Project Hamilton: Building a Hypothetical
   Central Bank Digital Currency' (n.d.).
8 World Bank. 'Defying Predictions, Remittance Flows Remain Strong
   During COVID-19 Crisis' (12 May 2021).
9 World Bank. Demirgüç-Kunt, Alsi, Klapper, Leora, Singer, Dorothe
   and Ansar, Saniya. 'The Global Findex Database 2021: Financial
   Inclusion, Digital Payments, and Resilience in the Age of COVID-19''
   (World Bank Group, Washington D.C.: 2022).
10 World Bank. 'Remittances Slowed in 2023, Expected to Grow Faster
   in 2024' (26 June 2024).
11 Bank for International Settlements. 'Central Bank Digital Currencies
   for Cross-Border Payments' (Bank for International Settlements,
   Basel, Switzerland: 2021).
12 United Nations Office on Drugs and Crime. 'Money Laundering'
   (n.d.).
13 Internet Crime Complaint Center. 'Internet Crime Report 2023'
   (Federal Bureau of Investigation, Washington, D.C.: 2024).

14 Smith, Josh. 'Crypto hacks stole record $3.8 billion in 2022, led by North Korea groups'. *Reuters* (6 February 2023).

15 Kemp, Simon. 'Digital 2024: Kenya'. *DataReportal* (23 February 2024).

16 Warsh, Kevin. 'Money matters: The US dollar, cryptocurrency, and the national interest'. In: *American Renewal: A Conservative Plan to Strengthen the Social Contract and Save the Country's Finances*, Paul Ryan and Angela Rachidi (eds.) (American Enterprise Institute, Washington, D.C.: 2022).

17 Tran, Hung and Matthews, Barbara C. 'CBDCs will further fragment the global economy – and could threaten the dollar'. *Atlantic Council* (16 November 2023).

18 Ibid.

19 Reback, Sheldon. 'Fed chair Powell told House Democrats US needs stablecoin bill: Politico'. *CoinDesk* (14 February 2024).

20 Roy, Avik. 'There's no such thing as an "American-style" central bank digital currency'. *Forbes* (14 April 2023).

21 Ibid.

22 Alden, Lyn. *Broken Money: Why Our Financial System is Failing Us and How Can We Make it Better* (Timestamp Press: 2023).

23 Ibid.

Bibliography

Acheson, Noelle. 'A CBDC alternative to SWIFT?'. *CoinDesk* (7 November 2023). Also available at: https://www.coindesk.com/opinion/2023/11/07/a-cbdc-alternative-to-swift/

Adams, Michael. 'Top 10 cryptocurrencies of July 16, 2024'. *Forbes Advisor* (16 July 2024). Also available at: https://www.forbes.com/advisor/investing/cryptocurrency/top-10-cryptocurrencies

Ainslie Bullion. 'The petrodollar is history. CBDCs are here' (14 June 2024). Also available at: https://ainsliebullion.com.au/News-Resources/Article/The-Petrodollar-is-History-CBDCs-are-here/ID/5367

Aizhu, Chen. 'Vast China-Russia resources trade shifts to yuan from dollars in Ukraine fallout'. *Reuters* (11 May 2023). Also available at: https://www.reuters.com/markets/currencies/vast-china-russia-resources-trade-shifts-yuan-dollars-ukraine-fallout-2023-05-11/

Alden, Lyn. *Broken Money: Why Our Financial System is Failing Us and How Can We Make it Better* (Timestamp Press: 2023).

Allison, Graham. 'Xi and Putin have the most consequential undeclared alliance in the world'. *Foreign Policy* (23 March 2023). Also available at: https://foreignpolicy.com/2023/03/23/xi-putin-meeting-china-russia-undeclared-alliance

Alpher, Stephen. 'Javier Milei wins Argentine presidency: Bitcoin gains nearly 3%'. *CoinDesk* (20 November 2023). Also available at: https://www.coindesk.com/markets/2023/11/20/javier-milei-wins-argentine-presidency-bitcoin-gains-nearly-3

Anthony, Nicholas. 'Nigeria restricts cash to push central bank digital currency'. *Cato Institute* (19 December 2022). Also available at: https://www.cato.org/blog/central-bank-digital-currency-war-cash

Areddy, James T. 'How China became the world's top development
    financier'. *Wall Street Journal* (6 November 2023). Also available
    at: https://www.wsj.com/world/china/how-china-became-the-wor
    lds-top-development-financier-08509fc9
Asif, Muhammad and Khan, Muhammad. 'Possible US-Iran military
    conflict and its implications upon global sustainable development'.
    Journal of Sustainable Development, 2/1 (2009). Also available
    at: https://doi.org/10.5539/jsd.v2n1p3
Atlantic Council. 'Dollar Dominance Monitor' (2024). Also available
    at: https://www.atlanticcouncil.org/programs/geoeconomics-center/
    dollar-dominance-monitor
Audu, Victoria. 'The back end of genocide: How the rush for Congo's
    cobalt is killing thousands'. *Republic* (19 November 2023). Also
    available at: https://republic.com.ng/october-november-2023/congo-
    cobalt-genocide
Austin, Greg. 'Can there be any winners in the US–China "tech
    war"?'. *International Institute for Strategic Studies* (20 January 2020).
    Also available at: https://www.iiss.org/online-analysis/online-analy
    sis/2020/01/csfc-any-winners-in-the-us-china-tech-war/
Baazil, Diederik, Koc, Cagan and Robertson, Jordan. 'ASML and
    TSMC can disable chip machines if China invades Taiwan'.
    Bloomberg UK (21 May 2024). Also available at: https://www.bloomb
    erg.com/news/articles/2024-05-21/asml-tsmc-can-disable-chip-machi
    nes-if-china-invades-taiwan
Bank for International Settlements. 'Central Bank Digital Currencies
    for Cross-Border Payments' (Bank for International Settlements,
    Basel, Switzerland: 2021). Also available at: https://www.bis.org/publ/
    othp38.pdf
Bank of England. 'Bank of England and HM Treasury Respond to
    Digital Pound Consultation' (25 January 2024). Also available
    at: https://www.bankofengland.co.uk/news/2024/january/boe-hmt-
    respond-to-digital-pound-consultation
———. 'New Prospects for Money'. Speech by Andrew Bailey,
    Governor of the Bank of England, London (10 July 2023). Also
    available at: https://www.bankofengland.co.uk/speech/2023/july/and
    rew-bailey-speech-at-the-financial-and-professional-services-dinner

————. 'The Digital Pound'. Speech by Jon Cunliffe, Deputy
    Governor of Financial Stability at the Bank of England, UK Finance
    (7 February 2023). Also available at: https://www.bankofengland.
    co.uk/speech/2023/february/jon-cunliffe-speech-at-uk-finance-upd
    ate-on-central-bank-digital-currency
Barrett, Jonathan. 'Silicon Valley Bank: Why did it collapse and is
    this the start of a banking crisis?' *Guardian* (13 March 2023). Also
    available at: https://www.theguardian.com/business/2023/mar/13/sili
    con-valley-bank-why-did-it-collapse-and-is-this-the-start-of-a-bank
    ing-crisis
Baskaran, Gracelin. 'What China's ban on rare earths processing
    technology exports means'. *Center for Strategic & International Studies*
    (8 January 2024). Also available at: https://www.csis.org/analysis/
    what-chinas-ban-rare-earths-processing-technology-exports-means
Bassino, Jean-Pascal, Broadberry, Stephen, Fukao, Kyoji, Gupta,
    Bishnupriya and Takashima, Masanori. 'Japan and the great
    divergence, 730–1874'. *Explorations of Economic History*, 72 (2019),
    pp. 1–22. Also available at: https://doi.org/10.1016/j.eeh.2018.11.005
BBC News. 'Bowie talks to Paxman about music, drugs and the
    internet'. *BBC Newsnight* (1999). Also available at: https://www.bbc.
    co.uk/news/av/entertainment-arts-35286749
————. 'Canada protests: Police push back demonstrators in Ottawa'.
    BBC News (19 February 2022). Also available at: https://www.bbc.
    co.uk/news/world-us-canada-60420469
Benchmark Mineral Intelligence. 'Analysis: Lithium industry needs $42
    billion to meet 2030 demand'. *Benchmark Source* (13 May 2022). Also
    available at: https://source.benchmarkminerals.com/article/analysis-
    lithium-industry-needs-42-billion-to-meet-2030-demand
Benrath, Bastian, Speciale, Alessandro and Condon, Christopher.
    'China sprints ahead in race to modernize global money flows'.
    Bloomberg UK (9 August 2023). Also available at: https://www.
    bloomberg.com/news/articles/2023-08-09/china-s-digital-yuan-mbri
    dge-plan-challenges-7-trillion-dollar-dominance
Bertaut, Carol, von Beschwitz, Bastian and Curcuru, Stephanie. ' "The
    International Role of the US Dollar" Post-COVID Edition'. FEDS
    Notes *Board of Governors of the Federal Reserve System* (Washington
    D.C: 2023). Also available at: https://doi.org/10.17016/2380-7172.3334

Bloomberg UK. 'China's oil demand outlook darkens as OPEC+ prepares to meet' (29 May 2024). Also available at: https://www. bloomberg.com/news/articles/2024-05-29/china-s-oil-demand-outl ook-darkens-as-opec-prepares-to-meet

Board of Governors of the Federal Reserve System. 'Money and Payments: The US Dollar in the Age of Digital Transformation' (Federal Reserve System, Washington, D.C.: 2022). Also available at: https://www.federalreserve.gov/publications/files/money-and-payments-20220120.pdf

Bown, Chad P. 'China bought none of the extra $200 billion of US exports in Trump's trade deal'. *PIIE* (Peterson Institute for International Economics) (19 July 2022). Also available at: https://www.piie.com/blogs/realtime-economics/china-bou ght-none-extra-200-billion-us-exports-trumps-trade-deal

BRICS Russia 2024. 'First BRICS meeting on finance ministers and central bank governors under Russia's chairship held in Brazil' (28 February 2024). Also available at: https://brics-russia2024.ru/en/ news/v-brazilii-sostoyalas-pervaya-v-ramkakh-rossiyskogo-predseda telstva-vstrecha-ministrov-finansov

Broadberry, Stephen, Guan, Hanhui and Li, David Daokui. 'China, Europe, and the great divergence: A study in historical national accounting, 980–1850'. *The Journal of Economic History*, 78/4 (2018), pp. 955–1000. Also available at: https://doi.org/10.1017/S0022050718000529

Brook, Anne-Marie, Sédillot, Franck and Ollivaud, Patrice. 'Channels for Narrowing the US Current Account Deficit and Implications for Other Economies'. OECD Economics Department Working Papers, 390 (OECD Publishing, Paris: 2004). Also available at: https://doi. org/10.1787/18151973

Brooker, Charlie, Schur, Michael and Jones, Rashida. 'Nosedive'. *Black Mirror*, series 4, episode 1, Netflix (2016).

Brown, Sheldon. 'Patent statistics'. *Patent Experts* (22 March 2023). Also available at: https://patentexperts.org/patent/statistics

Bull, Alister. 'South Africa's Kganyago plays down common African currency'. *Bloomberg UK* (4 July 2023). Also available at: https:// www.bloomberg.com/news/articles/2023-07-04/south-africa-s-kgany ago-plays-down-common-african-currency

Burwell, Frances and Propp, Kenneth. 'Digital sovereignty in practice: The EU's push to shape the new global economy'. *Atlantic Council*

(2 November 2022). Also available at: https://www.atlanticcouncil.
org/in-depth-research-reports/report/digital-sovereignty-in-practice-
the-eus-push-to-shape-the-new-global-economy

Carney, Richard. *China's Chance to Lead: Acquiring Global Influence via
Infrastructure Development and Digitalization* (Cambridge University
Press, Cambridge: 2023).

Carrington, Damian. 'Too late now to save Arctic summer ice,
climate scientists find'. *Guardian* (6 June 2023). Also available
at: https://www.theguardian.com/environment/2023/jun/06/
too-late-now-to-save-arctic-summer-ice-climate-scientists-find

Cassidy, Bill, M.D. 'Cassidy, Blackburn Introduce Bill to Crack Down
on China's Digital Currency'. *US Senator for Louisiana* (9 March
2022). Also available at: https://www.cassidy.senate.gov/newsroom/
press-releases/cassidy-blackburn-introduce-bill-to-crack-down-on-chi
nas-digital-currency/

Cassidy, Bill, M.D. 'Iran completes pre-pilot phase of central bank
digital currency' (6 March 2023). Also available at: https://
www.binance.com/en/square/post/2023-03-06-iran-comple
tes-pre-pilot-phase-of-central-bank-digital-currency-276960

CBUAE (Central Bank of the UAE). 'The CBUAE Successfully
Launches Project mBridge Minimum Viable Product Platform for
Early Adopters' (5 June 2024). Also available at: https://www.centralb
ank.ae/media/zo1jlmsq/the-cbuae-successfully-launches-project-mbri
dge-minimum-viable-product-platform-for-early-adopters-en.pdf

Chang, Shun-Chiao and Tsai, Pei-Hsuan. 'A hybrid financial
performance evaluation model for wealth management banks
following the global financial crisis'. *Technological and Economic
Development of Economy*, 22/1 (2016), pp. 21–46. Also available
at: https://doi.org/10.3846/20294913.2014.986771

Chin, Josh and Lin, Liza. *Surveillance State: Inside China's Quest
to Launch a New Era of Social Control* (St. Martin's Press,
New York: 2022).

China Daily. 'China's 5G subscribers exceed 850m in February'
(31 March 2024). Also available at:https://www.chinadaily.com.
cn/a/202403/31/WS6608e205a31082fc043bf99c.html

CIPS (Cross-Border Interbank Payment System). 'CIPS Participants
Announcement No. 95' (n.d.). Also available at: https://www.cips.
com.cn/en/2024-06/27/article_2024062719493697765.html

CoinDesk. 'Post Malone, Podcaster Joe Rogan Slam Prospects of a US Digital Dollar: That's "Game Over".' 'The Hash' team's reflection on comments from The Joe Rogan Experience podcast, episode #2018 – Post Malone, *Spotify* (August 2023). Also available at: https://www. coindesk.com/video/post-malone-podcaster-joe-rogan-slam-prospe cts-of-a-us-digital-dollar-thats-game-over/

Cruz, Ted. 'Sen. Cruz Introduces Legislation to Ban Central Bank Digital Currencies'. *US Senator for Texas* (26 February 2024). Also available at: https://www.cruz.senate.gov/newsroom/press-releases/ sen-cruz-introduces-legislation-to-ban-central-bank-digital-currencies

Crypto News. 'Russia-China CBDC payments may debut in 2024 – Moscow' (15 December 2023). Also available at: https://cryptonews. net/news/finance/28177791

Cyberspace Solarium Commission. 'Introduction' (n.d.). Also available at: https://www.solarium.gov/

Davidson, Helen and Hawkins, Amy. 'Western leaders give cool response to China's plan for Ukraine peace talks'. *Guardian* (24 February 2023). Also available at: https://www.theguardian.com/ world/2023/feb/24/china-calls-for-russia-ukraine-war-peace-talks

Dawson, Ian G. J. and Zhang, Danni. 'The 8 billion milestone: Risk perceptions of global population growth among UK and US residents'. *Risk Analysis* (2024). Also available at: 5995https://doi. org/10.1111/risa.14272

de Castro Camioto, Flávia and Pulitaáñ, Alícia Cristina. 'Efficiency evaluation of sustainable development in BRICS and G7 countries: A data envelopment analysis approach'. *Gestão & Produção*, 29 (2022), e022. Also available at: https://doi. org/10.1590/1806-9649-2022v29e022

Demirgüç-Kunt, Asli, Klapper, Leora, Singer, Dorothe and Ansar Saniya. 'The Global Findex Database 2021: Financial Inclusion, Digital Payments, and Resilience in the Age of COVID-19'. *World Bank Group* (Washington, D.C.: 2022). Also available at: https:// www.worldbank.org/en/publication/globalfindex

Deutsche Bundesbank. 'Bundesbank Survey: Widespread Acceptance of Digital Euro Among General Public' (4 June 2024). Also available at: https://www.bundesbank.de/en/press/press-releases/bundesb

ank-survey-widespread-acceptance-of-digital-euro-among-general-
public--933322

Digital Currency Initiative. 'Project Hamilton: Building a Hypothetical
Central Bank Digital Currency' (n.d.). Also available at: https://dci.
mit.edu/project-hamilton-building-a-hypothetical-cbdc

Dudley, Dominic. 'Russia and Iran eye up trade using cryptocurrencies
to avoid dollars and sanctions'. *Forbes* (18 January 2023). Also
available at: https://www.forbes.com/sites/dominicdudley/2023/01/18/
russia-and-iran-eye-up-trade-using-cryptocurrencies-to-avoid-doll
ars-and-sanctions/

Duesterberg, Thomas. 'US efforts to counter Huawei 5G dominance
making progress: Open RAN playing growing role'. *Forbes* (22 March
2021). Also available at: https://www.forbes.com/sites/thomasdues
terberg/2021/03/17/us-efforts-to-counter-huawei-5g-dominance-mak
ing-progress-open-ran-playing-growing-role/

Economic Affairs Committee. 'Central Bank Digital Currencies: A
Solution in Search of a Problem?' (House of Lords, London: 2022).
Also available at: https://committees.parliament.uk/publicati
ons/8443/documents/85604/default/

Economist Intelligence. 'Brazil Prepares to Launch Digital Currency
by Early 2025' (7 March 2024). Also available at: https://www.eiu.
com/n/brazil-prepares-to-launch-digital-currency-by-early-2025

———. 'Democracy Index 2023' (2024). Also available at: https://www.
eiu.com/n/campaigns/democracy-index-2023

Eichengreen, Barry. 'Bretton Woods after 50'. *Review of Political
Economy*, 33/4 (2021), pp. 552–69. Also available at: https://doi.
org/10.1080/09538259.2021.1952011

Ekins, Emily and Gygi, Jordan. 'Poll: Only 16% of Americans support
the government issuing a central bank digital currency'. *Cato Institute*
(31 May 2023). Also available at: https://www.cato.org/survey-reports/
poll-only-16-americans-support-government-issuing-central-bank-
digital-currency

ElBahrawy, Abeer, Alessandretti, Laura, Kandler, Anne, Pastor-Satorras,
Romualdo and Baronchelli, Andrea. 'Evolutionary dynamics of the
cryptocurrency market'. *Royal Society of Open Science*, 4/11 (2017).
Also available at: https://doi.org/10.1098/rsos.170623

ELCON (Electricity Consumers Resource Council). 'The Economic
    Impacts of the August 2003 Blackout' (ELCON, Washington,
    D.C.: 2004). pp. 1–2. Also available at: https://elcon.org/wp-content/
    uploads/Economic20Impacts20of20August20200320Blackout1.pdf
Emmer, Tom. 'Emmer's Flagship CBDC Anti-Surveillance State Act
    Passes House of Representatives'. *Congressman and Majority Whip*
    (23 May 2024). Also available at: https://emmer.house.gov/2024/5/
    emmer-s-flagship-cbdc-anti-surveillance-state-act-passes-house-of-
    representatives
European Central Bank. 'Eurosystem Launches Digital Euro Project'
    (14 July 2021). Also available at: https://www.ecb.europa.eu/press/pr/
    date/2021/html/ecb.pr210714~d99198ea23.en.html
——. 'Eurosystem Report on the Public Consultation on the Digital
    Euro' (European Central Bank, Frankfurt, Germany: 2021). Also
    available at: https://www.ecb.europa.eu/pub/pdf/other/Eurosystem_
    report_on_the_public_consultation_on_a_digital_euro~539fa8cd8d.
    en.pdf
——. 'For a Few Cryptos More: The Wild West of Crypto Finance'.
    Speech by Fabio Panetta, Member of the Executive Board of the
    ECB, Columbia University (25 April 2022). Also available at: https://
    www.ecb.europa.eu/press/key/date/2022/html/ecb.sp220425~643
    6006db0.en.html
——. 'The Digital Euro: Our Money Wherever, Whenever We
    Need It'. Speech by Fabio Panetta, Member of the Executive Board
    of the ECB, Committee of Economic and Monetary Affairs of the
    European Parliament, Brussels (23 January 2023). Also available
    at: https://www.ecb.europa.eu/press/key/date/2023/html/ecb.sp230
    123~2f8271ed76.en.html
Fabus, Jurai, Kremenova, Iveta, Stalmasekova, Natalia and Kvasnicova-
    Galovicova, Terezia. 'An empirical examination of bitcoin's halving
    effects: Assessing cryptocurrency sustainability within the landscape
    of financial technologies'. *Journal of Risk and Financial Management*,
    17/6 (2024), 229. Also available at: https://doi.org/10.3390/
    jrfm17060229
Federal Reserve. 'The Federal Reserve Payments Study 2022: Triennial
    Initial Data Release' (2023). Also available at: https://www.federalrese
    rve.gov/paymentsystems/fr-payments-study.htm

Finextra. 'Capgemini World Payments Report: Non-cash transactions to reach 1.3 trillion' (14 September 2023). Also available at: https://www.finextra.com/newsarticle/42951/capgemini-world-payments-report-non-cash-transactions-to-reach-13-trillion

———. 'China's digital yuan hits $250 billion milestone' (21 July 2023).

Frankel, Jeffrey. 'The Plaza Accord, 30 Years Later'. NBER Working Paper Series, 21813 (National Bureau of Economic Research, Cambridge, Massachusetts: 2015). Also available at: https://doi.org/10.3386/w21813

Fukuyama, Francis. 'The end of history?'. *The National Interest*, 16 (1989), pp. 3–18. Also available at: https://www.jstor.org/stable/24027184

Gajapathy, Manickam and Vasagan, V. T. 'Retrospect of gross domestic product of India and China: A comparative analysis'. *Asia–Pacific Journal of Management and Technology*, 4/3 (2024), pp. 31–44. Also available at: https://doi.org/10.46977/apjmt.2024.v04i03.004

Galati, Gabriele and Wooldridge, Philip. 'The euro as a reserve currency: A challenge to the pre-eminence of the US dollar?'. *International Journal of Finance & Economics*, 14/1 (2009), pp. 1–23. Also available at: https://doi.org/10.1002/ijfe.379

Gauba, Sucheta and Singh, Juhi. 'From geo-political to geo-economics: The significance of IMEC for India'. *VEETHIKA: An International Interdisciplinary Research Journal*, 10/1 (2024), pp. 42–9. Also available at: https://doi.org/10.48001/veethika.2024.10.01.005

Genov, Nikolai. 'Strong individualization in managing Asian societal transformations'. *Journal of Social Sciences Transformations & Transitions*, 2/5 (2022). Also available at: https://doi.org/10.52459/josstt25240323

Giancarlo, J. Christopher and Harper, Jim. 'Fight China's "surveillance coin" with a US "freedom coin"'. *The Hill* (13 March 2023). Also available at: https://thehill.com/opinion/finance/3897860-fight-china s-surveillance-coin-with-a-us-freedom-coin/

Glauben, Thomas and Duric, Ivan. 'BRICS: World heavyweight in agricultural trade'. *Intereconomics*, 59/3 (2024), pp. 160–6. Also available at: https://doi.org/10.2478/ie-2024-0033

Gould, Stephen Jay. 'Nonoverlapping Magisteria'. *Filozoficzne Aspekty Genezy*, 11 (2021), pp. 7–21. Also available at: https://doi.org/10.53763/fag.2014.11.95

Guida, Victoria. ' "Tyranny": Trump vows to block any Fed effort to
    launch digital currency'. *Politico* (18 January 2024). Also available
    at: https://www.politico.com/news/2024/01/18/trump-
    vows-to-block-any-fed-effort-to-launch-digital-currency-00136328

Hagens, Nate. 'Luke Gromen: "Peak Cheap Oil and the Global Reserve
    Currency PwC India". The Great Simplification #91'. *YouTube*
    (4 October 2023). Also available at: https://www.youtube.com/
    watch?v=bIq0040J080

Haime, Jordyn. 'China's Xi Jinping makes televised pledge to absorb
    Taiwan'. *Telegraph* (1 January 2024). Also available at: https://www.
    telegraph.co.uk/world-news/2024/01/01/china-xi-jinping-televised-
    pledge-absorb-taiwan-2029

Hamilton, Jesse. 'US Fed Chair Powell says "Nowhere near" pursuing
    CBDC, won't spy on Americans'. *CoinDesk* (7 March 2024).
    Also available at: https://www.coindesk.com/policy/2024/03/07/
    us-fed-chair-powell-says-nowhere-near-pursuing-cbdc-wont-spy-on-
    americans/

Hayley, Andrew. 'China's oil trade and investment in Venezuela' (12
    September 2023). *Reuters*. Also available at: https://www.reuters.com/
    business/energy/chinas-oil-trade-investment-venezuela-2023-09-12

He, Laura. 'China's exports jump thanks to demand from India, Russia
    and other emerging markets'. *CNN* (7 March 2024). Also available
    at: https://edition.cnn.com/2024/03/07/business/chinas-exports-
    surge-at-the-start-of-2024-intl-hnk/index.html

He, Qiang, Bertness, Mark D., Bruno, John F., Li, Bo, Chen, Guoqian,
    Coverdale, Tyler C., Altieri, Andrew H., Bai, Junhong, Sun, Tao,
    Pennings, Steven C., Liu, Jianguo, Ehrlich, Paul R. and Cui,
    Baoshan. 'Economic development and coastal ecosystem change
    in China'. *Scientific Reports*, 4 (2014), 5995. https://doi.org/10.1038/
    srep05995

Hegel, Georg Wilhelm Friedrich. *The Phenomenology of Spirit*
    (Cambridge Hegel Translations) (Cambridge University Press,
    Cambridge: 2019).

Hemingway, Ernest. *The Sun Also Rises* (Scribner's, New York: 1926).

Hobsbawm, Eric. *Age of Extremes: The Short Twentieth Century, 1914–
    1991* (Abacus, London: 1995).

Holland, Steve, Bose, Nandita and Hunnicutt, Trevor. 'US does not support Taiwan independence, Biden says'. *Reuters* (14 January 2024). Also available at: https://www.reuters.com/world/biden-us-does-not-support-taiwan-independence-2024-01-13/

Honorato, Felipe Antonio and de Freitas, Guilherme Silva Pires. 'Cobalt exploration is vital for the Democratic Republic of Congo and the world'. *London School of Economics* (4 April 2024). Also available at: https://blogs.lse.ac.uk/africaatlse/2024/04/04/cobalt-exploration-is-vital-for-the-democratic-republic-of-congo-and-the-world

Hotez, Peter J., Basáñez, María-Gloria, Acosta-Serrano, Alvaro and Grillet, Maria Eugenia. 'Venezuela and its rising vector-borne neglected diseases'. *PLOS Neglected Tropical Diseases*, 11/6 (2017), e0005423. Also available at: https://doi.org/10.1371/journal.pntd.0005423

Ibrahim, Ridwan Lanre, Al-mulali, Usama, Solarin, Sakiru Adebola, Ajide, Kazeem Bello, Al-Faryan, Mamdouh Abdulaziz Saleh, Mohammed, Abubakar. 'Probing energy transition-environmental sustainability hypothesis in post COP26 era: Do technological advancement, structural change, and demographic mobility matter for G7?' (4 November 2022), https://link.springer.com/article/10.1007/s11356-023-27472-6

IISS (The International Institute for Strategic Studies). *Cyber Capabilities and National Power: A Net Assessment* (IISS, London: 2021). Also available at: https://www.iiss.org/globalassets/media-library---content--migration/files/research-papers/cyber-power-report/cyber-capabilities-and-national-power---a-net-assessment___.pdf

IMF (International Monetary Fund). 'GDP Based on PPP, Share of World' (n.d.). Also available at: https://www.imf.org/external/datamapper/PPPSH@WEO/CHN/USA

Internet Crime Complaint Center. 'Internet Crime Report 2023' (Federal Bureau of Investigation, Washington, D.C.: 2024). Also available at: https://www.ic3.gov/Media/PDF/AnnualReport/2023_IC3Report.pdf

Jensen, Benjamin. 'When systems fail: What pandemics and cyberspace tell us about the future of national security'. *War on the Rocks* (9 April 2020). Also available at: https://warontherocks.com/2020/04/

when-systems-fail-what-pandemics-and-cyberspace-tell-us-about-the-
future-of-national-security/

Jiao, Wu. 'Xi in call for building of new "Maritime Silk Road"'. *China
Daily* (4 November 2013). Also available at: https://usa.chinadaily.
com.cn/china/2013-10/04/content_17008940.htm

John F. Kennedy Presidential Library and Museum. 'Address at Rice
University on the Nation's Space Effort'. Speech by John F. Kennedy,
President of the United States of America, Rice University, Houston,
Texas (12 September 1962). Also available at: https://www.jfklibrary.
org/archives/other-resources/john-f-kennedy-speeches/rice-univers
ity-19620912

Jones, Marc. 'Saudi Arabia joins BIS- and China-led central bank digital
currency project'. *Reuters* (5 June 2024). Also available at: https://
www.reuters.com/technology/saudi-arabia-joins-bis-led-central-bank-
digital-currency-trial-2024-06-05/

Kaaru, Steve. 'China integrates new blockchain consensus protocol
into mBridge cross-border CBDC project'. *CoinGeek* (21 October
2023). Also available at: https://coingeek.com/china-integrates-new-
blockchain-consensus-protocol-into-mbridge-cross-border-cbdc-
project

Kapron, Zennon. 'Cross-border CBDC focused project mBridge
moves forward'. *Forbes* (23 June 2024). Also available at:
https://www.forbes.com/sites/digital-assets/2024/06/23/
cross-border-cbdc-focused-project-mbridge-moves-forward

Kemp, Simon. 'Digital 2024: Kenya'. *DataReportal* (23 February 2024).
Also available at: https://datareportal.com/reports/digital-2024-kenya

Kennedy, Scott. 'Made in China 2025'. *Center for Strategic &
International Studies* (1 June 2015). Also available at: https://www.csis.
org/analysis/made-china-2025

Khanna, Parag and Srinivasan, Balaji S. 'Great protocol politics'. *Foreign
Policy* (11 December 2021). Also available at: https://foreignpolicy.
com/2021/12/11/bitcoin-ethereum-cryptocurrency-web3-great-proto
col-politics/

Kihara, Leika. 'G7 to discuss digital currency standards, crypto
regulation'. *Reuters* (11 April 2023). Also available at: https://www.
reuters.com/markets/currencies/g7-discuss-digital-currency-standa
rds-crypto-regulation-2023-04-11

Kirch, Wilhelm (ed.). *Encyclopaedia of Public Health: Purchasing Power Parity* (Springer, Dordrecht, Germany: 2008), p. 1220. Also available at: https://doi.org/10.1007/978-1-4020-5614-7_2880

Klare, Michael T. *Resource Wars: The New Landscape of Global Conflict* (Henry Holt & Company, New York: 2002).

———. *Rising Powers, Shrinking Planet: The New Geopolitics of Energy* (Henry Holt & Company, New York: 2008).

Kroeber, Arthur. 'Digital renminbi will not help Russia evade sanctions'. *Financial Times* (16 March 2022). Also available at: https://www.ft.com/content/cb13c87c-90d5-4266-8d62-e7e50be14f01

Kumar, Ananya. 'A report card on China's Central Bank Digital Currency: The e-CNY'. *Atlantic Council* (1 March 2022). Also available at: https://www.atlanticcouncil.org/blogs/econographics/a-report-card-on-chinas-central-bank-digital-currency-the-e-cny/

———. 'Practice makes perfect: What China wants from its digital currency in 2023'. *Atlantic Council* (24 April 2024). Also available at: https://www.atlanticcouncil.org/uncategorized/practice-makes-perfect-what-china-wants-from-its-digital-currency-in-2023/

Kumari, Ishika. 'Elon Musk slams US dollar again, compares it to a "scam coin"'. 'Digital Sovereignty: Review of Macron's Term and Debates in the 2022 Presidential Campaign' *AMB Crypto* (14 March 2024). Also available at: https://ambcrypto.com/elon-musk-slams-u-s-dollar-again-compares-it-to-a-scam-coin/

Kwok, Yun-Kwong and Zhang, Yanchun. 'Impacts of external oil supply shocks on the Chinese economy'. Refereed paper presented at the ACESA 2006 Conference – Emerging China: Internal Challenges and Global Implications, Victoria University, Melbourne, 13–14 July (2006). Also available at: https://citeseerx.ist.psu.edu/document?repid=rep1&type=pdf&doi=0199f2fbce374a5fc02413c493694eee8f00275b

LawInfoChina. 'Cybersecurity Law of the People's Republic of China'. Order No. 53 of the President, as adopted at the 24th Session of the Standing Committee of the Twelfth National People's Congress of the People's Republic of China (7 November 2016). Also available at: https://www.lawinfochina.com/Display.aspx?Id=22826&Lib=law&LookType=3

Ledesma, Lyllah. 'Chon, Jake Jiang, Eddy Suzuki, Ryosuke. BlackRock CEO Larry Fink seeing client demand for crypto "around the world"'. CoinDesk *Journal of Student Research* (17 October 2023). Also available at: https://www.coindesk.com/business/2023/10/17/blackrock-ceo-larry-fink-seeing-client-demand-for-crypto-around-the-world

Ledger Insights. 'Russia to start using CBDC for cross border payments in 2025' (11 June 2024). Also available at: https://www.ledgerinsights.com/russia-to-start-using-cbdc-for-cross-border-payments-in-2025

Leonard, Mark. 'China is ready for a world of disorder: America is not'. *Foreign Affairs* (20 June 2023). Also available at: https://www.foreignaffairs.com/united-states/china-ready-world-disorder

LePan, Nicolas. 'The final frontier: How Arctic ice melting is opening up trade opportunities'. *World Economic Forum International Journal of Science and Research Archive* (13 February 2020). Also available at: https://www.weforum.org/agenda/2020/02/ice-melting-arctic-transport-route-industry

Lin, Chengyi. '3 drivers of China's booming electric vehicle market'. *Harvard Business Review* (3 January 2024). Also available at: https://hbr.org/2024/01/3-drivers-of-chinas-booming-electric-vehicle-market

Lowery, Jason P. *Software: A Novel Theory on Power Projection and the National Strategic Significance of Bitcoin* (Independently published: 2023).

Madden, Payce. 'People's Bank of China Africa in the news: Russia-Africa summit, Botswana's election, and Africa's new growth projections *Payment System Report (2023)*'. Brookings *Payment System Report (2023)* (26 October 2019). Also available at: https://www.brookings.edu/articles/africa-in-the-news-russia-africa-summit-botswanas-election-and-africas-new-growth-projections-russia-hosts-first-africa-heads-of-state-summit

Maharrey, Mike. 'The petrodollar is dead and that's a big deal'. *FXStreet* (14 June 2024). Also available at: https://www.fxstreet.com/analysis/the-petrodollar-is-dead-and-thats-a-big-deal-202406141938

Mann, Yossi. 'The global oil market and the status of the Suez Canal'. In: *The Suez Canal: Past Lessons and Future Challenges*, Carmela Lutmar and Ziv Rubinovitz (eds.) (Palgrave Macmillan, Cham: 2023), pp. 95–114. Also available at: https://doi.org/10.1007/978-3-031-15670-0_5

McCarthy, Niall. 'China now boasts more than 800 million internet users and 98% of them are mobile [infographic]'. *Forbes* (23

August 2018). Also available at: https://www.forbes.com/sites/
niallmccarthy/2018/08/23/china-now-boasts-more-than-800-million-
internet-users-and-98-of-them-are-mobile-infographic

McCauley, Robert N. 'Does the US dollar confer an exorbitant
privilege?'. *Journal of International Money and Finance*, 57 (2015), pp.
1–14. Also available at: https://doi.org/10.1016/j.jimonfin.2015.06.005

McElwee, Lily, Snegovaya, Maria, Chopenko, Alexandra and Dolbaia,
Tina. 'Xi goes to Moscow: A marriage of inconvenience?'. *Center
for Strategic & International Studies* (28 March 2023). Also available
at: https://www.csis.org/analysis/xi-goes-moscow-marriage-inconv
enience

McKinsey & Company. 'Quantum Technology Monitor: April 2023'
(McKinsey & Company, New York City: 2023). Also available
at: https://www.mckinsey.com/~/media/mckinsey/business%20
functions/mckinsey%20digital/our%20insights/quantum%20
technology%20sees%20record%20investments%20progress%20
on%20talent%20gap/quantum-technology-monitor-april-2023.pdf

Michel, Norbert. 'Central bank digital currencies, under any name,
threaten privacy and freedom'. *Cato Institute* (2 May 2023). Also
available at: https://www.cato.org/commentary/central-bank-digital-
currencies-under-any-name-threaten-privacy-freedom

Miller, Chris. *Chip War: The Fight for the World's Most Critical
Technology* (Scribner, New York: 2022).

Ministry of Foreign Affairs of the People's Republic of China. 'A Journey
of Friendship, Cooperation and Peace That Attracts Worldwide
Attention' (22 March 2023). Also available at: https://www.mfa.gov.
cn/mfa_eng/zxxx_662805/202303/t20230324_11048606.html2023

Money and Banking. 'The extraordinary failures exposed by Silicon
Valley Bank's collapse' (20 March 2023). Also available at: https://
www.moneyandbanking.com/commentary/2023/3/20/
the-extraordinary-failures-exposed-by-silicon-valley-banks-collapse

Moritsugu, Ken. 'Russia, China push back against US in pre-Olympics
summit'. *Associated Press* (4 February 2022). Also available at: https://
apnews.com/article/winter-olympics-putin-xi-meet-0e9127176250c0c
ab19b36e75800052e

Munroe, Tony, Osborn, Andrew and Pamuk, Humeyra. 'China, Russia
partner up against West at Olympics summit'. *Reuters* (4 February
2022). Also available at: https://www.reuters.com/world/europe/

russia-china-tell-nato-stop-expansion-moscow-backs-beijing-tai
wan-2022-02-04/

NATO (North Atlantic Treaty Organization). *Cyber Defence* (n.d.). Also
available at: https://www.nato.int/cps/en/natohq/topics_78170.htm

Newton, Scott. 'Sterling, Bretton Woods, and Social Democracy, 1968–
1970'. *Diplomacy & Statecraft*, 24/3 (2013), pp. 427–55. Also available
at: https://doi.org/10.1080/09592296.2013.817931

New Zealand Ministry of Foreign Affairs and Trade. 'Regional
Comprehensive Economic Partnership' (n.d.). Also available
at: https://www.mfat.govt.nz/en/trade/free-
trade-agreements/free-trade-agreements-in-force/
regional-comprehensive-economic-partnership-rcep/rcep-overview

Pannier, Alice. 'Digital Sovereignty: Review of Macron's Term and
Debates in the 2022 Presidential Campaign'. *French Institute of
International Relations* (Paris: 2022). Also available at: Reuters
https://www.ifri.org/sites/default/files/atoms/files/pannier_digital_
sovereignty_2022.pdf

Pardee School of Global Studies. 'Assessing China's Belt & Road
Initiative (BRI)'. Center for the Study of Asia, Boston University
(n.d.). Also available at: https://www.bu.edu/asian/resources/
assessing-chinas-belt-road-initiative-bri

Park, Hail and Son, Jong Chil. 'Dollarization, inflation and foreign
exchange markets: A cross-country analysis'. *International Journal
of Finance & Economics*, 27/3 (2022), pp. 2724–36. Also available
at: https://doi.org/10.1002/ijfe.2295

Park, Zachary, Chon, Jake, Jiang, Eddy and Suzuki, Ryosuke. 'The
effects of foreign direct investments on major economic metrics: A
case study of post-colonialism Republic of Korea'. *Journal of Student
Research*, 11/4 (2022). Also available at: https://doi.org/10.47611/jsrhs.
v11i4.3671

Parks, Bradley C., Malik, Ammar A., Escobar, Brooke, Zhang, Sheng,
Fedorochko, Rory, Solomon, Kyra, Wang, Fei, Vlasto, Lydia, Walsh,
Katherine and Goodman, Seth. 'Belt and Road Reboot: Beijing's Bid
to De-Risk its Global Infrastructure Initiative'. *AIDDATA at William
& Mary* (Williamsburg, Virginia: 2023). Also available at: https://
www.aiddata.org/publications/belt-and-road-reboot

Pemmaraju, Satya Prem. 'Marine trading sector in Singapore'.
International Journal of Science and Research Archive, 11/1 (2024),

pp. 1562–72. Also available at: https://doi.org/10.30574/ijsra.2024.
11.1.0192

People's Bank of China. Shen, Samuel Wee, Rae. 'Payment System
Report (2023)' (People's Bank of China, Beijing: 2023). Also available
at: http://www.pbc.gov.cn/en/3688110/3688172/5188125/5327700/2024
041216580199504.pdf

Pessarlay, Wahid. 'Indonesia's central bank eye CBDC trial for 2024'.
CoinGeek (5 January 2024). Also available at: https://coingeek.com/
indonesia-central-bank-eye-cbdc-trial-for-2024

Pitron, Guillaume. *The Rare Metals War: The Dark Side of Clean Energy
and Digital Technologies* (Scribe UK, London: 2021).

Pok, Caden. 'Donald Trump promises to "never allow" CBDCs
during New Hampshire speech'. *Benzinga* (30 January
2024). Also available at: https://www.benzinga.com/markets/
cryptocurrency/24/01/36852864/donald-trump-promises-to-never-
allow-cbdcs-during-new-hampshire-speech

Ponomarev, S. V., Bukhonova, N. M., Saifutdinova, L. R. and Garayeva,
C. R. 'Comparative analysis of the scientific, educational and digital
potential of the BRICS and G7 countries: Conclusions for public
administration systems'. *Proceedings of the Southwest State University.
Series: Economics. Sociology. Management*, 13/2 (2023), pp. 39–52. Also
available at: https://doi.org/10.21869/2223-1552-2023-13-2-39-52

Pozsar, Zoltan, Berman, Noah. 'Bretton Woods III'. *Credit Suisse*
(Zürich: 2022). Also available at: https://static.bullionstar.com/blogs/
uploads/2022/03/Bretton-Woods-III-Zoltan-Pozsar.pdf

———— 'Great power conflict puts the dollar's exorbitant privilege
under threat'. *Financial Times* (20 January 2023). Also available
at: https://www.ft.com/content/3e05b491-d781-4865-b0f7-777bc
95ebf71

Prasad, Eswar S. *The Dollar Trap: How the US Dollar Tightened its Grip
on Global Finance* (Princeton University Press, NJ: 2015).

President of Russia. 'Article by Vladimir Putin "Russia and Africa:
Joining Efforts for Peace, Progress and a Successful Future".'
(24 July 2023)

————. 'Joint Statement of the Russian Federation and the People's
Republic of China on the International Relations Entering a New
Era and the Global Sustainable Development' (4 February 2022).

Press Trust of India. 'States must uphold territorial integrity, says Delhi G20 declaration'. NDTV World (9 September 2023). Also available at: https://www.ndtv.com/india-news/ukraine-conflict-g20-declaration-calls-on-all-states-to-uphold-principles-of-territorial-integrity-and-sovereignty-4375287

Prokopenko, Alexandra. 'Ramírez-Melgarejo, Monserrat.What are the limits to Russia's "Yuanization"?' *Carnegie Politika* (27 May 2024). Also available at: https://carnegieendowment.org/russia-eurasia/politika?lang=en

PwC India. 'Trends in the APAC Payments Landscape' (n.d.). Also available at: https://www.pwc.in/industries/financial-services/fintech/payments/trends-in-the-apac-payments-landscape.html

Ramani, Arjun. 'The roll-out of central-bank digital currencies will slow in 2024'. *Economist* (13 November 2023). Also available at: https://www.economist.com/the-world-ahead/2023/11/13/the-roll-out-of-central-bank-digital-currencies-will-slow-in-2024

Rao, Sujata and Jones, Marc. 'Russia's economic defences likely to crumble over time under sanctions onslaught'. *Reuters* (25 February 2022). Also available at: https://www.reuters.com/world/europe/russias-economic-defences-likely-crumble-over-time-under-sanctions-onslaught-2022-02-25/

Rasheed, Moshin. 'Renewable energy adoption and CO2 emissions in G7 economies: In-depth analysis of economic prosperity and trade relations'. *Journal of Environmental Science and Economics*, 3/2 (2024), pp. 41–66. Also available at: https://doi.org/10.56556/jescae.v3i2.839

Reback, Sheldon. 'Fed chair Powell told House Democrats US needs stablecoin bill: Politico'. *CoinDesk* (14 February 2024). Also available at: https://www.coindesk.com/policy/2024/02/14/fed-chair-powell-told-house-democrats-us-needs-stablecoin-bill-politico/

Reuters. 'China ramps up yuan internationalisation under Belt and Road Initiative' (19 October 2023). Available at: https://www.reuters.com/markets/currencies/china-ramps-up-yuan-internationalisation-under-belt-road-initiative-2023-10-19/

———. 'China sets up third fund with $47.5 bln to boost semiconductor sector' (27 May 2024). Also available at: https://www.reuters.com/technology/china-sets-up-475-bln-state-fund-boost-semiconductor-industry-2024-05-27

————. 'Russian 2024 GDP growth seen matching 2023 at 3.6%,
   finance minister says' (19 April 2024). Also available at: https://www.
   reuters.com/world/europe/russian-2024-gdp-growth-seen-matching-
   2023-36-finance-minister-says-2024-04-19/

Roten, Ivan C. and Mullineaux, Donald J. 'Equity underwriting spreads
   at commercial bank holding companies and investment banks'.
   SSRN (December 2020). Also available at: https://doi.org/10.2139/
   ssrn.261736

Roubini, Nouriel. 'A bipolar currency regime will replace the dollar's
   exorbitant privilege'. Financial Times (5 February 2023). Also
   available at: https://www.ft.com/content/e03d277a-e697-4220-a0ca-
   1f8a3dbecb75

————. ' "Flatcoins" are the way forward'. Financial Times (14
   December 2024). Also available at: https://www.ft.com/cont
   ent/7774da77-048d-4e75-8350-4fec136cb18f

Roy, Avik. 'There's no such thing as an "American-style" central
   bank digital currency'. Forbes (14 April 2023). Also available
   at: https://www.forbes.com/sites/theapothecary/2023/04/12/the
   res-no-such-thing-as-an-american-style-central-bank-digital-
   currency/

Ruzima, Martin and Boachie, Micheal Kofi. 'Exchange rate uncertainty
   and private investments in BRICS economies'. Asia–Pacific Journal
   of Regional Science, 2 (2018), pp. 65–77. Also available at: https://doi.
   org/10.1007/s41685-017-0062-0

Sandle, Paul. 'BT warns of 500 million pounds hit from British limits
   on Huawei'. Reuters (30 January 2020). Also available at: https://
   www.reuters.com/article/world/bt-warns-of-650-million-hit-from-
   british-limits-on-huawei-idUSKBN1ZT0MI/

Sanoski, Steve. 'Li, Chang Brou, Ettien Fulgence Kassi, Diby Francois
   Gnangoin, Yobouet Thierry.Trans-Pacific Partnership would benefit
   La. ports and economy, US ag secretary says'. Business Report
   (26 January 2015). Also available at: https://www.businessreport.com/
   article/trans-pacific-partnership-big-la-ports-economy-us-ag-
   secretary-says

Savage, Rachel. 'What is a BRICS currency and is the US dollar in
   trouble?'. Reuters (24 August 2023). Also available at: https://www.
   reuters.com/markets/currencies/what-is-brics-currency-could-one-be-
   adopted-2023-08-23/

Scott, Rick. 'Sen. Rick Scott Introduces Bill to Combat CCP Influence in Digital Banking'. *US Senator for Florida* (8 November 2023). Also available at: https://www.rickscott.senate.gov/2023/11/sen-rick-scott-introduces-bill-to-combat-ccp-influence-in-digital-banking

SecureWorld. 'How Bruce Schneier sees security in 2019'. SecureWorld News Team (16 May 2019). Also available at: https://www.securewo rld.io/industry-news/bruce-schneier-on-security

Shen, Samuel and Wee, Rae. 'Cheap yuan catapults China to second-biggest trade funding currency'. *Reuters* (17 November 2023). Also available at: https://www.reuters.com/markets/currencies/cheap-yuan-catapults-china-second-biggest-trade-funding-currency-2023-11-17

Shumba, Camomile. 'Digital pound consultation received over 50,000 responses, with privacy a major concern'. *CoinDesk* (27 October 2023). Also available at: https://www.coindesk.com/pol icy/2023/10/27/digital-pound-consultation-received-over-50000-responses-with-privacy-a-major-concern/

Siddiqui, Kalim. 'The political economy of growth in China and India'. *Journal of Asian Public Policy*, 2/1 (*Deng Xiaoping and the Transformation of China* Harvard University Press Cambridge, Massachusetts 2009), pp. 17–35. Also available at: https://www.researchgate.net/publication/249057799_2009

Singh, Amitoj. 'UAE unveils CBDC strategy: First phase to be completed by mid-2024'. *CoinDesk* (24 March 2023). Also available at: https://www.coindesk.com/policy/2023/03/24/uae-unveils-cbdc-strategy-first-phase-to-be-completed-by-mid-2024/

Sinha, Saurabh and Getachew, Melat. 'As Africa's population crosses 1.5 billion, the demographic window is opening; getting the dividend requires more time and stronger effort'. *United Nations Economic Committee for Africa* (12 July 2024). Also available at: https://www.uneca.org/stories/%28blog%29-as-africa%E2%80%99s-population-crosses-1.5-billion%2C-the-demographic-window-is-opening-getting

Siripurapu, Anshu and Berman, Noah. 'The dollar: The world's reserve currency'. *Council on Foreign Relations* (19 July 2023). Also available at: https://www.cfr.org/backgrounder/dollar-worlds-reserve-currency

Smith, Josh. 'Crypto hacks stole record $3.8 billion in 2022, led by North Korea groups'. *Reuters* (6 February 2023). Also available

at: https://www.reuters.com/technology/crypto-hacks-stole-rec
ord-38-billion-2022-led-by-north-korea-groups-report-2023-02-01/

Statista. 'Number of Mobile Payment Transactions in China Between
2009 and 2023' (2024). Also available at: https://www.statista.com/
statistics/244538/number-of-mobile-payment-transactions-in-china

———. 'Oil Consumption in the United States From 1998 to 2023'
(2024). Also available at: https://www.statista.com/statistics/282716/
oil-consumption-in-the-us-per-day

Stognei, Anastasia. 'Russia embraces China's renminbi in face of
western sanctions'. *Financial Times* (26 March 2023). Also available
at: https://www.ft.com/content/65681143-c6af-4b64-827d-a7ca6
171937a

Stringer, Thomas and Ramírez-Melgarejo, Monserrat. 'Nearshoring to
Mexico and US supply chain resilience as a response to the COVID-
19 pandemic'. *Findings Press* (22 December 2023). Also available
at: https://doi.org/10.32866/001c.91272

Swift. 'Swift reports strong annual growth' (3 February 2022).
Also available at: https://www.swift.com/news-events/news/
swift-reports-strong-annual-growth

Tang, Hsin-Wei and Feng, Yuan. 'International anarchy in perpetuity?
A re-examination based on the perspectives of classical political
thinkers and ancient historical experience'. *Issues & Studies*,
52/3 (2016), 1650012. Also available at: https://doi.org/10.1142/
S1013251116500120

TASS. 'Kremlin announces creation of blockchain-based payments
system in BRICS' (5 March 2024). Also available at: https://tass.com/
politics/1755521

Tett, Gillian. 'Quantum computing: Investment surges as talent gap
persists'. *Financial Times* (12 June 2023). Also available at: https://
www.ft.com/content/a8204a7d-2922-4944-bdff-5449a8f3aee9

The Bitcoin Standard Podcast. '194. The Debt Bubble with Luke
Gromen'. *YouTube* (November 7 2023). Also available at: https://
www.youtube.com/watch?v=zNVO6aejrYY

The Business Standard. 'Saudi Arabia's petro-dollar exit: A
global finance paradigm shift' (12 June 2024). Also available
at: https://www.tbsnews.net/world/global-economy/
saudi-arabias-petro-dollar-exit-global-finance-paradigm-shift-875321

The Dialogue. 'China-Latin America Finance Databases' (n.d.). Also available at: https://www.thedialogue.org/map_list

The Global Economy. 'Venezuela: Inflation Forecast' (n.d.). Also available at: https://www.theglobaleconomy.com/Venezuela/inflation_outlook_imf

Tran, Hung and Matthews, Barbara C. 'CBDCs will further fragment the global economy – and could threaten the dollar'. *Atlantic Council* (16 November 2023). Also available at: https://www.atlanticcouncil.org/blogs/econographics/cbdcs-will-further-fragment-the-global-economy-and-could-threaten-the-dollar/

Tuo, Siele Jean, Li, Chang, Brou, Ettien Fulgence, Kassi, Diby Francois and Gnangoin, Yobouet Thierry. 'Estimating carbon dioxide emission levels of G7 countries: A count data approach'. *Energy & Environment*, 35/4 (2022). Also available at: https://doi.org/10.1177/0958305X221143416

Turrin, Richard. *Cashless: China's Digital Currency Revolution* (Authority Publishing, Gold River, CA: 2021).

UK Government. 'G7 Foreign and Development Ministers' Meeting: Communique, London, 5 May 2021', policy paper (UK Foreign, Commonwealth & Development Office, London: 2021). Also available at: https://www.gov.uk/government/publications/g7-foreign-and-development-ministers-meeting-may-2021-communique/g7-foreign-and-development-ministers-meeting-communique-london-5-may-2021

———. 'Government Sets Out Plan to Make UK a Global Cryptoasset Technology Hub' (4 April 2022). Also available at: https://www.gov.uk/government/news/government-sets-out-plan-to-make-uk-a-global-cryptoasset-technology-hub

———. 'Mansion House Speech 2021'. Speech by Rishi Sunak, UK Chancellor, Mansion House, London (1 July 2021). Also available at: https://www.gov.uk/government/speeches/mansion-house-speech-2021-rishi-sunak

———. 'Response to Petition: "Prevent the Introduction of Any 'Programmable' CBDC in the UK"' (21 December 2022). Also available at: https://petition.parliament.uk/petitions/624159

United Nations Office on Drugs and Crime. 'Money Laundering' (n.d.). Also available at: https://www.unodc.org/unodc/en/money-laundering/overview.html

United States Census Office. 'Twelfth Census of the United States Taken in the Year 1900, Population, Part 1' (United States Census Office, Washington: 1901). Also available at: https://www2.census. gov/library/publications/decennial/1900/volume-1/volume-1-p2.pdf

US Department of Defense. 'DoD News Briefing – Secretary Rumsfeld and Gen. Myers'. Speech by Donald Rumsfeld, US Secretary of Defense (12 February 2002). Also available at: https://web.archive. org/web/20160406235718/http://archive.defense.gov/Transcripts/Tra nscript.aspx?TranscriptID=2636

US Department of the Treasury. 'The Future of Money and Payments: Report Pursuant to Section 4(b) of Executive order 14067' (US Department of the Treasury, Washington, D.C.: 2022). Also available at: https://home.treasury.gov/system/files/136/Future-of-Money-and-Payments.pdf

US Government. 'Economic and Trade Agreement Between the Government of the United States of America and the Government of the People's Republic of China'. Office of the United States Trade Representative, Executive Office of the President of the United States (2022). Also available at: https://ustr.gov/countries-regions/china-mongolia-taiwan/peoples-republic-china/phase-one-trade-agreem ent/text

———. 'H.R.5403 (CBCD Anti-Surveillance State Act)'. Union Calendar No. 409, 118th Congress, 2D Session (US Government Publishing Office, Washington, D.C.: 2024). Also available at: https://emmer.house.gov/_cache/files/1/b/1b5d3 177-a835-4d7f-857c-8eaa765dc2ec/C9A5E6203EC89BFB3F9DEF702 726560B.cbdcs-final.pdf

Van Veen, Kelsi and Melton, Alex. 'Rare Earth Elements Supply Chains, Part 1: An Update on Global Production and Trade'. *Executive Briefing on Trade* (United States International Trade Commission, Washington D.C.: 2020). Also available at: https://www.usitc.gov/ publications/332/executive_briefings/ebot_rare_earths_part_1.pdf

Vogel, Ezra F. *Deng Xiaoping and the Transformation of China* (Harvard University Press, Cambridge, Massachusetts: 2011). Also available at: https://doi.org/10.4159/harvard.9780674062832

Wang, Yan and Yao, Yudong. 'Sources of China's economic growth 1952–1999: incorporating human capital accumulation'. *China*

Economic Review, 14/1 (2003), pp. 32–52. Also available at: https://doi.org/10.1016/S1043-951X(02)00084-6

Warsh, Kevin. 'Money matters: The US dollar, cryptocurrency, and the national interest'. In: *American Renewal: A Conservative Plan to Strengthen the Social Contract and Save the Country's Finances*, Paul Ryan and Angela Rachidi (eds.) (American Enterprise Institute, Washington, D.C.: 2022). Also available at: https://americanrenpr.wpengine.com/wp-content/uploads/2022/11/AR-final.pdf

Weinland, Don. 'China is rapidly rolling out its new digital currency'. *Economist* (18 November 2022). Also available at: https://www.economist.com/the-world-ahead/2022/11/18/china-is-rapidly-rolling-out-its-new-digital-currency

White House. 'Executive Order on Ensuring Responsible Development of Digital Assets' (9 March 2022). Also available at: https://www.whitehouse.gov/briefing-room/presidential-actions/2022/03/09/executive-order-on-ensuring-responsible-development-of-digital-assets/

———. 'International Strategy for Cyberspace: Prosperity, Security and Openness in a Networked World' (White House, Washington, D.C.: 2011). Also available at: https://obamawhitehouse.archives.gov/sites/default/files/rss_viewer/international_strategy_for_cyberspace.pdf

———. 'Joint Statement from India and the United States' (8 September 2023). Also available at: https://www.whitehouse.gov/briefing-room/statements-releases/2023/09/08/joint-statement-from-india-and-the-united-states/

Williamson, John. 'A short history of the Washington Consensus'. In: *The Washington Consensus Reconsidered: Towards a New Global Governance*, Narcís Serra and Joseph E. Stiglitz (eds.) (Oxford University Press, Oxford: 2008), pp. 14–30. Also available at: https://doi.org/10.1093/acprof:oso/9780199534081.003.0002

Winder, Davey. 'Trump declares national emergency as foreign hackers threaten US power grid'. *Forbes* (2 May 2020). Also available at: https://www.forbes.com/sites/daveywinder/2020/05/02/trump-declares-national-emergency-as-foreign-hackers-threaten-us-power-grid/

Witte, Michelle. 'Xi Jinping calls for regional cooperation via new Silk Road'. *Astana Times* (11 September 2013). Also available at: https://

astanatimes.com/2013/09/xi-jinping-calls-for-regional-cooperation-via-new-silk-road

Wolf, Martin. 'The time to embrace central bank digital currencies is now'. *Financial Times* (20 July 2021). Also available at: https://www.ft.com/content/7a93fb0a-ae95-44fc-a3d2-1398ef0ce1af

World Bank. 'Africa's Pulse: An Analysis of Issues Shaping Africa's Economic Future', volume 8 (2013). Also available at: https://www.worldbank.org/content/dam/Worldbank/document/Africa/Report/Africas-Pulse-brochure_Vol8.pdf

———. 'Defying Predictions, Remittance Flows Remain Strong During COVID-19 Crisis' (12 May 2021). Also available at: https://www.worldbank.org/en/news/press-release/2021/05/12/defying-predictions-remittance-flows-remain-strong-during-covid-19-crisis

———. 'GDP (Current US$) – United States'. World Bank national accounts data, and OECD National Accounts data files (n.d.). Also available at: https://data.worldbank.org/indicator/NY.GDP.MKTP.CD?name_desc=false&locations=US

———. 'Gross Domestic Product 2022'. World Development Indicators Database (2023). Also available at: https://databankfiles.worldbank.org/public/ddpext_download/GDP.pdf

———. 'Patent Applications, Residents – United States'. World Intellectual Property Organization (WIPO) Patent Report: Statistics on Worldwide Patent Activity (n.d.). Also available at: https://data.worldbank.org/indicator/IP.PAT.RESD?end=1999&locations=US&skipRedirection=true&start=1990&view=chart

———. 'Remittance Prices Worldwide Quarterly: An Analysis of Trends in Cost of Remittance Services', 48 (World Bank Group, Washington, D.C.: 2023). Also available at: https://remittanceprices.worldbank.org/sites/default/files/rpw_main_report_and_annex_q423_final.pdf

———. 'Remittances Slowed in 2023, Expected to Grow Faster in 2024' (26 June 2024). Also available at: https://www.worldbank.org/en/news/press-release/2024/06/26/remittances-slowed-in-2023-expected-to-grow-faster-in-2024

———. 'Trade (% of GDP)'. World Bank national accounts data, and OECD National Accounts data files (n.d.). Also available at: https://data.worldbank.org/indicator/NE.TRD.GNFS.ZS

World Gold Council. 'Gold Demand Trends Q1 2024: Central Banks'
(2024). Also available at: https://www.gold.org/goldhub/research/
gold-demand-trends/gold-demand-trends-q1-2024/central-banks

Wright, Robin. 'Russia and China unveil a pact against America and the
West'. *New Yorker* (7 February 2022). Also available at: https://www.
newyorker.com/news/daily-comment/russia-and-china-unveil-
a-pact-against-america-and-the-west

Xiao, Yijia, Chen, Yanming, Liu, Xiaoqiang, Yan, Zhaojin, Cheng,
Liang and Li, Manchun. 'Oil flow analysis in the Maritime Silk Road
region using AIS data'. *International Journal of Geo-Information*, 9/4
(2020), p. 265. Also available at: https://doi.org/10.3390/ijgi9040265

Zeng, Wendy, Johnson, William and Davis, James C. 'United States
and Global Macroeconomic Projections to 2033' (US Department of
Agriculture, Washington, D.C.: 2024). Also available at: https://doi.
org/10.32747/2024.8374830.ers

Zhang, Pepe and Prazeres, Tatiana Lacerda. 'China's trade with Latin
America is bound to keep growing. Here's why that matters'. *World
Economic Forum* (17 June 2021). Also available at: https://www.
weforum.org/agenda/2021/06/china-trade-latin-america-caribbean

Acknowledgements

This book would not have come about without our agent, Andrew Gordon, whose instinctive interest in the subject matter and intuition for the shape it should take helped to find the best publisher we could possibly wish for.

Special thanks go to the brilliant team at Bloomsbury: first and foremost to Ian Marshall for taking on the project, helping to guide its narrative voice and having continued faith that we'd get there in the end; and to Faye Robinson, Elisabeth Denison, Anna Massardi, Shanika Hyslop, James Nightingale, Martin Bryant and Youssef Khaireddine for their professional support and dedication, and whose efforts in editing, designing and marketing have been instrumental in bringing this book to life.

BRUNELLO ROSA

Smart Money is the result of decades of study and research on all the disciplines involved in its realisation, including macroeconomics, economic history, history of economic thought, financial and monetary economics and history, geo-strategy and politics, banking and financial markets. It wouldn't have been possible to write it without the fundamental contributions of all the people I encountered along the way in various capacities, who taught me those disciplines, or provided invaluable insights on them. Making a complete list of these people to acknowledge their contributions would be simply impossible, and therefore I will only mention the pivots of my professional and academic career, in inverse chronological order.

This list needs necessarily to start with Nouriel Roubini, my long-standing business partner and friend, for his endless support and guidance throughout the many years we have been working together in various settings. Rarely do we find people who think alike, and this I believe has been the glue of our professional relationship and friendship.

In academia, I want to thank the people who supported and accompanied the growth of my role throughout the years. At the London School of Economics and Political Science (LSE), I want to thank Ricardo Reis of the Centre for Macroeconomics; Jean-Pierre Zigrand and Jon Danielsson of the Systemic Risk Centre; David Webb of the Financial Markets Group; and especially my thesis supervisor, Hyun Song Shin, with whom I have remained in constant contact, even when our professional paths brought us to different parts of the world. At Bocconi University, impossible not to start with Mario Monti, for decades its President before becoming Italian Prime Minister; and then Gianmario Verona, Francesco Billari, Carlo Altomonte, Stefano Caselli and Alessandro Minichilli. At City, University of London, I want to thank especially Anastasia Nesvetailova, Ronen Palan, Charles Lees and Inderjeet Parmar for their continued support and guidance. At Siena University, my deepest gratitude goes to Alessandro Vercelli, who first discovered my talent for macroeconomics and believed in me, launching my career as a professional economist. Our friendship has evolved over the decades into what I consider to be a very solid intellectual relationship. Also from the University of Siena, I would like to remember and thank Nicola Dimitri, Alberto Dalmazzo, Mario Tonveronachi, Giuseppe Della Torre and Riccardo Fiorito.

On the specific issue of digital assets, a necessary mention goes to Michael Mainelli, Riccardo Tordera Ricchi, Kunal Jhanji, Paul Sisnett and Eugenia Lichakhina, Tony Craddock and Robert Courtneidge, Ruth Wandhöfer and Maurizio Ghirga. A special mention goes to Piero Cipollone, for our insightful conversations on policymaking over the years.

On a personal note, I also need to thank all those who have always believed in me, and have been kind enough to put up with my impossible schedule and working hours, which don't spare weekends and holiday periods, and who have sacrificed their valuable time to assist me in the process.

CASEY LARSEN

This book owes a debt to the work of some exceptional thinkers and builders from the spheres of business, technology, macroeconomics, bitcoin, digital assets and venture capital, such as Lyn Alden, Luke Gromen, Michael Saylor, Saifedean Ammous, Nic Carter, Nik Bhatia, Balaji Srinivasan, Paul Sisnett, Richard Turrin, Michael R. Klare and others.

We have tried to place central bank digital currencies in their appropriate context, by arguing that they are important to take seriously not because they are a natural evolution – let alone the apotheosis – of the revolution that was started by Satoshi Nakamoto and the advent of Bitcoin and blockchain technology, but because they are a technological and geopolitical inevitability that will soon affect all of our lives in ways that we can't yet fully apprehend.

The book's section on the new era for money sought to make clear that 'smart money', to whatever extent that might be considered a positive term, is the outcome of individual and private-sector innovation, and that governments need to handle its invention with care. The idea that governments will not – or should not – avail themselves of these technologies, however, has always seemed fanciful.

I am grateful to a number of people who have been great to me and without whom this would not have been possible: Michael Farrant and Peter Headden at Farrant Group for their continued support both professional and personal; Henry Porter, who sparked my interest in the tech industry and couldn't have been a better journalistic mentor and friend during my time at *Vanity*

Fair; Paul Sisnett for his continued (if intermittent) faith in my communications advice, and whose indefatigable efforts to build 'the internet for money' I'm confident will soon yield a solution to many of the problems outlined in this book; and of course the brilliant Brunello Rosa, whose life's work undergirds this book's thesis and who is always fun to work with. Thank you also to Riccardo Tordera Ricchi for introducing me to Paul and Brunello.

On a personal note, thank you to my parents for always being there for me. My contribution is dedicated to my late father, Sven, who inspired me to read and write, and who would have been pleased to see my name on a book.

Note on the Authors

BRUNELLO ROSA is a financial economist and geopolitical strategist who advises market participants, policy-makers and institutions. He is the CEO and head of research of Rosa & Roubini Associates, a visiting professor at City St George's, University of London, and a Senior Executive Fellow at the School of Management of Bocconi University in Italy. He is the coordinator of the executive education course in Global Macroeconomic Challenges at the London School of Economics, where he has taught in various capacities for the last twenty years. Having previously worked at the Bank of England, he is an active member of the Chief Economists Advisory Board of the European Investment Bank. More recently he has advised several institutions, including the UK Parliament, on the geopolitical aspects of CBDCs.

CASEY LARSEN is a British–Swiss writer and strategic communications consultant. Casey advises political and business leaders on geopolitics, technology and international affairs. He started his career at *Vanity Fair* and occasionally writes for newspapers and magazines in the United Kingdom and United States. Casey holds an MA (Hons) in Philosophy from the University of St Andrews.

Note on the Type

The text of this book is set Adobe Garamond. It is one of several versions of Garamond based on the designs of Claude Garamond. It is thought that Garamond based his font on Bembo, cut in 1495 by Francesco Griffo in collaboration with the Italian printer Aldus Manutius. Garamond types were first used in books printed in Paris around 1532. Many of the present-day versions of this type are based on the *Typi Academiae* of Jean Jannon cut in Sedan in 1615.

Claude Garamond was born in Paris in 1480. He learned how to cut type from his father and by the age of fifteen he was able to fashion steel punches the size of a pica with great precision. At the age of sixty he was commissioned by King Francis I to design a Greek alphabet, and for this he was given the honourable title of royal type founder. He died in 1561.